Balancing Acts:

The Scholarship of Teaching and Learning in Academic Careers

Mary Taylor Huber

A collaboration of The Carnegie Foundation for the Advancement of Teaching and the American Association for Higher Education

A collaboration of The Carnegie Foundation for the Advancement of Teaching and the American Association for Higher Education

The mission of the Carnegie Foundation for the Advancement of Teaching as expressed in our founding charter is, "to do and perform all things necessary to encourage, uphold, and dignify the profession of the teacher and the cause of higher education." Foundation programs, headed by a small group of distinguished scholars, aim to reinvigorate education by renewing the connections between teaching and research. These programs seek to foster forms of reflection and inquiry that will raise the level of attention to educational issues throughout American academic life.

AAHE is an independent, membership-based, nonprofit organization dedicated to building human capital for higher education. AAHE is the source of choice for information about higher education on issues that matter in a democratic multiracial society. AAHE promotes and disseminates examples of effective educational practice to address those issues. AAHE members are a national talent pool willing and ready to share their expertise with colleagues in higher education, policymakers, media professionals, and the public at large.

Recommended Bibliographic Listing
Huber, M. T. (2004). Balancing acts: The scholarship of teaching and learning in academic careers. Washington, DC: American Association for Higher Education and The Carnegie Foundation for the Advancement of Teaching.

For information about additional copies of this publication, call AAHE's fulfillment center at (301) 645-6051 or order online at www.aahe.org/pubs.

ISBN 1-56377-065-2

Contents

About the Author

Mary Taylor Huber is a senior scholar at The Carnegie Foundation for the Advancement of Teaching, where she works with the Carnegie Academy for the Scholarship of Teaching and Learning (CASTL) and Carnegie's Initiatives in Liberal Education. Trained as a cultural anthropologist, Huber directed the research program on Cultures of Teaching in Higher Education, which gave birth both to *Balancing Acts* and to her co-edited volume, *Disciplinary Styles in the Scholarship of Teaching and Learning* (2002). Huber is a coauthor of *Scholarship Assessed* (1997), the Foundation's follow-on report to *Scholarship Reconsidered* (Boyer, 1990), to which she also contributed.

Four-word: Against the Grain

Lee S. Shulman

President, The Carnegie Foundation for the
Advancement of Teaching

M ary Huber's provocative monograph, *Balancing Acts*, is a set of case
studies of four individual scholars who had to make serious career
choices. A humanist, a psychologist, a mechanical engineer, and a chemist,
the choice of how they would make a difference in their respective fields
was often not easy. They were confronted with the compelling and often
competing goals of engaging in mainstream forms of disciplinary inquiry
or giving primacy to inquiry responsive to their roles as educators in those
disciplines. *Balancing Acts* explores the essence of these dilemmas, the
challenge of trading off competing goods in the service of higher ends.
Indeed, this book can be read as an account of four academic journeys in
which values, choices, actions and their consequences are in continuing
interaction and competition. How does one represent this kind of intersection of values, choices and their outcomes? For me, the essential tool is
the 2×2 or "four-fold table." If that seems like a puzzling observation, permit me to digress a bit.

Four-fold tables are powerful ways of representing the intersection
among alternative actions (often moral or strategic choices) on the one
hand, the possible states of nature on the other hand, and the likely consequences of those interactions. Thus, imagine a situation where a driver is
approaching a railroad crossing without signal warnings. He can either
stop and look in both directions or he can proceed across without stopping. The state of the world also has two possibilities: there is either a train
coming or there is not. The cells of the four-fold table now summarize the
possibilities. If he stops and there is indeed a train coming, he avoids
injury and keeps himself safe. If he stops and there is no train coming, he
has experienced a slight delay, and remains safe. If he fails to stop and
there is no train nearby, he remains safe. But if he fails to stop and a train

is coming, he is likely to be badly injured or killed. Given the four alternatives, and the very low cost of stopping briefly to check for trains, the best decision is clear.

DECISION: Stopping at Railroad Crossing

		DRIVER ACTION	
		Stop	Proceed
TRAIN	Not Coming	safe	safe
CONDITION	Coming	safe	death or injury

Now, however, imagine that the driver is trying to escape from an assassin who is intent on murdering him. Suddenly, the contingencies change rather dramatically. Now stopping has a serious cost associated with it as well. The decisions are much less clear.

DECISION: Stopping at Railroad Crossing While Escaping from Assassin

		DRIVER ACTION	
		Stop	Proceed
TRAIN	Not Coming	death or injury	safe
CONDITION	Coming	death or injury	death or injury

There are many famous examples of the uses of four-fold tables as ways of representing human choices in the world. Three of my favorites are Pascal's Gamble, Bacon's Skeptic, and Pasteur's Quadrant.

Pascal was encountered by a friend coming out of church. Knowing that Pascal was a nonbeliever, the friend chided Pascal for his hypocrisy. Pascal replied that the decision was quite straightforward. There were two possibilities: God exists, or God does not exist. And he had two actions he could take: Go to church or stay away from church. The intersection yields a four-fold set of possibilities. If there is a God, and he goes to church, all is well. If there is no God, and he stays away, the consequences are benign. Similarly, if there is no God and he attends church, he has wasted a few hours each Sunday and holy day, but is merely inconvenienced. But if there is a God and he fails to act with reverence, the consequences could be unfortunate for him for all eternity. Hence, "Pascal's Gamble" is to attend church.

Bacon's Skepticism is also related to religion, but leads to doubt rather than acts of faith. In his discourse on "the idols of the mind," Bacon describes a visitor to a church who is shown a fresco depicting those fortunate souls who were shipwrecked, and when drowning prayed to be saved, and indeed were rescued. Bacon's question was, Where are the frescoes showing those who prayed under the same conditions and were not saved? Once again, we have a four-fold table, in which the cells represent those who pray and are saved, those who do not pray and drown, those who do not pray and are saved, and those who pray but nevertheless drown. The skeptic suspects that most shipwrecked souls drown whether or not they pray, and that the painter of the fresco selects only from the "off-diagonal" cell a set of cases that are distinctly nonrepresentative. Bacon's table is a cautionary tale for us. Are the four scholars who are the subjects of Mary Huber's careful analysis all residents of the same cell as those who prayed and were rescued from drowning? Are they, thus, potentially misleading examples, representing a small but unlikely set of exceptions to a quite different general rule?

Pasteur's quadrant was Donald Stokes' (1997) representation of the choices of conducting basic or applied research and the consequences of outcomes that had some practical value. He argued that Pasteur's cell was the one in which basic questions were asked in the context of pursuing applied ends. In that situation, the scholar simultaneously pursues the ends of both knowledge and application, and when things go well she attains a modicum of each.

PASTEUR'S QUADRANT: Research is inspired by:

		CONSIDERATIONS OF USE?	
		No	Yes
QUEST FOR FUNDAMENTAL UNDERSTANDING?	Yes	Pure basic research (Bohr)	Use-inspired basic research (Pasteur)
	No		Pure applied research (Edison)

So, rather than serving as potentially misleading and nonrepresentative members of an odd cell, are the four cases harbingers of "Carnegie's Quadrant," of scholarship that achieves both disciplinary and pedagogical virtue?

By this time in the essay, my readers will be quite legitimately asking themselves how all this is relevant to the foreword to this book on the work of university scholars who opted to make questions of teaching and learning occupy the heart of their scholarly agendas. Good question. I believe that Mary Huber's case studies can be illuminated by means of a four-fold table. The underlying logic of this book is that there are two kinds of scholars in the world of higher education, those who behave as most of their disciplinary colleagues expect them to, and those who elect to go against the grain.

Thus, one might say that there are four kinds of scholars. There are those who do what is expected of them and succeed thereby. There are also those who do the expected, but nevertheless are not deemed successful. Then there are those who do not do what is expected and, not surprisingly, fail. Finally, and most interesting, I believe, are those who do not behave as their disciplinary community expects them to behave, yet succeed nevertheless—as illustrated in the next four-fold table, for which I adapt the terms "pathfinders," and "pathfollowers" from Patricia Gumport's pathbreaking work (2002).

CARNEGIE QUADRANT: Scholarship

		CONFORMS TO DISCIPLINARY CONVENTION?	
		Yes	No
LEADS TO ACADEMIC ADVANCEMENT?	Yes	Successful Pathfollowers	Successful Pathfinders (Carnegie)
	No	Unsuccessful Pathfollowers	Unsuccessful Pathfinders

This book is about the fourth category or cell in the four-fold table. Dan Bernstein, Brian Coppola, Sheri Sheppard, and Randy Bass each elected to violate the extant norms of their academic disciplines and devote themselves to the scholarship of teaching and learning within psychology, chemistry, mechanical engineering, and English, respectively. Nevertheless, they succeeded in the academic world at public and private institutions of higher education of the highest level—Nebraska (and later, Kansas), Michigan, Stanford, and Georgetown.

What can be learned from studying Pascal's Gamble, Bacon's Skepticism, Pasteur's Quadrant, or the Carnegie Quadrant? What is the value of carefully investigating the "off-diagonal" cell? Shall we approach the work of our four case-study scholars as equivalents of Pasteur's Quadrant, as evidence that one can (and should) strive to make contributions to both a discipline and its teaching? Is the lesson of this book that we need to create a vision of the possible, an academic world in which the Carnegie Quadrant is not so underpopulated? Or shall we view the account through the lenses of Bacon's skeptic, asking for another, much longer book, about those who opt for the scholarship of teaching and learning and are rewarded with the academic equivalent of drowning? And is there an equivalent of Pascal's Gamble (shall we call it Andrew's Bet?) wherein, like most of Huber's cases, it remains most prudent to conduct just enough traditional research in one's discipline to retain a modicum of conventional legitimacy, and then strive for distinctive excellence in the scholarship of teaching?

We learn from Huber's studies that we can nurture a vision of the possible in which serious scholars in their disciplines make fundamental contributions to the health and development of those fields by taking the path not normally taken, the off-diagonal cell of the scholarship of teaching and learning in their disciplines. But we should not kid ourselves. In order to succeed with this strategy in our era, it is probably necessary to be not just very good but distinctively excellent in one's unconventional (in this case, scholarship of teaching) inquiries and career. While being "good enough" may be sufficient for many engaged in traditional research in their discipline, it is probably not going to be sufficient for work in education.

In our family delicatessen while growing up, I learned a lesson from my immigrant mother that is almost as valuable as the four-fold table. "When slicing a brisket" she explained, "always cut against the grain." The advice generalizes admirably for the slicing of all meats, I later learned. And as Mary Huber demonstrates in this provocative monograph, it's not bad advice for scholars of courage and talent. Cut against the grain. You take a serious risk, but your impact may be profound.

Bobby Kennedy once observed, "There are those who look at things the way they are and ask, Why? . . . I dream of things that never were and ask, Why not?" Indeed, the world need not remain as it presents itself to us. There may in fact be limits to the uses of four-fold tables with their either-or logic and clearly bounded cells. The decision need not remain forever between the options of engaging exclusively in traditional forms of inquiry and in the scholarship of teaching and learning in one's discipline. It is within our power as an academic community to choose a new route, a route in which the two roads no longer diverge, but converge into a powerful new conception of the scholarly career, in which the scholarships of the discipline, of teaching and learning, and of service to humanity achieve parity and mutual enhancement.

REFERENCES

Gumport, P. (2002). *Academic pathfinders: Knowledge creation and feminist scholarship.* Westport, CT: Greenwood Press.

Stokes, D. E. (1997). *Pasteur's quadrant: Basic science and technological innovation.* Washington, DC: The Brookings Institution.

Preface and Acknowledgments

The pedagogical landscape of higher education is changing. College still involves a familiar mix of lectures, laboratories, and seminars. But across the country, faculty are redesigning courses and curricula to engage students in more active, collaborative, and community-based learning; exploring the best ways to make good use of new media; and providing opportunities for undergraduates to experience real research. Teaching initiatives in higher education are gaining visibility, innovation is on the upswing, and a new scholarship of teaching and learning has been forming as "regular" faculty join education specialists in asking questions and sharing answers about classroom practice with colleagues on campus and beyond.

What might these changes mean for scholars who wish to rethink their role as educators? This book addresses that question through the experience of four faculty members who have been innovators in their own classrooms, leaders of education initiatives in their institutions or disciplines, and pioneers in the scholarship of teaching and learning. It looks at the pathways through which these scholars became involved in this work, the issues they have taken up over time, and the communities with which they have become engaged. It also explores the consequences that these scholars' efforts to understand and improve undergraduate education have had for their own careers, especially (though not only) with regard to tenure and promotion.

This concern about consequences is one that we at the Carnegie Foundation hear often from people who are thinking about taking up the scholarship of teaching and learning, from those interested in mentoring them, and from faculty and administrators who wish to change institutional policies and practice to better support their work. Indeed, it is a concern that resonates with faculty who get involved in virtually *any* emergent area of work, including the "newer" forms of scholarship identified in the Carnegie Foundation's influential report, *Scholarship Reconsidered: Priorities of the Professoriate* (Boyer, 1990): the scholarships of integration, application (outreach or engagement), and teaching. Most faculty take up new lines of work because they are intrinsically interesting or valuable in use. But new fields, like established ones, can progress only if they become what Lee Shulman calls "community property" (1996). They only become "community property" in colleges and universities when the reward system allows practitioners to stay in the academy and advance to senior positions.

Strong leadership and supportive policy are essential. But whether they will prevail—whether this new work will *really* "count" for academic advancement—is a question that is now being answered case by case. These early cases are influencing academic careers in two ways, first, by deciding the fate of individuals for appointment, reappointment, tenure, or promotion, and second, by the messages these decisions send to faculty who are setting their own scholarly agendas or helping others do so through "corridor talk" and formal advice. The faculty featured in this book were each told by caring and responsible mentors that they were undertaking a fool's errand in treating teaching so seriously. But they persisted; they have been tenured and promoted to associate professor, and two so far have been further advanced to full professor. Their stories now circulate in their communities as signs that the scholarship of teaching and learning can be woven successfully into an academic career.

Indeed, it was with the purpose of highlighting such stories and extending their reach that chemist Brian Coppola of the University of Michigan first suggested that the Carnegie Foundation prepare a set of case studies of people who, like himself, had recently been tenured with records rich in the scholarship of teaching and learning. How are scholars presenting this work in their dossiers? What issues is it provoking in the committees that make decisions about academic advancement? What arguments are winning the day? Because considerations of confidentiality prevent too deep a probe into committee deliberations, my colleagues and I broadened the scope of the inquiry to include the role of the scholarship of teaching and learning in the larger sweep of an academic career.

My biggest debt of gratitude is to the four scholars who generously agreed to share their stories here: Dan Bernstein, a psychologist who has moved from the University of Nebraska– Lincoln (where most of his story takes place) to the University of Kansas; Brian Coppola, the chemist at the University of Michigan; Sheri Sheppard, a mechanical engineer at Stanford University; and Randy Bass, in English and at the Center for New Designs in Learning and Scholarship at Georgetown University. All four talked with me at length about the history of their academic lives, walked me through their tenure and promotion experiences, invited me into their professional networks, and introduced me to the pedagogical developments and debates in their institutions and fields. I am in awe of their commitment to advancing the scholarship of teaching and learning and especially their extraordinary generosity in sharing with me—to share with you—the ups and downs of their remarkable careers.

Naturally, all four of these scholars could have written about their own careers, and they have in other venues. I decided early on, however, that these cases would be most valuable if I included a variety of voices and perspectives from within their own departments and institutions and from their academic communities beyond. Thus I am also grateful to the 41 colleagues who agreed to talk to me about the institutional and disciplinary contexts in which Bernstein's, Coppola's, Sheppard's, and Bass's work on teaching and learning has taken place. Each of them took time away from busy schedules to speak to me in person or by telephone for half an hour or more. All illuminated important issues in the conduct, recognition, and reward of teaching and learning as scholarly work.

My thanks to Alice Agogino, Rick Bevins, George Bodner, Dorothy Brown, Bill Buskist, Lawrence Carlson, Stephen Chew, M. David Curtis, Mark Cutkosky, Denice Denton, Michael Doyle, Clive Dym, Seyhan Ege, Arthur Ellis, Leona Fisher, Calvin Garbin, James Gibbons, John Glavin, Edie Goldenberg, Roald Hoffmann, Anthony Ingraffea, Gregory Jay, Joseph Krajcik, Robert Kuczkowski, Larry Leifer, Lucy Maddox, Craig Nelson, John O'Connor, W.C. Reynolds, Bernard Roth, John Carlos Rowe, Anita Salem, Paul Savory, Bassam Shakhashiri, Lee Shulman, James Slevin, James Sosnoski, Ross Thompson, Barbara Walvoord, Kristin Wood, and one colleague who prefers to remain anonymous. All who are named and quoted in the text have seen and agreed to having these excerpts from our conversations appear in this book. The interpretation of their remarks and those of the case study scholars is, of course, my own.

My understanding of the cultures of teaching and learning in which Bernstein, Coppola, Sheppard, and Bass are engaged has benefited from simultaneous involvement in two other projects. One was co-editing *Disciplinary Styles in the Scholarship of Teaching and Learning: Exploring Common Ground*, a collection of essays by teams of scholars in 10 fields (Huber & Morreale, 2002). I owe thanks to all of these authors for insights into the ways that the disciplines provide different homes for the scholarship of teaching and learning, and I have drawn extensively on their essays, especially the ones on the fields considered here—psychology, chemistry, engineering, and English.

The other project that has informed and inspired this work is the higher education program of the Carnegie Academy for the Scholarship of Teaching and Learning (CASTL). In particular, this book reflects lessons learned from working with CASTL's national fellowship winners between 1998 and 2003—137 scholars of teaching and learning, including Bernstein, Coppola, and Bass, at different stages in their careers, in different types of colleges and universities, and in different fields. Collectively, these

Carnegie Scholars and their colleagues in CASTL's associated campus program and work with scholarly societies have become my touchstone for comparison. I am very grateful to them all.

My closest colleague in developing these case studies has been Rebecca Cox, a graduate student in higher education at the University of California, Berkeley, who has worked as my research assistant throughout. Becky and I have met twice or more weekly for three years to discuss issues and identify research needs. She kept the interview transcripts organized and accessible; assembled material on the people, places, programs, and projects mentioned in the interviews; and wrote background papers in which her knowledge of the scholarly literature on higher education proved invaluable. Two earlier research assistants, Eric Van Duzer and Julie Kerekes, also deserve thanks.

I cannot imagine a more congenial intellectual community in which to work than The Carnegie Foundation for the Advancement of Teaching. President Lee Shulman and vice presidents Pat Hutchings and John Barcroft generously supported the program on Cultures of Teaching in Higher Education under whose auspices this study took place. Special thanks to Lee and Pat, too, for their leadership of CASTL and for including me among its staff, and to my other CASTL colleagues at Carnegie, Marcia Babb and Richard Gale, and at the American Association for Higher Education (AAHE), Barbara Cambridge, director of CASTL's campus program. Thanks also to the many senior scholars, research associates, and visiting scholars at the Carnegie Foundation who have listened to my presentations on this project and provided such patient and perceptive advice.

A few people have played especially important roles in moving this project to completion: Lindsay Turner helped prepare the manuscript; Pat Hutchings and Cheryl Fields read and critiqued it; Gay Clyburn orchestrated publication arrangements and public relations; and Jane Hamblin at AAHE edited and oversaw the production of the book, with Nancy O'Neill as copyeditor. Margaret Miller encouraged me to write a preview of these case studies for *Change* magazine in August 2001, and the publisher of *Change*, Heldref Publications, has allowed me to use that material in the introduction and conclusion of the book. *Balancing Acts: The Scholarship of Teaching and Learning in Academic Careers* has benefited from many good critical friends, but I alone am responsible for what errors remain.

Finally, these acknowledgments would not be complete without a grateful nod to Ernest Vigdor, my fellow traveler from beginning to end.

1

Introduction: The Scholarship of Teaching and Learning in Academic Careers

· ·

Poised on the cusp of a new century, in a world that wrestles with a multitude of difficulties, the university must fulfill a more well-rounded mission. . . . American higher education has to demonstrate the imagination and creativity to support and reward both scholars uniquely gifted in research and those who excel in other uses of knowledge.[1]

"Balance" is a blessing that many faculty members seek in their professional lives, but it is one that few believe they can achieve without serious risk to the advancement of their academic careers. An elusive idea with resonance in physics, politics, justice, and morals, "balance" also has an aesthetic sense that may come closest to what faculty usually mean by the term. John Ruskin, arbiter of artistic opinion in 19th-century England, captured it well when he noted, "In all perfectly beautiful objects, there is found the opposition of one part to another, and a reciprocal balance" (cited in *Oxford English Dictionary*, 1971, p. 158). It may seem futile to seek beauty in a 21st-century profession that values the parts of its work so unevenly. But the recent movement to broaden the idea of scholarship in the academy is beginning to bear fruit and show that differently balanced careers can indeed be designed and successfully pursued.

It should not be necessary to dwell long on the national conversation about faculty priorities, a vigorous discussion that has traveled far since the early 1990s when Ernest Boyer urged that the nature of academic scholarship be "creatively reconsidered." Convinced that a narrow focus on research productivity had *unbalanced* the work of the academy, Boyer and his Carnegie Foundation colleagues argued that colleges and universities would not be able to meet the challenges of the 21st century unless they began to recognize and reward a wider range of scholarly activity (Boyer, 1990; Glassick, Huber, & Maeroff, 1997). Higher education's traditional missions of research, teaching, and service will be strengthened when faculty are encouraged to approach work across disciplines, in the classroom, and in the community with the same care and curiosity that they bring to research at the frontiers of knowledge in their own fields. Further, the Carnegie reports concluded, faculty taking advantage of opportunities to develop varied scholarly interests and talents will enjoy more balanced professional lives.

These promises retain their timeliness and appeal. Market forces continue to raise the bar for institutional, departmental, and individual success in the academy's prestige economy, pushing pressure for research productivity to new heights.[2] At the same time, new students, new technologies, and new social and cultural developments require more systematic attention to teaching and learning, broader interdisciplinary thinking and collaboration, and closer engagement with the larger community. By now, many institutions have revised their guidelines to include a wider range of scholarship in their systems of faculty roles and rewards. The question remains as to whether individual faculty, departments, and institutions will take the risks that embracing new work inevitably entails (see Gumport, 2002a).

Everyone has heard discouraging tales of tenure denial that publicize such risks to innovative young scholars. Now that more hopeful stories are also beginning to circulate, it is possible to ask how people are weaving new kinds of work into their careers and making the case for "scholarship" writ large. Chronicling the experience of four scholars, in four disciplines, from four universities, this book examines the pathways they have traveled through the scholarship of teaching and learning, the issues with which they engage, the communities this work brings them in touch with, and the consequences (so far) for their careers. Since careers take place in time, this approach also provides unique perspectives on the history of innovation and reform in college and university teaching, including the emergence of a scholarship of teaching and learning, over the past 40 years.

The lessons to be learned from the experience of these scholars are not simple. As Joan Wallach Scott writes of academic freedom, "Specific cases are always complex, and they always involve contestation: differences of interpretation and therefore debate about what has happened and why. It is the debate about cases . . . that articulates historical meanings" (Scott, 1995, p. 44). "Scholarship," like "academic freedom," is always historically circumscribed and defined. The case studies presented here tell us how individuals are beginning to gain institutional recognition for new kinds of work, and how the move to broaden scholarship is influencing specific scholarly milieus. It is my hope that these cases will also prove useful to those who wish to undertake new kinds of scholarship themselves, to their advisors and supporters, and to all those who recognize that in the long run, the work of the academy will be balanced only when work that matters also becomes work that counts.

MAKING WORK THAT MATTERS WORK THAT COUNTS

How does the academy change its sense of what work matters? How does newly valued work actually come to count—to be funded, recognized, rewarded, taught? These elusive questions have been the concern of sociologists of knowledge and historians of higher education for some time. Certainly, some of these changes are a matter of national priorities—as one can see with the establishment of the National Science Foundation (NSF) after World War II and the growth of research funding for academic science during the Cold War. This largesse circuitously benefited many fields beyond the sciences, from my own of cultural anthropology to English literature. But money could not do the magic by itself. In *Scholarship Assessed*, my co-authors and I recalled, "In the late 1950s, shortly after Sputnik extended the Cold War to space, sociologist Robert Merton argued that America's capacity to respond to the Soviets depended on the nation's ability to encourage scientific development by recognizing excellence in research" (Glassick, Huber, & Maeroff, 1997, p. 6).[3] To advance fields of knowledge, new priorities must gain an effective presence in higher education through the academy's systems of peer review and faculty roles and rewards.

The same is true for more contentious changes in the sense of what knowledge matters enough to count. Consider, for example, the emergence of new interdisciplinary scholarship in the 1960s, 1970s, and 1980s. As sociologist Patti Gumport shows in her study of the academic history of feminist scholarship, even when the climate was friendly to the creation of special centers, new programs, and new departments, it often was not easy for "pathfinders" to establish the legitimacy (and excellence) of their work (2002a). Feminist scholars eventually succeeded in creating the infrastructure needed to advance the field that has become known as gender studies—faculty lines, graduate and undergraduate programs, research funding, conferences, journals, and book publishers. Yet many younger faculty fell by the wayside in unfavorable tenure and promotion decisions before debates were resolved about the quality and importance of these lines of research.

A similar drama is playing out today in the effort to broaden the kinds (not just the content) of faculty work. The sense that recognizing and rewarding not only the scholarship of discovery but also the scholarships of integration, application, and teaching would be worthwhile has a broad constituency—well beyond those influenced by any of the Carnegie reports.[4] Since the 1990s, faculty members and campus administrators, higher education associations and scholarly societies, and accrediting bodies and foundations have worked on several fronts to reach agreement about the kinds of work that should matter and to get this work to count (Huber, 2002). They have also worked tirelessly on pilot projects, infrastructure-building, and changing rules and regulations, tasks that can take years of planning, persuading, fundraising, and committee work fueled by untold amounts of energy, commitment, elation, tedium, and tears.

Early reports from the field indicated uneven change. In a 1994 Carnegie Foundation survey, almost 80 percent of the chief academic officers at four-year colleges and universities reported that their institutions either had recently reexamined their systems of faculty roles and rewards or planned to do so, and the most widely embraced goal of these reviews was to redefine traditional faculty roles such as teaching, research, and service (Glassick, Huber, & Maeroff, 1997, p. 12). However, change does not happen evenly on all fronts. For example, *The Chronicle of Higher Education* studied all 48 tenure cases decided in Ohio State University's five colleges of the arts and sciences during the 1993–1994 academic year and concluded, "recent talk in the academy about the need to broaden the definition of scholarship and to better reward teaching did not appear to greatly influence most cases at Ohio State [that] year" (Lederman & Mooney, 1995, p. A17). The authors report that attention was paid to classroom performance in all cases, and that most people said it was given more attention than would have been paid in the past. But, they note, "in almost every negative tenure case, inadequate research was cited as the major reason . . . no candidate was denied tenure solely because of inadequate teaching" (p. A17).

In the research university setting this is perhaps not surprising, and the authors found that in branch campuses where teaching loads were higher, faculty up for tenure that year were not expected to have been as productive in research (Mooney, 1995, p. A22). However, if one distinguishes *teaching* from the *scholarship of teaching*, one notes that Ohio State apparently had no candidate make a case for the latter that year. Of course, when such cases do come up at colleges and universities around the country, they do not necessarily sail right through. As Richard Chait observed in 1995, recognizing different forms of scholarship involves "less certainty about the qualities and characteristics of scholarship—about what should count" (1995, p. 7).

The ways in which people were managing uncertainty about "scholarship" in the mid 1990s is beautifully documented in a case study by Louise Wetherbee Phelps of Syracuse University (1997). Phelps noted that the chancellor of her institution had announced in 1992 that over the next four years, the university would become a "student- and learning-centered research university," and that "scholarship at Syracuse will encompass discovery, integration, application and teaching, and faculty members in every unit will be rewarded for the unique contributions they will make" (p. 1). This set the stage for the local version of a transition that Phelps saw rolling through higher education at large: a period of "turbulence and uncertainty . . . during which the new paradigm is being invented and negotiated even as it displaces the old research paradigm" (p. 6).

According to Phelps, debates and decision-making for promotion and tenure in the Committee of the College of Arts and Sciences included lengthy discussions about the scholarship of teaching and how it should be valued given the university's new policies. These discussions were "filled with confusion, ambivalence, ambiguity, ignorance, and frustration. They showed a tremendous desire to be fair and principled but great uncertainty about what principles applied and how to apply them" (1997, p. 2). Hard questions came up—as they should in such debates: How is *scholarly* teaching different from or related to *good* teaching? What is meant by the "scholarship" or "intellectual work" of teaching? How should the scholarly dimension of teaching be valued relative to its quantity (number of courses or students), effectiveness, popularity with students, difficulty, or importance to a particular department? (p. Overhead 2)

In complicated or borderline cases, Phelps noted, faculty who were confused or ambivalent about the new forms of scholarship, "ignored the new standards, in most cases not because they categorically opposed them, but because faculty were unsure what they meant, whether they were rigorous in ways comparable to the old criteria, and how to determine that individuals met such new standards" (1997, p. 3). At Syracuse, she concluded, the transition from one paradigm to another was generating "interference patterns . . . that carry significant risks and dangers, especially for young faculty" (p. 1).

Another example of what can happen when a mission changes comes from the University of Colorado at Denver. This institution spent two years in the early 1990s redefining its mission and inviting its faculty to integrate their work in teaching, research, and service toward solving important urban problems and improving the quality of urban life (University of Colorado at Denver, n.d.). In a 1998 conference session, a team from Denver described the case of Doris Kimbrough, an assistant professor with broad interests in chemistry education, who took up the challenge and became, in her words, the university's new "poster child." When it was time for tenure and she received the official notebook for presenting her case, she tore out the dividers still labeled "teaching," "research," and "service" and reorganized her material to emphasize the integrated nature of her work. Unfortunately, the presenters noted, while her scholarship embodied official university ideals, it challenged the existing tenure criteria, which were still written in terms of excellence in research, teaching, and service. The case became highly contentious, generating much discussion about the nature of scholarship at the institution, and Kimbrough won only after her work was dis-integrated and the dividers between research, teaching, and service put back in. When asked whether she would advise others to follow her path, she said, "No, not in a thousand years."[5]

Even when new missions are matched by new guidelines, it can be daunting to face evaluation in a case resting on achievement in one of the "new" scholarships. Portland State University, well-known in higher education circles for its embrace of community engagement, now defines discovery, integration, interpretation, and application as "four expressions of scholarship" that apply equally to research, teaching, and community outreach. The university stipulates that quality and significance can be evaluated by the "clarity and relevance of their goals," "mastery of existing knowledge," "appropriate use of methodology and resources," "effectiveness of communication," significance of results," and "consistently ethical behavior" (Portland State University, 1997).[6] Still, as two faculty members from Portland State observe, "Many faculty members are fearful that the commitment to be engaged scholars could jeopardize their chances for tenure and promotion, particularly related to how their peers will evaluate their work" (Gelmon & Agre-Kippenhan, 2002, p. 7). The authors' experiences with their individual reviews, they write, were "still fraught with anxiety, tension, and concerns" (p. 7).

This time-series of tales may suggest progress both in clarifying the concept of "scholarship" and in the alignment of mission, guidelines, and practice. The most remarkable thing about such stories is that seemingly against the odds, some faculty members are eager to pursue these "new" kinds of scholarly work. To be sure, there are senior faculty who are taking them up without risking rank or tenure, and some for whom the work is a small if stimulating sideline to an otherwise conventional career. Clearly it is too early (and may never be possible) to collect statistics on the frequency with which cases for tenure, promotion, or annual merit reviews are submitted with substantial work flying under the flag of one or another kind of new scholarship. Tracking these developments is made even harder by the fact that so much of this work crosses the conventional categories of scholarly work.

Since 1998, when the Carnegie Academy for the Scholarship of Teaching and Learning (CASTL) was established, the Carnegie Foundation has offered fellowships to more than 130 faculty to "explore their own teaching practice and the character and depth of student learning that result (or do not) from that practice" (CASTL, 1999, p. 9). Over the years, several of these faculty members have been tenured or promoted by their institutions. Some have used their projects as rich evidence of how they approach "teaching" as serious intellectual work; some have categorized portions of their activities in support of the scholarship of teaching and learning on campus or in their fields as "service"; some have submitted their more substantial initiatives and presentations on teaching and learning as "research" or "scholarship" in the more conventional sense of the term.

Not surprisingly, those of us working with CASTL, including the scholars themselves, are often asked about the consequences faculty face when they take up the scholarship of teaching and learning. Most often these questions concern tenure and promotion. As the stories above suggest, steps have been taken in many settings to encourage and reward scholars who widen their scholarly sights. Still, it is hard to give general answers in a transitional situation, when so many particulars of institutional and individual history influence the outcome of what are still extraordinary cases. It seems, therefore, that it would be most helpful at this moment to look *in depth* at the experience of a few faculty members who have crafted careers in which the scholarship of teaching and learning is playing a major role.

LEARNING FROM EXTRAORDINARY CASES

Four colleagues we know well at the Carnegie Foundation generously agreed to become "subjects" for case studies about how the scholarship of teaching and learning is playing out in academic careers. Three have been members of the pioneer class of Carnegie scholars, and one is directing a Carnegie study in our program on preparation for the professions.[7] They are not typical scholars of teaching and learning, but people who have achieved national and even international recognition for their work. Dan Bernstein, a psychologist now at the University of Kansas (but for most of his career at the University of Nebraska–Lincoln), is best known for mastery learning and faculty course portfolios. Brian Coppola, a chemist at the University of Michigan, has focused his efforts on innovation in chemical education and the development of future faculty. Sheri Sheppard, a mechanical engineer at Stanford University, has made major contributions to engineering education reform. Randy Bass, in English and American studies at Georgetown University and also director of Georgetown's Center for New Designs in Learning and Scholarship, has made his reputation through experimentation with new media in teaching the humanities.

These case studies are based on extensive interviews with these four scholars, as well as on interviews with over 40 of their colleagues—about 10 each, half from within their departments or institutions and half from other academic communities to which they belong. These are not the distilled sketches that are sometimes offered as "cases" or prompts for discussion, nor are they full biographies. They also do not explore such important issues as the relationship between academic and family life or the many ways in which gender (or race or class) affects the progress of professional life.[8] Rather, the two chapters devoted to each scholar focus on the history of his or her involvement with the scholarship of teaching and learning. I have chosen to focus on faculty at research universities because their careers illustrate most dramatically the tensions inherent in efforts that do not fit neatly into the conventional categories of academic work.

One lesson to be learned from these cases is that the scholarship of teaching and learning is not a simple or single thing. Our case study scholars' work in this area has the characteristics that Pat Hutchings and Lee Shulman outline in "The Scholarship of Teaching: New Elaborations, New Developments" (1999). Hutchings and Shulman noted:

> It is not (only) excellent classroom teaching, carefully prepared, well-designed and enacted, engaging for students, and productive of important learning. Nor is it (only) scholarly teaching, in which faculty consult the literature on teaching and learning in their field, and document their work, and invite peer collaboration and review. The scholarship of teaching and learning is *also* teaching gone "meta." It is teaching that involves inquiry into learning, and that is being made public in a way that can be critiqued, reviewed, built upon, and improved. (p. 13)

Like any body of creative intellectual work, however, this kind of scholarship is varied in content and form. For many, it may begin and end with inquiry into and documentation of teaching and learning in a single course, or iterations of that course, shared and discussed with campus or disciplinary colleagues. For faculty who have achieved prominence in the scholarship of teaching and learning, like those considered here, it *also* includes well-documented classroom innovation, curriculum development, new resources for students and colleagues, grantsmanship, publication in peer-reviewed journals, presentation at conferences and other universities, Web activities, workshops for fellow faculty, participation on national panels and curriculum projects, and elaborations, collaborations, new initiatives, and the like.

Consider as an example of this wide range of work the activities of Sheri Sheppard, who is perhaps best known for developing "mechanical dissection," an activity in which her first- and second-year students at Stanford participate in hands-on investigations of the relationship between the form and function of various mechanical devices. Designed as a way to provide a meaningful foundation for future mechanics courses, dissection activities involve teams of students taking apart and studying bicycles, hair dryers, disk drives, and other small machines, to develop an understanding of the engineering design process. The course includes dissection labs, student presentations, multimedia resources, redesign activities, and in some cases, even prototyping. A set of formal evaluations, including interviews with students and video analysis of their teamwork, has consistently demonstrated the effectiveness of these activities. Through conference presentations, articles, websites, and workshops, mechanical dissection has spread to other schools in NSF's Synthesis Engineering Coalition (during which it was developed) and beyond. Sheppard is now writing a textbook on mechanics that will include mechanical dissection, and she is also engaged in many other engineering education initiatives.

This leads to another important lesson. When people take up new forms of scholarship, old ideas about "balance" are best placed in quotes. Faculty work has long been represented as some specified proportion of teaching, research, and service, including academic citizenship and outreach. When faculty members take a scholarly approach to teaching and learning, or to service in its various forms, the boundaries between the conventional parts of academic life can easily blur. For our subjects, "balance" is less about the relationship between different kinds of work, and more about their integration. Sheppard's traditional engineering research applies concepts and theory to real systems, and she developed mechanical dissection so that students too can apply the concepts and theories they are learning to an understanding of how real things work. Her experience with mechanical dissection has fed new understandings about learning into her courses, which have in turn informed an array of projects in the scholarship of teaching and learning.

Still, our featured scholars and the colleagues who support them have also had to find ways to translate new kinds of scholarship into systems of evaluation that privilege established forms of research. Of course, their scholarly achievements can be represented in conventional terms, but making such a case—dividing the work between teaching and research and service—requires special effort on the part of the candidate. At the same time, committees must first agree to broaden the definition of scholarship used normally in their department and institution and then make a special effort to discern the degree of distinction of an unusual and often unfamiliar body of work. Many candidates who try are unsuccessful. Those who do gain tenure or promotion at respected universities make a double contribution. In addition to the contributions to teaching and learning that these extraordinary scholars make through their work, the stories about their careers become a beacon to others, enlarging the academy's capacity to nurture and value faculty whose scholarship is both sound *and* broadly defined.[9]

ROUTES INTO THE SCHOLARSHIP OF TEACHING AND LEARNING

Our scholars' stories map many routes into academic careers that include significant work in the scholarship of teaching and learning. Some paths are purely personal, involving interests and insights that they variously trace to childhood, college, graduate school, and beyond. Some are circumstantial, involving opportunities sought or grasped *because* of their interest in the general domain of teaching and learning. For example, while an undergraduate, Randy Bass served for three years on a committee to reform his college's general education program. Because the college was part of a consortium concerned with general education, Bass was able to attend national conferences and publish an article on the student's view of reform. During his sophomore, junior, and senior years, he worked closely with faculty who cared about teaching and learning. He watched the process go through its entire arc, from exciting, new ideas to a program only slightly different from what they had before. Fortunately, Bass found this experience to be eye opening rather than embittering and considers it valuable preparation for his subsequent roles as national reformer and campus leader in teaching, learning, and technology.

Opportunities for intellectual exchange about teaching and learning multiply during graduate school, because that is where most future faculty actually began to teach. Until very recently, few programs took this part of professional development seriously, although students who were determined or lucky could still nourish their pedagogical imagination. For psychologist Dan Bernstein, a graduate student in the late 1960s and early 1970s, the spark came from his dissertation advisor and from a fellow graduate student, whose unconventional views on assessment led Bernstein to a career-long interest in mastery learning in his own psychology classes. Chemist Brian Coppola, funded as a graduate student by research fellowships, looked outside his department for teaching experience. Responding to a call for volunteer tutors, Coppola wound up working with a graduate student in education who introduced him to literature on peer-tutoring, methods for classroom observation, and the benefits of interdisciplinary collaboration in education research.

As these scholars' graduate experiences indicate, opportunities to engage in the scholarship of teaching and learning are shaped in part by the disciplines themselves (Huber & Morreale, 2002). While there are many crosscutting issues, scholarly work on teaching and learning is not the same across fields. Each field has its own intellectual history as well as agreements and disputes about subject matter and methods, which then influence who is taught what, when, how, and why. Each has a set of traditional pedagogies, like lab instruction and problem sets in the sciences, and its own discourse of critique and reform. Each has its own community of scholars interested in the teaching and learning *of that field*, with one or more journals, associations, and face-to-face forums for pedagogical reflection and exchange. For good and for ill, scholars of teaching and learning must engage what Joseph Schwab (1964) so elegantly described as the substantive and syntactic structures of their disciplines, that is, the "conceptions" that "guide inquiry" (p. 25) and the "pathways of enquiry [disciplines] use, what they mean by verified knowledge and how they go about this verification" (p. 21).

From this perspective, chemists, psychologists, American literature professors, and engineers look at the world through different lenses and undertake intellectual inquiry into the teaching and learning of their subjects in somewhat different ways. In some corners of academe, the model of scholarly discourse is the highly theorized critical essay, while in others it is an account of statistical results from a quasi-experimental research design. Some fields, such as composition and interdisciplinary studies, are dense with discussion about college pedagogy while others, such as literature and history, are not. Some disciplines have large stores of intellectual capital from which their scholars of teaching and learning can draw and to which they can contribute. Communication scholars can see teaching as a communicative act; management scholars can see the classroom as an organization; psychologists can see teaching as an inquiry into learning. Some fields, especially in the sciences, have developed somewhat specialized communities of educators, who draw on ideas and methods from other fields, but whose relatively well-funded curricular and pedagogical initiatives have brought wide attention to educational issues within their fields.[10]

Like most scholars who turn to teaching and learning, then, our subjects' early educational agendas developed in conversation with different disciplinary worlds. Dan Bernstein's advisor in graduate school was a maverick who "really was interested in viewing education as a legitimate subject of psychological interest in behavior change. And so, of course he was interested in the way you teach, and dedicated to the idea that you would do it better, the same way you'd do anything better." Early in his career, Bernstein's interest in mastery learning connected well with his experimental research on human motivation, while his later work on the peer review of teaching has kept a focus on student learning as its signature theme.

Randy Bass's fields of literature and American studies were not as open to pedagogical discussion as Bernstein's corner of psychology, but Bass soon found allies in other disciplinary neighborhoods. His dissertation research on the literatures of 19th-century America led him into interdisciplinary efforts to design new media educational resources, a brave and exciting new world at the time, while his later development of new media pedagogies as "engines of student inquiry" were inspired in part by writing across the curriculum models circulating on the composition side of English studies.

For scientists, education reform agendas in their fields come very prominently into play. As mentioned, Sheri Sheppard's innovative efforts to provide a design experience for freshman and sophomore engineers was made possible by her participation through one of NSF's Engineering Education Coalitions. Brian Coppola's first professional opportunity to focus on issues in chemistry education came through an invitation to participate in the University of Michigan's initiative to design an undergraduate chemistry curriculum, which subsequently became well known for its focus on organic, rather than physical, chemistry; laboratories emphasizing student inquiry; and honors sections with peer instruction. Coppola saw his later development of a fellowship program for graduate students interested in teaching as part of a larger effort to build a scholarship of teaching in chemistry that is accessible and engaging to students and faculty at all stages of their careers.

WHAT COUNTS AS WHAT

While most scholars of teaching and learning develop agendas that tie into their disciplines' histories, pedagogies, and investigative styles, they also live and work in specific departments in particular institutions that have traditions, divisions, aspirations, and rules. The scholarship of teaching and learning may find warmer welcome in this or that department or this or that institution, such as a department or campus where a lively community has formed around teaching and learning with support from key academic leaders.

Indeed, there are examples of both friendly and not-so-friendly campuses across the map of institutional types. Bernstein, Bass, Coppola, and Sheppard are all from doctoral and research intensive universities where the challenges are considerable, but their stories have resonance for people at master's colleges and universities, baccalaureate colleges, and community colleges, as well.

While all of our scholars have successfully negotiated their way through tenure (and in Bernstein's and Coppola's cases, promotion) at their institutions, it has not been easy. Even though each has had the advantage of working in a department open to their interests in teaching and learning, they have also faced ambivalence about the scholarly status of their work.

For Bernstein, who was hired to take on his department's large introductory psychology course and awarded tenure in the late 1970s on a "balanced" portfolio of teaching and research, institutional ambivalence about the value of teaching was registered in his paycheck and in other, less tangible ways. For those tenured more recently, however, the question has turned out to be less about the value of teaching versus research than about the status of the *scholarship of teaching* itself. Is it something untenured faculty should pursue? How should it be counted, as "research," "teaching," or "service"?

Early warning signs came through loud and clear, as they would to any scholar fortunate enough to have knowledgeable and street-smart mentors who care about their progress through academe. For example, Sheri Sheppard came to the Design Division of Stanford's Department of Mechanical Engineering with a research focus on weld fatigue and impact failures, fracture mechanics, and applied finite element analysis. Her strong interest in teaching led her to take on challenging courses, like Strength of Materials, with histories of low student ratings. "From the very beginning," one of her colleagues told me, "she was very stubborn about what she wanted to do and against my better advice, did certain things which really wouldn't serve the goal of getting promoted—like teaching certain undergraduate classes that she didn't have to teach." A few years later, when Sheppard began working with NSF's Synthesis Coalition for undergraduate engineering education reform, her closest colleagues again expressed concern, and she actually received a formal letter from her chair advising against it at that stage of her career. However, she went ahead with both her traditional research *and* the work on teaching and learning that the Synthesis Coalition gave her the opportunity to pursue.

Bass, too, took risks. As a pioneer in teaching with technology at Georgetown, he introduced students to new media pedagogies, which ran afoul of their expectations and suffered the predictable low ratings as a result. Bass himself tells the story of this "fall" and his later redemption by means of the scholarship of teaching and learning (1999a). This recovery was particularly important for his tenure decision, because he had also taken risks with his record of research.

He had known, of course, that the safest and wisest path to tenure would be to publish articles or a book about his dissertation topic, 19th-century documentary narratives. He began to do so, but traditional scholarship receded as attractive new media projects kept coming his way. A senior colleague from another university advised Bass to "keep your hand in the traditional American literary scholarship" but to also go ahead with "the more innovative electronic ones." His departmental mentor advised—begged—Bass to publish at least some conventional work. As the tenure decision came closer, however, Bass came to believe that "to try to do both was a trap," and he shifted his focus to the electronic domain where he was already gaining international renown.

Coppola's situation was different in fundamental ways. He had made his major break with expectations for a conventional career as an academic scientist while still in graduate school, and he began work at the University of Michigan in a typical (for the sciences) teaching-intensive non-tenure-track line. When after several years it seemed that a tenured position might become available, Coppola and his mentors determined that his case would be strongest if his work on teaching and learning could be judged by the usual standards for research. He implemented a familiar strategy right away. He won external grants to support research on the effectiveness of his teaching innovations; published articles in refereed journals about his pedagogical research; organized conferences, lectured, and led workshops around the country; networked extensively; and achieved national recognition as a chemistry educator. He also gave a lot of thought as to how best to present his case.

In these tenure documents, Coppola noted that for scholars like himself, "instructional and research activities are naturally intertwined," and that "ironically, sorting through these issues is also part of what I consider to be included in my professional and scholarly purview." He divided his pedagogical contributions into three descriptive categories: (a) day-to-day teaching practices (chemistry teaching and learning), (b) the structure of an educational program (chemical education), and (c) assessment and evaluation practices (examination-related activities, as well as chemical education research). While admitting that many of his activities "defy clean separations," he stated that he would include work within the first two categories in his teaching statement, leaving those in the last category for his statement on research. For example, the redesigned introductory chemistry curriculum and specific features that he developed or co-developed (including, for example, its interactive format and peer instruction options) are elaborated under "teaching," while his publications in the area of philosophy and epistemology, teaching and learning skills, preparation and training, and assessment and evaluation are offered as "research."

Scholars do not, of course, always have the last word over the way their work is counted, a critical point where questions of weighting come to the fore. Sheppard's contributions to the traditionally defined engineering area of welding and fracture clearly constituted research in the eyes of her evaluators, but her grants, research, and publications in engineering education did not seem to count in the same way. In some fields and some departments, scholarship on teaching and learning is a relatively new and still marginal venture, and colleagues have a strong sense that work *on* teaching should count *as* teaching, regardless of the specific activities it entails.

Bass's colleagues appear to have grappled less with what was "teaching" and what was "research," and more with the inadequacy of old notions of genre (article, book) or role (author, editor) when faced with electronic scholarship. Consider the American Studies Crossroads Project, which Bass describes as "a set of online resources for the study of the United States, including professional resources for the international American studies community, the organization of indexes to scholarly resources, the creation of curriculum and faculty development materials, and the coordination of an ongoing research project in which 30 faculty developed case studies documenting their experimentation with new technologies in the teaching of culture and history." Bass himself presented this work as a project that crosscut the scholarships of teaching, application, and integration, as defined in *Scholarship Reconsidered*. But what his colleagues wanted to know, it seemed, was whether it could be considered a book (Bass, 1999a). This was not a simple counting exercise, but a search for familiar models by which to evaluate the quality of unfamiliar work.

DISCERNING DISTINCTION

Committees must not only resolve basic questions about what counts as what when they are operating within the research, teaching, and service model of faculty work. They must also discern the level of distinction of the scholar's achievements. How good is it? Has it had an impact? Here again, when work crosses traditional boundaries, old ways of doing business do not necessarily apply. Every case is unique, deliberations are confidential, and decisions about a scholar's past performance and future promise are made on the picture that his or her whole record provides. These specifics are not our concern.[11] What is relevant here is what our subjects and their colleagues could tell us about the *general* questions that arise in assessing the quality of scholarly work on teaching and learning.

First, it is important to note that the current evaluation system works best for the scholarship of teaching and learning when "the standard metric" can be used virtually unchanged. The chemists who spoke to us about Brian Coppola's work were quite clear on this point. As Arthur Ellis at the University of Wisconsin put it, "I like to tell my colleagues in the research community that the metrics are all the same. You're looking for papers published in peer-reviewed, high profile journals; you're looking for funding brought in from competitive sources like National Science Foundation; you're looking for speaking invitations; you're looking for adoption or adaptation of the work in other people's programs."

The department chair at the time of Coppola's tenure decision acknowledged that Coppola's success depended upon building a "portfolio of some substance," including "a record of scholarship . . . a publishable record." Coppola's then-dean emphasized the importance of having "national visibility beyond classroom performance, which we expect of all of our faculty." In Coppola's case, this included "contributions that move the educational effort in a larger field and have promise of doing so beyond the [discipline]." Sheppard's colleagues at Stanford took a similar stance; distinction in the scholarship of teaching and learning in engineering would mean the same thing as distinction in any other specialty. For tenure candidates, this meant the promise of national and international leadership in that field.

This standard puts a special burden on a faculty member like Sheppard, who came up for tenure with both a traditional and nontraditional record of scholarly work, and it glosses over other difficulties as well. First, the metric by which these records are judged may be the same, but the application is different. This difference exists not so much in principle as in practice, because while engineers know very well how to evaluate work in, say, welding and fracture, they have less experience in judging the signs of "promise" for educational leadership. Letters from external reviewers are important in both cases.[12] But this creates a second problem in that these endorsements can be problematic if the community qualified to interpret the candidate's achievements is not well known to the committee members. As one colleague said, "it doesn't have the power of somebody saying, 'Oh yes, I know this character. He's a really tough cookie, and if he says this person's good, then they must be'." In emerging research areas with "buzz" this is not likely to be a serious problem, but engineering education has a lower profile.

In some cases, the metric itself is much harder to apply. As Bass notes in reflections on his own case, faculty who work with new technologies and their supporters are often in the strange position of arguing that the key to assessing this work is that it is both like and unlike other kinds of work. Certainly the American Studies Crossroads Project is in some says like a book. "Unfortunately," Bass pointed out, "as a publication, the Crossroads Project (like many others I could show you in digital form) commits all kinds of sins: it is . . . 'self-published'; it is highly collaborative; it is never 'finished' but ongoing; and it is very difficult to locate in its boundaries and extent" (1999a, p. 9).

As a departmental colleague explained, "The hard thing is for people to know how you . . . considered achievement that didn't come in the form of some kind of juried print. I think people are sincere. They [just] don't know what the equivalent is in order to make sure that what you were getting was material that in effect had been peer reviewed. I think that's the big issue. You know how a university press goes about choosing a book; you know how a journal does it. It's very hard to know what the equivalent evaluation process is for stuff that is coming out [on the Web]."

Web-based resources are not the only forms of scholarship on teaching and learning to challenge both the social and technical adequacy of the academy's standard "metrics" for measuring the quality of scholarly work. Classroom teaching, for example, is notoriously hard to submit for peer review. In recent years, however, progress has been made in finding ways of making teaching more public and therefore amenable to informed critique.

Dan Bernstein's recent work in faculty development focuses on the preparation and review of course portfolios, one of the most promising ways of capturing the full range of activities and reflection involved in teaching a college course. The goal, as Bernstein says, is to "create a model community of scholars who engage in regular substantive peer review to derive benefit from both reviewing and being reviewed. . . . We hope that this project will both generate renewed enthusiasm for teaching and provide a vehicle for review that will enhance the standing of teaching as a serious part of professional life."

BALANCING ACTS

Let me conclude by returning to that elusive concept of "balance," the organizing theme for the case studies that follow. The introduction and conclusion to this book focus on issues that all four scholars have faced because of their engagements with the scholarship of teaching and learning. The case studies themselves, however, focus on the particular circumstances in which each scholar's career has taken shape, and on each scholar's unique ways of balancing his or her various lines of work. The order is roughly chronological, beginning with Chapters 2 and 3 on Dan Bernstein, who began as an assistant professor at the University of Nebraska–Lincoln in 1973; Chapters 4 and 5 are about Brian Coppola, who started as an instructor at the University of Michigan in 1986; Chapters 6 and 7 are about Sheri Sheppard, who began teaching as an assistant professor at Stanford University, also in 1986; and Chapters 8 and 9 take up the story of Randy Bass, appointed as an assistant professor at Georgetown in 1991.

Balance, in its aesthetic sense, concerns symmetry. While there may be universals in the human sense of symmetry, there are also many ways of achieving a symmetrical, that is, balanced, effect (Gombrich, 1984; Grieder, 1996).[13] Dan Bernstein's pattern has been to alternate periods of special attention to teaching and learning with periods devoted to experimental psychological research. However, Bernstein's approach to teaching and learning is deeply rooted in his disciplinary perspective, and so these phases in his career have each contributed to the other. Brian Coppola's balance has been more "distributed" within his department. He maintains a small line of laboratory research in his particular branch of organic chemistry, but he has been able to negotiate a tenured position that allows him to spend most of his time in discipline-based pedagogical projects and research.

It is possible to see every part of Sheri Sheppard's work as a balancing act. Describing herself as a "bridge person," Sheppard has worked in both industry and the academy, converting abstract theory into useful mathematical tools. Just as she studies the strength of welds and solders that join materials, she sees the scholarship of teaching and learning as a way of strengthening connections between engineering education and design. Finally, there is Randy Bass, for whom new media pedagogy seems less a bridge than a center where several professional interests in history and culture converge. Digital technologies make it possible to put "novices in the archive," and Bass has devoted his career to exploring how scholars can help students make the most of that opportunity to connect text and context, read with more care, and interpret with more sophistication. In fact, all four scholars connect "teaching" and "research" by developing ways of teaching that engage undergraduates with the habits of mind of professionals in their respective fields.

Of course, the careers of these four scholars are not yet complete. They have all taken from and given back to the teaching and learning communities in which they have participated. Their careers, and the scholarship of teaching and learning itself, are still works in progress. Dan Bernstein, Brian Coppola, Sheri Sheppard, and Randy Bass, and others like them, are contributing to the development of a larger discourse community around teaching and learning. What lessons can be learned from these case studies about how we, as individuals and a community, can help people weave the scholarship of teaching and learning into successful academic careers?

NOTES

1. This quotation is from *Scholarship Assessed: Evaluation of the Professoriate* (1997), by Charles E. Glassick, Mary Taylor Huber, and Gene I. Maeroff, p. 10.

2. There is much anecdotal evidence about this "rising bar." For example, a trio of recent articles in *The Chronicle of Higher Education* refers to the pressures on institutions, departments, and individual scholars (Arnone, 2003; Graham & Diamond, 1999; Wilson, 2001). Survey data also suggest that pressures for research increased throughout the 1990s. In the Carnegie Foundation's 1997 Survey of the Academic Profession, for example, 42 percent of faculty at doctoral universities, 41 percent at master's colleges and universities, and 35 percent at baccalaureate colleges reported that research counts more than it did five years ago (Huber, 2002, p. 78).

3. See Merton's essay, "Recognition and Excellence: Instructive Ambiguities" (1973), first published in 1960.

4. There is no question that the Carnegie reports have been influential, entering into and helping shape a much larger debate about the character, quality, and recognition of faculty work. See Lazerson, Wagener, & Shumanis (2000), on "Teaching and Learning in Higher Education, 1980–2000."

5. The team presenting this case at AAHE's 1998 Conference on Faculty Roles and Rewards included the associate vice chancellor, the faculty head of the campus-wide promotion and tenure committee, chair of the chemistry teaching and research committee, and Kimbrough herself.

6. The preamble to Portland State's mission statement says, "As part of the Oregon University System, Portland State University's vision is to enhance recognition of the value of higher education by continually strengthening the metropolitan environment and utilizing that strength for its own growth toward standards of excellence in accessible high quality research, teaching and outreach programs. As a microcosm of the global society, the metropolitan environment becomes a

laboratory for Portland State in this vision. It is the vision of a university that will set the standard for institutions located in an urban setting" (Portland State University, 1999).

7. Teaching and learning communities share with other academic communities that "small world" quality, where people come to know each other through participation in a variety of meetings, projects, and institutions. Thus, before CASTL, all four of these scholars participated in an earlier AAHE project, directed by Lee Shulman and Pat Hutchings before Shulman and Hutchings became president and vice president, respectively, of the Carnegie Foundation. Further, Shulman had come to know of Sheppard when he headed the Stanford University committee that heard her tenure case. These kinds of ties are further elaborated in the case studies as part of the story about how participation in the scholarship of teaching and learning has influenced their careers.

8. Anne Colby (1994) has outlined some of the benefits and limitations of an approach to using case studies similar to the one chosen for this book in her essay, "Case Studies of Exceptional People: What Can They Teach Us?" Clearly, work and family issues are as important to scholars of teaching and learning as they are to other faculty and can be exacerbated by taking on additional work of any kind; the issues do not appear to be specific to the scholarship of teaching and learning. The interplay of gender and the scholarship of teaching and learning may be more complicated, because of the possibility that the tendency of the academy to marginalize women may intensify the tendency to marginalize the work (and vice versa). It would take a different kind of study to know how and when these dynamics come into play.

9. Indeed, two of the four scholars featured in this book, Brian Coppola and Randy Bass, make their careers a topic for oral presentation and publication (see Bass, 1999a; Coppola 1998, 1999).

10. See the essays on individual fields in the edited collection, *Disciplinary Styles in the Scholarship of Teaching and Learning: Exploring Common Ground* (Huber & Morreale, 2002). In the humanities, these include history, English studies, and interdisciplinary studies; in the social sciences, they are communication, management, sociology, and psychology; and in the sciences, mathematics, chemistry, and engineering.

11. After some consideration, I decided not to delve into these confidential depths. First, open access to university records, especially faculty personnel files, is a much-debated question (see Baez & Centra, 1995; Galle & Koen, 1993; Glidden, 1997), and AAUP does not favor access to promotion records by "outside requesters" (American Association of University Professors, Committee A on Academic Freedom and Tenure, 1997, p. 47). Second, many of the focus scholars' colleagues with whom I spoke had been involved in their tenure or promotion proceedings as committee members and external referees, and I did not want to ask them to compromise the confidentiality of these proceedings and communications.

12. For some of the ways in which external reviewers can even unwittingly damage a case, see Baron (2003).

13. Grieder notes, for example, "Art tells us things by the way it is balanced" (1996, p. 121). I thank Diane Losche and Rebecca Cox for help with, and references to, the concept of "balance" in art.

2

Teaching as Inquiry Into Learning
· ·

Faculty teaching practices . . . have their influence on learning in part by arranging a context in which students engage in productive learning activities with greater intensity or focus than previously.[1]

For many faculty, an invitation to look seriously at student learning promises entry to an intriguing dimension of classroom teaching, but it can prove daunting because most college professors are unschooled in the teaching and learning of their own and other fields. This is no surprise. As psychologist Howard Gardner points out, faculty and students in school and college are all parties to an "unwritten agreement" about what kinds of performances signal understanding in the classroom, and seldom stop to ask whether students *really* understand the material they are supposed to have learned. According to Gardner, "The gap between what passes for understanding and genuine understanding remains great. It is noticed only sometimes . . . and even then, what to do about it remains far from clear" (1991, p. 6).

Looking anew at learning is one of the first and most basic steps involved in the scholarship of teaching and learning. This can be as seemingly simple as asking whether one's students understand what one wants them to understand. But that same question can also be complex, engaging faculty with new literatures, new colleagues, and new styles of inquiry into the ways and means of teaching and learning in college. Some fields, of course, have more to say about learning than others, and psychology, with its long history of theory and research on learning, is an obvious case (Huber & Morreale, 2001). This is not to say that academic psychologists typically draw on this legacy when teaching their own college courses. However, when they *do* decide to ask questions about their students' learning, they have the tremendous advantage of a familiar set of theories, concepts, and methods (Nummedal, Benson, & Chew, 2001). Psychologist Dan Bernstein of the University of Kansas has been making connections

Case Study: Daniel Bernstein

Dan Bernstein is professor of psychology and director of the Center for Teaching Excellence at the University of Kansas. He is also project coordinator of a multi-university grant from Pew Charitable Trusts to build a community for peer review of the intellectual work in college teaching. This project uses electronic course portfolios to communicate the effectiveness of teaching to colleagues on other campuses. Bernstein teaches graduate and undergraduate courses in the history of psychology, learning processes, and the psychology of social behavior. A professor of psychology at the University of Nebraska–Lincoln before moving to the University of Kansas in 2002, he is winner of the University of Nebraska System's Outstanding Teaching and Instructional Creativity Award and is a Carnegie Scholar in CASTL. Bernstein received his baccalaureate degree from Stanford University and his doctorate in social and experimental psychology from the University of California, San Diego. Visit http://csumb.edu/ready2net/speakers/2002/program4/bio_bernstein.html for more information.

between his field's perspectives on learning and his own classroom teaching for a long time.

I had known Bernstein for a couple of years before asking him if he would be willing to participate in this study, in part because I admired his work, but also because I thought that he, like many scholars of teaching and learning, had only taken up this work after tenure and promotion. I later found out that a number of his colleagues thought the same thing. To my surprise, it turned out that Bernstein had been an innovator in teaching and learning in his early years as a college professor and that he had been tenured taking that into account. During my work with him in CASTL, I had been charmed by Bernstein's trenchant observations about education, observations that drew on psychology's analytic tools.[2] When we began our formal interviews in January 2001, our conversations underscored the fact that when Bernstein says things like "teaching is inquiry into learning," he is not just speaking cant. For him, the phrase evokes an attitude and a position rooted in the research traditions that have defined his identities as a social psychologist, behavior analyst, and college teacher since the time of his graduate work.

In fact, Bernstein's case is a good one with which to begin this book, because his career reflects such an important period in the history of teaching and learning in higher education. Entering the profession in the 1970s, at the height of higher education's expansion, Bernstein began his career in a climate of educational ferment. The number of students had grown from 2.3 million in 1950 (or 14.2 percent of the 18- to 24-year-old population) to 7.9 million in 1970 (or 32.1 percent of the 18- to 24-year-old population). The number of institutions and faculty also dramatically increased. In 1950, there were about 1,823 colleges and universities with 190,000 faculty members, while in 1970, the numbers were 2,525 with 532,000 faculty.[3] This period saw the development of scholarship on policy issues in higher education and of a "public sphere" for dissemination, discussion, and debate. The Carnegie Commission (later, Council) began to publish an extraordinarily influential series of studies in 1969, while *The Chronicle of Higher Education, Change* magazine, and Jossey–Bass Publishers all began publishing news, commentary, and books at about the same time.[4]

Within this climate of expansion, educational innovation was further inspired by the political and cultural upheavals of the time. Reforms of the era ranged from the creation of experimental programs and colleges, to large-scale curricular revisions, to pedagogical projects, like the Keller Plan for "individualized" learning in which Bernstein was heavily involved.[5] At Bernstein's first institution, the University of Nebraska–Lincoln, the increase in student enrollment from 1959 to 1969 (150 percent) exceeded that of postsecondary enrollments in the nation as a whole (120 percent). During that period at Nebraska, innovations included the establishment of a distinct cluster college (Centennial College), an interdisciplinary program encouraging independent studies (University Studies Program), a program to adapt ideas from developmental psychology to college teaching (ADAPT), and the creation of a teaching council to complement the already-existing research council (Knoll, 1995).[6]

Yet this was also a time when emphasis on research productivity was building steam across the academy, and the story of Bernstein's early career registers the tensions this provoked even (or especially) in institutions that were eager to compete in the cold war world of big science and federally funded research.[7] At Nebraska, a key mission for its postwar chancellors was to strengthen the university's position as a prestigious research university. According to historian Robert Knoll, Chancellor M. Hardin (1953–1968) pushed heavily for federal funds; he wanted to "bring the University into the magic circle of research universities" and did not want the various colleges to "be content with undergraduate teaching" (1995, p. 127). By the time of his departure, Hardin had instituted a series of research-related changes and expanded the university's external research funding. In 1973, when the first Carnegie Classification of Institutions of Higher Education came out, Nebraska was among the top 100 universities in terms of federal financial support and was classified as a Research University II. Its continuing determination to advance its research mission also set the stage for Bernstein's career.

INFLUENTIAL TEACHERS

In our conversations, Bernstein readily looked back on his professional life as a series of engagements with influential teachers and changing views on the nature and responsibilities of college teaching. The earliest and most influential of Bernstein's teachers were his parents, to whom he traces his calling as a college teacher—around the age of 12! Both of his parents taught English in Newark, New Jersey, at Weequahic High School, a public school that served a thriving mostly middle class Jewish community and a smattering of less affluent ethnic groups.[8] When Bernstein's father was principal, Weequahic produced such luminaries as Philip Roth, whose novels often include scenes from 1950s Newark, and Columbia University anthropologist Sherry Ortner, who has written about ethnicity and class through a study of the high school's graduating seniors of 1955.[9]

Family lore had it that Bernstein's parents, who came of age during the depression, finished college but couldn't afford to complete graduate school. But they certainly wanted their children to do so. At the dinner table, Bernstein recalled, the conversation was, "of course, you'll go to college. And understand that we will support you through a Ph.D., as long as you stay in school." Bernstein admired his parents, their friends who were teachers, and the teachers he had in school. Indeed, Bernstein suggested that in the 1950s and early 1960s, when he was growing up, "high school teachers were a pretty interesting lot. The folks who now teach in the Cal State system, in those days were teaching high school. There wasn't this other tier of higher education to take up that kind of person."

Bernstein realized from childhood that he was destined for college teaching, but understands now that his ideas about the profession were romanticized and vague. He knew from his parents' aspirations that the academic goal was a doctorate, and that with this degree one gets to teach not high school, but college. His parents spoke "almost reverentially" about professors, whom they regarded as a cut above high school teachers, primarily for the books they wrote. To Bernstein, therefore, college professors were teachers who wrote books on the side. If he had known how the profession would actually develop, how much more important than teaching the writing and books would actually become, he isn't sure whether he would have pursued it. But back then, "It was just real clear to me that I wanted to teach, that I loved school," he said. "I liked being in school. I liked the teachers. And the best kind of teaching was college teaching. So the only question then became, well, what?"

This question was answered shortly after Bernstein went to Stanford University. Arriving at college with an interest in mathematics and a facility in German, he soon found out that neither field was a particularly good fit with his talents and intellectual style. He could do math *after* it was explained, but the really good students appeared to just intuit the material, and Bernstein realized that he was unlikely to reach the top edge without prodigious amounts of work. During a semester in Vienna in his sophomore year, Bernstein realized that he had a good ear for German, and could speak and interact with German speakers very well. But he also realized that to be a professional in German meant being a specialist in German literature, and literary criticism, even in the 1960s, was not for him. Bernstein recalled, "the [Stanford] professor who was with us in Austria had these very well-formed ideas about literature, but I was constantly fighting with him because when I tried to ask him his reasons, he didn't give me good ones."

Psychology was different. According to Bernstein:

> . . . the Stanford psychologist Al Hastorf was in Austria then, too, and offered a side seminar in social psychology.[10] I was amazed at his analysis of certain kinds of interpersonal interactions. What really grabbed me was something called attribution theory. What are the characteristics of context that lead people to form judgments or attributions about the qualities of people—their abilities, their interests, giving them credit and blame. It's about everyday psychology, but it was not just post hoc guessing. It involved interesting conceptions and experiments. It was the first time anybody used a conceptual language that informed my understanding of human experience. It really made sense. It was an instant and deep understanding of something. There was an intellectual connection with the material and the ideas and an intellectual style.

When Bernstein returned to Stanford at the end of his sophomore year, he had decided on psychology as his major.

Stanford was a wonderful place to be an undergraduate in psychology in the 1960s, especially for a serious student like Bernstein. He actually sat through the same social psychology course that he had taken in Austria, in both his junior and senior years. "I just went to [Hastorf's] lectures to listen," he recalled, "and interestingly, I discovered that each time I got more out of it." While Hastorf was technically his honors advisor, Bernstein actually worked with graduate students, one of whom supervised his honors project and another of whom was an informal mentor. So he had, for the next two years, that "kind of a beginning graduate school experience" that can happen if one's advisors:

> ... think you're bright and you're connected to the research enterprise. If you get to be an insider in that system, an undergraduate can get the best by being like a mini-graduate student. There were maybe half a dozen of us who cracked that circle and went on to professional careers in social psychology. At the time, though, none of us really understood or appreciated that we had stumbled into the number one psychology department in the United States.

Indeed, the psychology department at Stanford was named the number one department in the country in 1964 and in 1969 by the American Council on Education, shortly before and just after Bernstein was an honors student there.[11] Chaired from 1922 to 1942 by Lewis Terman, best known for his work in intelligence testing for schoolchildren, the department had maintained a stellar reputation in the midst of the field's turbulent postwar years. Bernstein's specialty, social psychology, was thriving nationally as well. Before the war, academic psychology had been dominated by behavioral investigations into learning, often with animals. After the war, applied and clinical psychology expanded, while the number of theoretical approaches within academic psychology grew. Behavioral perspectives continued to thrive during the 1950s and 1960s, but the early to mid 1960s also saw the publication of some of the landmark works in cognitive psychology, which would soon take the lead. At the same time, social psychology had emerged reinvigorated by wartime work with other social scientists and was developing "into a productive and diverse area of study" (Gilgen, 1982, p. 129; see also Leahy, 1991).

The reputation of the Stanford psychology department rested heavily on its faculty's research and theoretical contributions to knowledge in the field. However, while research "trumped" teaching at Stanford and other elite universities early in the 20th century (Cuban, 1999), teaching itself was still a respected part of academic life. Bernstein, at any rate, recalled discussions among the graduate students about teaching, and wasn't aware of "people doing student bashing or complaining or referring to people who were teaching as victims, which I hear all the time now." He admitted that teaching at that time was "hopelessly archaic, as I see it now," but the graduate students Bernstein knew were devoted to discussing ideas and being clear in their teaching and being fair. Good teaching was a matter of identifying the important phenomena, presenting them in an organized fashion, writing fair tests, having office hours, talking to students. It was very conventional teaching, but people were serious about doing it well. "They felt that if they had organized it right, then good students would be able to get it. If they talked at the wrong level, if they used the wrong terms, if they were too theoretical or too abstract, then undergraduates would miss it. They also valued talking to students one-on-one, and treating them with respect."[12]

The power of one-on-one mentoring is still widely recognized in higher education and Bernstein recognizes its value, although he is mindful of its limits. Bernstein himself was particularly influenced by one of the graduate students with whom he "hung out" in the lab. "Where he was a great teacher," Bernstein recalled, "were the hours and hours he spent talking with me, and talking about his research, and talking about my ideas about psychology, and just treating me like a grownup whose ideas were worthy of conversation and respect. I was around the lab doing my research project, and he took me seriously, looked at what I did." Bernstein agreed that this is a wonderful way of encouraging students who show a special interest in one's subject, but is impatient with those who see it as the highest form of teaching. "I now see it as, in a way, the easiest form of teaching. It's easy because if you've found a student who's well enough prepared to be able to talk to you about what you know best, what could be nicer? Especially if at the same time that student is offering to help you with your research, which is often the case. Those are the people who get the attention. And I was the beneficiary of that."[13]

QUESTIONING RECEIVED OPINION

It was in graduate school at the University of California, San Diego, that Bernstein first began to question received opinion about teaching, especially its focus on identifying the "best and brightest." It was at this time too that he first encountered college instructors who thought about their practice as college teachers with tools from their own field. He credits his awakening, first, to bitter arguments about teaching philosophy among the graduate students assigned as teaching assistants in a large social psychology lecture class. In particular, Bernstein recalled an abrasive but influential operant psychologist,[14] who over the course of the semester convinced him to view teaching in a different light. The fundamental questions Bernstein's colleague posed were, "Why are you teaching? Are you teaching to maximize the amount of learning that takes place? Or are you teaching in the sense that you lay out a learning opportunity and you see how well people do at it?"

This second position, to lay out a learning opportunity and see how people do, was, of course, the received view. It had served generations of bright students well, and although Bernstein, like many of its beneficiaries, had never really embraced it, he had never questioned it either. Bernstein's fellow graduate student argued against this position from two points of view, both characteristic of behavioral psychology. "One," Bernstein explained, "is seeing nurture as the dominant variable over nature. The other is that there's no necessary benefit to rank ordering. That's one function you might have in teaching, but it's a higher benefit to the society to have more people learn. The people who learn more slowly, still learn."

Our culture's esteem for fast learning was underlined for Bernstein by his own experience in calculus:

> I was a B student in calculus in a very fast group. What I realized when I studied for tests by looking at old tests, was that it wasn't that I couldn't learn calculus because the tests from three or four weeks ago always looked easy to me. It was that I wasn't learning it as fast as the fast guys, and that what the system was doing was selecting out on rate of acquisition. And that may be what our culture calls intelligence. Now, it may be that when you're picking somebody to get your rocket to the moon, you might use that characteristic to make that selection. But it doesn't follow from that fact that you design your whole education system only to sort out on that characteristic.[15]

How then, do you design education? As Bernstein explained, his fellow graduate student (the operant psychologist) was not just inventing these ideas on his own. In fact, he introduced Bernstein to a body of research on how these ideas could actually be carried out. This is how Bernstein learned about Fred Keller, a distinguished behavioral psychologist, then recently retired from Columbia University, who saw teaching and learning as belonging "in the domain of science, more specifically in the domain of experimental psychology, especially in the analysis of behavior" (Gallup, 1998). Father of the "personalized system of instruction" developed in the early to mid 1960s, Keller advocated a kind of course design that allowed students to move through units of instruction at their own pace. In Keller Plan teaching, lectures, if given at all, were supplementary. The basic protocol was for students to study materials on their own, take and retake tests on each unit until they achieved mastery, work with a tutor to review their performance immediately after each test, move on to the next unit's materials, and start the process again. Indeed, Keller's initial presentation of this method was provocatively titled "Good-Bye, Teacher . . . ." (1968).[16]

This was not a position that would appeal to all psychologists. But in the late 1960s and early 1970s, the so-called "cognitive revolution," which eventually displaced behavioral psychology, was far from complete. Some social psychologists worked more or less openly in the behavior analysis tent. According to Bernstein:

> What had transformed me from being a straight social psychologist is that I used some ideas from the operant conditioners [i.e., behavior analysts] in my work with nurses at the hospital in San Diego, where I did "alternative service" during the Vietnam War. I had been trying for six months to have any effect whatsoever on the nurses in terms of their relations with certain kinds of patients. Got nowhere. But then I enlisted the nurses as behavioral shapers of difficult patients. Used their attention as a reward for patients who behaved well. Boom! The behavior of the patients changed instantly. I didn't care whose model it was. I just suddenly saw people who were fighting with each other getting along well. It impressed me that it worked in noisy, real-world environments, just like the Keller Plan.

Bernstein sympathized with the basic idea that lay behind Keller's work, "that learning, like much of behavior, is connected to its outcomes." Bernstein's advisor, social psychologist Ebbe Ebbesem, also liked the logic of the Keller Plan and used its methods of multiple testing and mastery requirements in the way he taught.[17] Thus, Bernstein's teaching experiences as a graduate student were informed by a literature and a practice that clearly embraced "maximizing learning" as the goal of teaching, a perspective that has grounded Bernstein's approach to teaching ever since. As he explained, "You can use what tools and understanding you have of the relation between behavior and its consequences to maximize the amount of progress people make, rather than simply sort them out on the steepness of their learning curves."[18]

KELLER PLAN TEACHING

Bernstein got an opportunity to develop his own version of Keller Plan teaching when he took his first faculty position at the University of Nebraska–Lincoln in 1973. During his job interview in the department of psychology, when asked what kind of teaching he would like to do, Bernstein said that he would like to design an introductory course in psychology based on mastery teaching ideas. The climate was right, as a growing number of faculty were experimenting with mastery teaching in the early 1970s, both at Nebraska and beyond. Bernstein recalled his excitement at discovering this community of scholars early on.

A particularly important moment occurred during a visit to Florida State University, where Bernstein had been invited to give a presentation on his research. While there, he attended a colloquium on teaching by Jack Michael, a well-known behavior analyst then at Western Michigan University.[19] For Bernstein, this "colloquium was like magic. There were a half a dozen really good ideas about how to improve what I was doing. And I went home and put all those things into my Keller Plan. It included things that a lot of college teachers in those days, and probably some still, think of as cheating: telling students ahead of time the structure of the knowledge you'd like them to understand, making a clear alignment between intellectual goals and assessment. Ideas that are all the rage now, Jack Michael was saying very articulately in 1973."

It was at this point that Bernstein, still a social psychologist, realized that his neighbors in the behavior analytic community were quite committed to teaching:

> They were not embarrassed about it. But in some sense it was arrogance, although not a bad arrogance. They believed that they understood behavior and that learning is a form of behavior. They believed that what you're trying to do with students is change how they act, and that ought to be amenable to the same kind of analysis. And it turned out that there was a written scholarship of teaching from the behavioral perspective. What [they] were saying very early was to articulate your goals clearly. Bring the known principles of motivation and performance to bear on a class. Provide prompts. Let students know what the target is. Provide multiple opportunities. Provide encouragements so that they don't quit on you. And build a system. If you build that system, many people will stay in it and you'll have a higher level of achievement, although the grades will no longer reflect differences in the rate of learning.[20]

This was an argument that mattered as higher education began to deal with a much larger, more diverse, student population than ever before. There were more first-generation college students and a smaller proportion was well prepared. Certainly it was a critical time at the University of Nebraska–Lincoln, where student enrollment had more than doubled in 1960s, growing from approximately 8,000 in 1959 to nearly 20,000 in 1969, the year of the university's centennial. In 1973, when Bernstein arrived in Lincoln, the university was scrambling to educate 21,160 students (University of Nebraska, 2001, 2002).

Psychology departments of that era felt the crunch. Since World War II, the number of degrees earned in psychology had been growing dramatically, in part because of the field's emergence as a gateway to careers in counseling, business, and social service fields.[21] From 1959 to 1969, the number of baccalaureate degrees earned in psychology increased by 318 percent, while the total number of baccalaureate degrees increased by only 102 percent. At the University of Nebraska–Lincoln, the number of faculty positions did not grow in proportion to the number of students, but Bernstein credits the vision and astute politicking of his chair, David Levine, for the fact that the psychology department was able to add nine faculty members, including Bernstein, during the early 1970s.

In his department, Bernstein was given the resources he needed to fully develop a large, introductory psychology course taught according to his own understanding of Keller principles. Another colleague in Bernstein's department also believed that he was doing Keller Plan teaching because students studied on their own and the tests were repeatable. However, this course did not use tutors, a component Bernstein and his chair believed to be central to Keller's vision, and they felt that more challenging questions should be asked on the exams. In Bernstein's course, students also studied on their own and took and retook tests to show mastery before moving on to the next unit. Bernstein's tests were open-ended and students received immediate feedback and tutoring. "The first semester, I had 30 students; second semester, I had 200," he recalled. "When I hit 350, my chair convinced the university to give me a second room, which I had 24 hours a day—two big rooms with a TA room in the middle. We had it staffed day and night. Students would come in to one room, take their tests, hand them to the TAs for grading, meet with the TAs in the next room, and leave."

At the height of this course's popularity, Bernstein was teaching 1,000 students per semester, with seven graduate teaching assistants, and 50 undergraduate TAs whom he prepared "richly and thoroughly" for their task of grading the open-ended exams. Bernstein could guarantee the reliability and validity of their judgment. "We did blind reliability checks. We could pass exams through the system and grade them 20 times, because graders did not write on the exams themselves, but on separate grading sheets. We had a really excellent quality control system." Bernstein also had a full-time computer programmer, who gave a weekly report on every test. "We knew the percent correct on every question; percent by every TA. And we had an appeal system. Double appeal. They could appeal to the graduate student first, and then to me. We knew which questions got appealed the most, which TAs got appealed the most, which TAs got overturned on appeal the most, and the waiting time to get a test graded every hour of the day."

Clearly, Keller Plan teaching could be organizationally complex, but it could also be highly efficient. Bernstein believed that his course was making $100,000 a year "profit," after expenditures for his salary, and for tuition for the TAs. It was also, of course, quite at odds with the usual way of doing things in the university. Perhaps most disturbing was that grades were handled so differently. Bernstein recalled being:

> . . . called in front of the College of Arts and Sciences grade inflation committee because my students were doing too well. So I had my first peer review, although we didn't call it that. I went to the committee, and I presented the nature of the exams, the nature of the readings, showed them the content and my intellectual goals. I described to them the teaching method, and gave them two typical student records showing that to reach mastery of a unit, they would often have to take the test three, four, or five times. And the committee said, "the students keep doing that?" I said, "Yes." And when I showed them the end result, the quality of the work, and the amount of work students did, they said, "Oh, that's great." And then they asked me to join their committee. Which I did.

Bernstein not only made his teaching public to colleagues at his university, but also gave them evidence about student learning, both important characteristics of what, 20 years later, would be called the scholarship of teaching and learning. In Bernstein's case, this came about through another invitation to explain his work. In Bernstein's third or fourth year, the dean sent a memo to the chair asking about all the resources that were being spent on the course. Bernstein wrote a memo in return, where he:

> compared the learning in the lecture section, which I also taught, with the learning in the Keller section, because it was an unusual case. You have the same instructor, same examinations, same books, the same semester . . . the difference being the structure of the course. In one case, students would go through the material in units and have to master each one. In the other, it was broken down into three big exams, though each of the exams was repeatable. In an alternate version of the lecture course, students were graded by the same TAs as those in the Keller section. They had access to the same tutoring. I had very high evaluations as a lecturer. But it was really clear. The Keller Plan section totally outperformed the lecture, even though the lecture students liked the class slightly better. One reason they liked the lecture class better is that in the Keller Plan, you don't have the option of doing "C" work. You have to do "A" work for 70 percent of the course to get a "C." That's much harder than doing "C" work the whole time. That was clearly annoying to students. But there's no magic to why the Keller Plan produces learning. You set the standards high, but you provide a lot of help. A student gets immediate conversation with the person who graded his or her test a minute

ago. And if a student does this work, he or she gets the same grade as the person who learned it well the first time. So you get motivation, you get certification of achievement, but you lose differentiation.

TEACHING VS. RESEARCH

Interest in Keller Plan teaching rose throughout the country in the 1970s but eventually ebbed. Its supporters today cite several reasons, including the time and effort it took from faculty to do it well, its departure from conventional expectations of the professor's role ("Good-Bye, Teacher"!), unusual use of grades, constant demands from colleagues and administrators for explanation, and the fact that some faculty and some publishers designed courses and materials that emphasized efficiency over quality, tarnishing the reputation of the approach (Gallup & Allan, 1996). Perhaps the realization that there were diminished rewards for teaching also played a role. This was true for Bernstein, who stopped teaching introduction to psychology altogether in the late 1970s, largely because of tensions between teaching and research in his institution's system of faculty roles and rewards.

Although fissures were beginning to show by the time of Bernstein's tenure decision, it was really only after tenure that he became aware that the balance he had struck between teaching and research, which had been acceptable for tenure, would delay his promotion to full professor and diminish his salary and his stature in the department. A very distinguished senior chair with great influence at the university had hired Bernstein and told him that while his research would be supported, his tenure would be decided on the success of this teaching project. Unfortunately, the agreement was never put in writing, and this chair stepped down the next year and died a year later. This placed Bernstein out of step with the trajectory of his university, which, in the mid-to-late 1970s, was eager to build and sustain its position as one of the smaller research-oriented state universities.[22]

Bernstein's department continued to support him, and he got through the tenure decision unscathed, although he does believe that his tenure case was critically assisted by the dean's assurance to the department that his unusually teaching-heavy portfolio would be acceptable to the university's executive committee. "I think most of my colleagues thought I was OK," Bernstein said. "They did not think I would have a great research career, but I had a lead article in the best journal in my field and people whom they had invited praised my work. It wasn't the quality that was an issue. It was the rate at which it was turning into publication. I knew that.

It wasn't an intentional sort of career trajectory choice. It was just that I so loved that course that I was willing to give it all the time it needed."[23]

Bernstein's teaching, however, was not the sole reason for his slow rate of publication. Bernstein's research on human motivation was very labor intensive and actually benefited from the access to students that his large Keller Plan course provided. With a laboratory that ran 24 hours a day, and people who lived in the laboratory for two months at a time, Bernstein explained, "You've got to have somebody there all the time. Fifteen hours a day, watching through a window. Recording everything they do. In graduate school, I did all that myself. Having this cadre of undergraduates meant I could pick the best of them to work with me on my research, which I did. So, the teaching and the research helped each other. I don't think I could have run my research without having that large a base within the undergraduate population."

Still, Bernstein knew he was underperforming according to conventional publication standards. After tenure, he said, the next chair told him many times, "'You've got to stop being such a perfectionist. You've got to be willing to work the system a little more.'" Bernstein continued:

> Actually, my most esteemed colleague at Kansas University, a very senior guy who is quite well known, was having a chat with me about that one time, and I said, "I realize that I don't put things out as often as I could." He said to me, "But whenever I see something that comes out by you, I'm always eager to read it." Now, that's an old-fashioned model, that once every five years there's something worth reading. In my old age, I've made some peace with that. What I've published, I think, is worth reading even if the numbers aren't that high.

Of course, Bernstein's chair was trying to help him, "make sure that I made full professor more quickly. He was afraid it would take a long time. And he was right. It did take a long time. So he was just trying to say, 'This is what you have to do.'" Bernstein experienced something similar earlier in his career. "I had had a Polonius-like conversation with a wonderful experimental psychologist at San Diego who was on my dissertation committee," Bernstein said:

> As I was leaving, he said, "You've got to stop doing that research you're doing. It's too slow. You know, each person is in the study for two months. You run a couple of people a year. Do something quick. Do it. Get it out. Get tenure, and then you can go back and do the things you think are important." Meant to be very helpful. Meant to save me from myself. You know, telling me that rate was more important than quality. But this is something that diminishes and demeans our work.

This preoccupation with rate over quality is, of course, at the core of Bernstein's critique of conventional attitudes toward student learning, as well.

Not long after Bernstein received tenure, he finally concluded that his work was not appreciated in his department. Convinced that he was paid less than colleagues who had served the same length of time, and suspecting that he was on the wrong side of departmental politics, Bernstein announced, to some opposition, that he would no longer teach the department's introductory course. He became convinced that his enthusiasm for the course "labeled me as somebody who had something wrong with him. Look at how much time and energy he's putting into teaching. I also felt that my opinions on key matters in the department were being dismissed and that I was not meaningfully participating in department governance. I was becoming marginalized."

Another complication was the gradual eclipse of behavioral psychology by other approaches. The tensions could be intense. For example, there was a person of influence in the Nebraska department who had begun his career as a behaviorist. "But about three or four years before I arrived in Lincoln," Bernstein said:

> . . . he had a life-changing transformation, in which he became a constructivist, rejected positivism, and began running seminars for the faculty to try to get them to abandon the scientific model of psychology. One of the people whom he most influenced was another social psychologist, who made it his major research agenda to demonstrate that any operant learning with humans was a complete artifact; it was all volitional change, and the mechanistic model couldn't possibly be right. But I was doing operant conditioning with humans, and my research was appearing in the Skinnerian journal. Some of those folks may not have wanted to see this kind of influence continue in the department.

RESEARCH YEARS

In 1982, then, determined to gain relief, Bernstein took a sabbatical that engaged him more centrally in the operant community in psychology, heightened his profile as a researcher and, for a while, changed the course of his career. Indeed, when you talk to people in his department today who were not around during Bernstein's first decade in the department, you quickly come to suspect that the man who had been known primarily for his pioneering work in undergraduate teaching had apparently disappeared from collective memory. The "old Dan" that they knew or had heard of was a dedicated and successful researcher, whose new work on teaching was seen as a somewhat surprising detour in a standard academic career. For example, his colleague Rick Bevins arrived in the mid 1990s, "after Bernstein went from a typical research program to a teaching program." Indeed, when selecting Bernstein for this study, I, too, assumed that he had taken up the scholarship of teaching after tenure and promotion. While there is some justification for this view, as we shall see in the next chapter, Bernstein did go through a very deliberate process of reinvention in this second, post-tenure and pre-promotion phase of his career.

Bernstein began his period of concentration on research by arranging to work with two well-known operant psychologists located in Baltimore, an easy commute from Washington, DC, where he was staying for family reasons. Although the operant community was increasingly embattled in the larger world of academic psychology in the 1980s, it was still vigorous and becoming a more clearly bounded subgroup within the larger discipline, with its own journals and its own section in the American Psychological Association. Bernstein's colleagues in Baltimore, one a specialist in behavioral biology at Johns Hopkins medical school, and the other at the University of Maryland Baltimore County (UMBC), were central figures in this community. Bernstein explained, "Charlie Catania at UMBC was unbelievably smart and well-read, and operant psychologists would make the pilgrimage just to be around him. And I was two doors down from his office, so I just met more great operant psychologists and got lots and lots of ideas about what was current and what was hot and what was interesting in our field. He was doing both animal and human work, so it was an unbelievable intellectual renewal. But that wasn't all. Over at the behavioral biology lab at Johns Hopkins, it was said that if there's one grant left in psychology, Joe Brady will have it. So working with Joe, I learned everything I needed to know about how to interact with the money world. We became co-principal investigators on a big grant, and he invited me to join his group at the end of the year. But I wasn't ready to give up tenure for soft money."[24]

Based on research he had conducted earlier, Bernstein launched into the new project, designing laboratory procedures to test the effects of marijuana on human motivation. Funded by a $250,000 grant over a period of three years (through the Johns Hopkins Medical School), Bernstein was able to produce conditions in which even a good deal of marijuana did not interrupt motivation. These results were something of a surprise to his colleagues. The National Institute on Drug Abuse, which had funded the study, was interested in finding out the conditions in which the expected anti-motivational effects of marijuana could be demonstrated. So, for the next several years, Bernstein and his colleagues in Baltimore explored variations in levels of motivation and drug use to find out when and how much they interacted (see, for example, Foltin, Fischman, Brady, Bernstein, Capriotti, et al., 1989; Foltin, Fischman, Brady, Bernstein, Nellis, et al., 1990).

For a while, teaching was completely off the agenda. As Bernstein explained, "The whole point of doing it was that I realized that if I continued to focus on teaching, I was going to continue to get the wrong end of everything in my department." It did make a difference, because he returned to Nebraska as recipient of a large research grant, and even though the grant went to Johns Hopkins, the outside recognition it marked brought Bernstein much needed prestige. It also bought him time. He taught one night course that first semester, assembled some undergraduates, and had a very active research lab for a number of years. "I kept up my old research, but added another kind that turned over much faster. For the first time, I started getting a stream of graduate students who were recommending me to each other. And I did very little teaching—only some advanced undergraduate courses. During the three years of the grant I hardly taught at all."

The quality of Bernstein's new work, his new string of publications, and his connections in the operant conditioning community in the 1980s and early 1990s brought invitations to give research colloquia across the country and a Fulbright to work with colleagues in Trier, Germany on a new line of research. He was appointed to the board of editors of *Behavior Analyst*, *Social Psychology Quarterly*, and the field's premiere journal, *Journal of the Experimental Analysis of Behavior*, for which he also served as associate editor from 1991 to 1994. "What was interesting," Bernstein said, "was if you were to predict my research life from what I did pre-tenure, you would not have predicted what happened afterward. It kept getting richer and bigger, not diminishing." Indeed, looking at Bernstein's vitae, Craig Nelson, a biologist at Indiana University and a colleague in the scholarship of teaching, remarked, "He really picked the research up after he quit teaching all those students. He developed a normal research career."

For a while, too, Bernstein remained aloof from departmental affairs:

> During the year in Washington it was as though nothing that happened in Lincoln, Nebraska, mattered. This is pre-email. I talked on the phone to the chair once. Gave him my vote on a hire. Other than that, I didn't even know what was going on. They didn't ask me. I didn't ask them. I wasn't writing to people. I just had no contact. I was gone. That mentality lasted four or five years after I got back. I didn't care what happened in department politics. I had my grant. I had research. I was connected to this national research community. I had journal work to do. I was starting to get better raises. The less I did for the university, the higher my standing. The less I was there, the more I was elsewhere.

Bernstein had, it seemed, finally proved himself by the rules of the modern research game.

. . . .

RESEARCH UBER ALLES

The story of Bernstein's return to teaching in the mid 1980s will be the subject for the next chapter, but let us end this one with a vignette from Bernstein's promotion to full professor in 1993. By that time, according to Bernstein's colleagues, it is quite likely that Bernstein could have made a strong case on the basis of his new teaching activities, including his participation in several important departmental and campus teaching projects. However, there was some uncertainty about whether this would persuade the levels beyond the department, since Bernstein's promotion came up before the change in climate at the university that he helped to bring about. According to Bernstein's departmental colleague Ross Thompson, the issue therefore became "how to make a sufficiently satisfactory research case so that it would pass if somebody at a higher level were still applying a research *uber alles* approach."

But there were also Bernstein's own preferences or, as Thompson phrased it, his "self-presentation" to take into account. Bernstein, who worked so hard to establish himself by the most stringent academic standards after years as an assistant professor known more for teaching than research, insisted that promotion papers give prominence to his research accomplishments. Indeed, Bernstein is impatient with younger faculty who sometimes assume, with his current high profile in teaching, that teaching rather than research played the major role in his promotion. As his colleague Cal Garbin said, "I've heard from some people that Bernstein decided that he was going to get promoted, started publishing, and got full professorship. But other people said, 'You can call it publication, but he got it because he's a great teacher.' Now, the second one seems to annoy him. I'm not sure why."

Bernstein's reasons, of course, include his desire to be recognized as a research scholar. But they also register his sense that teaching is often not appreciated in the academy for the intense intellectual effort that it can involve. "Great teachers" may be lauded for many reasons, but usually not for the quality of thinking that underlies the design and teaching of a course. However, gaining recognition for the intellectual work in teaching—not just his own, but everyone's—is the very problem to which Bernstein turned his considerable talents in the later part of his career.

NOTES

1. This quotation is from Bernstein, Jonson, and Smith (2000), pp. 77–78.

2. I found this same facility among Bernstein's departmental colleagues. Perhaps it reflects the field's commitment to defining concepts operationally in terms that can be explored experimentally. The early practice of American psychology, as represented by the work of William James and G. Stanley Hall, highlighted the

importance of tangible behaviors, both as the visible evidence of an individual's thoughts, and as the means of adapting to environmental conditions. As American psychology emerged as a distinct and increasingly popular discipline at the turn of the 20th century, its original contributions were scientific experiments that examined the concrete behavioral components of adaptation. See Leahey (1991).

3. Data regarding students and percents and numbers of institutions are from the U.S. Census Bureau's *Historical Statistics of the United States* (1975, pp. 382–383). Information on the increase of faculty numbers from 1950 to 1970 is located in Metzger (1987) as cited in Rosovsky and Hartley (2002), p. 2.

4. Jossey-Bass was actually established in 1967, but began publishing on higher education in 1969.

5. Notable examples of large-scale curricular revision from this period include those at Brown University, Sterling College, and Alverno College; innovative programs and colleges include the new University of California Experimental College (1965), Hampshire College (1970), Kresge College at the University of California, Santa Cruz (1970), New College at the University of Alabama (1971), the College of Human Services (1970), and Metropolitan State University (1972). As a whole, such experimentation offered new program formats, different course scheduling, expanded subject foci, increased access for nontraditional students, and new educational providers (Grant & Riesman, 1978; Kerr, 1993; Levine, 1978). While Kerr (1993) and Levine (1978) provide descriptive taxonomies of these innovations, Grant and Riesman (1978) offer a different analytical approach. They distinguish between "telic" reforms ("attempts at change that embody a distinctive set of ends or purposes") and "popular" reforms, resulting from "increases in student autonomy, new patterns of organization, and attempts to respond to the demands of minorities and other previously disenfranchised groups" (p. 2). See Hannan and Silver (2000) for developments in England at the same time.

6. According to Knoll (1995), Centennial College opened in 1969 with a curriculum defined by student interests and responsive to student concerns. At the same time that Centennial College was proposed to the regents, the vice chancellor for academic affairs also proposed a Teaching Council for "the encouragement, support, and coordination of innovation and experimentation in the teaching program" (Knoll, 1995, p. 150). The University Studies program began in 1970 as a nonresidential, interdisciplinary program encouraging independent studies and tutorials. ADAPT (Accent on Developing Advanced Processes of Thought) originated in the early 1970s from informal faculty lunch discussions focused on alternative teaching strategies.

7. Throughout the 1950s and 1960s, government funding of research contributed to the increased resources available to postsecondary institutions. During this period, federal funding increased incrementally until the launching of Sputnik in 1957, at which point increases in state funding and huge jumps in federal resources directed support to basic research. While defense-related research was the first priority, resources were also extended to other areas through the Department of Health, Education, and Welfare, and later through the National Endowment for the Arts and the National Endowment for the Humanities. Although this support was disproportionately concentrated in the highest status institutions, it represented an important source of funds for others as well (Freeland, 1992).

8. According to Sherry Ortner, the ethnic backgrounds of the 1955 graduating class of Weequahick High School was approximately "80% Jewish, 13% other white ethnic groups, and 7% black" (see Levine, 1996, p. 5).

9. For recent examples from Roth, both of which include teachers in the Newark schools as important characters, see *American Pastoral* (1997) and *I Married a Communist* (1998). Ortner's book on Weequahick High School is *New Jersey Dreaming: Capital, Culture, and the Class of '58* (2003). See also Ortner, 1993, 1996, and 1998. Curiously, I was amazed to find out that Weequahick High School was also the alma mater of my sister-in-law, Lilian Vigdor, who graduated in 1940, and recalled Bernstein's father fondly as her homeroom teacher and head of the English department. She still treasures the poem he wrote for her in her yearbook—something he did then for many of his homeroom students.

10. Albert H. Hastorf received a Ph.D. in social psychology from Princeton University. In addition to being a professor of psychology and professor of human biology at Stanford University (now emeritus), he served as a vice president at Stanford, as well as provost and dean of the School of Humanities and Sciences. His research has explored social interaction and social perception, and includes a famous study with Hadley Cantril of a college football game between Princeton and Dartmouth. When interviewed later, fans for each team shared their reactions, and described distinctly different versions of the same event. From this study, they conclude that:

> There is no such "thing" as a "game" existing "out there" in its own right which people merely "observe." The "game" "exists" for a person and is experienced by him only in so far as certain happenings have significances in terms of his purpose. Out of all the occurrences going on in the environment, a person selects those that have some significance for him from his own egocentric position in the total matrix. (Hastorf & Cantril, 1954, p. 133)

11. Bernstein was an undergraduate from 1964 to 1968. Stanford's "History of the School of Humanities and Sciences" notes that for 1964, "Psychology is ranked as the number one department in the nation by the American Council on Education. This position is sustained for 35 years (and counting)." This was the time when Bernstein was an undergraduate (1963–1967). Based on a reputational survey of department chairs in 1964, Stanford was tied for first on the quality of its graduate faculty with Harvard University (Cartter, 1966). In a follow-up reputational survey of faculty in leading departments, Stanford was ranked first on the quality of its graduate faculty and on the effectiveness of its graduate program (Roose & Andersen, 1970). The National Research Council ranked Stanford's psychology department first in 1982 and 1993 for both the scholarly quality of its faculty and the effectiveness of its graduate program (Goldenberger, Maher, & Flatteau, 1995, p. 607). Today, Stanford's graduate program in psychology still ranks at the top according to *U.S. News & World Report* (2001).

12. Bernstein has gone back to Stanford over the years to visit his former professors:

> There's a political scientist I still keep up with, whom I recently asked about his perception of what he was doing then as a teacher. I would have charac-

terized his teaching as just straight out of the mill. But he talked for two hours about his intentional and planful forms of teaching, the way he structured things. He had given a great deal of thought to which ideas would work as teaching ideas. I've had similar conversations with Al Hastorf.

For stark contrast, consider Sylvia Nasar's description of the disturbed mathematical genius and Nobel laureate John Nash's undergraduate courses in calculus at MIT in the 1950s: "His lectures were closer to free association than exposition." A colleague commented, "He didn't care whether the students learned or not, made outrageous demands, and talked about subjects that were either irrelevant or far too advanced" (1998, pp. 139–140).

13. The same John Nash, whose lectures were disorganized and whose classroom behavior former students describe as "flamboyant" and even "mischievous" (Nasar, 1998, p. 140) could be quite different one on one. According to Nasar:

> Nash could be charming to students he regarded as mathematically talented, and such students found much to admire. To a select few, often undergraduates, Nash made himself "very, very available for chatting about mathematics," Barry Mazur, a number theorist at Harvard who first encountered Nash during his freshman year at MIT, recalled. "It was amazing what he was willing to talk about. There was a sense of infinite time in every conversation." (p. 141)

14. Operant conditioning is an approach to behavioral psychology that highlights the importance of the consequences that result from specific, voluntary behaviors. In essence, an individual's experience of the consequences of a certain behavior affects the likelihood that he or she will engage in that behavior again. From this perspective, learning consists of modifying one's behavior in accordance with the anticipated outcomes. Theorists associated with the development of this approach in psychology include Edward Thorndike and B. F. Skinner.

15. Psychologist Howard Gardner made a similar point in a *New York Times* op-ed on SAT testing policies entitled, "Test for Aptitude, Not for Speed." He wrote, "Nothing of consequence would be lost by getting rid of timed tests by the College Board or, indeed, by universities in general. Few tasks in life—and very few tasks in scholarship—actually depend on being able to read passages or solve math problems rapidly" (2002, p. A23). Perhaps the connection Americans make between rate of acquisition and intelligence is related to their penchant for attributing intelligence to innate ability—as opposed to, say, the Japanese, who are more likely to attribute intelligence to hard work (see, e.g., chapter five of the cross-cultural study by Stevenson & Stigler, 1992).

16. Keller himself identified the essential features of a personalized instruction course as: "(1) The go-at-your-own-pace feature, which permits a student to move through the course at a speed commensurate with his ability and other demands on his time. (2) The unit-perfection requirement for advance, which lets the student go ahead to new material only after demonstrating mastery of that which preceded. (3) The use of lectures and demonstrations as vehicles of motivation, rather than sources of critical information. (4) The related stress upon the written word in teacher-student communications; and, finally: (5) The use of proctors, which per-

mits repeated testing, immediate scoring, almost unavoidable tutoring, and a marked enhancement of the personal–social aspect of the educational process" (1968, p. 83).

17. Ebbe Ebbeson has continued as a professor of social psychology at UCSD. His interests include cognitive psychology, learning and motivation, and the organization of social systems. He has also done work regarding psychology and the law, including the reliability of eyewitness reports and the influence on jurors of pre-trial bias.

18. Bernstein added, "I sometimes joke with students. I say, 'Hey, you know, if I thought that's what I was doing, I'd just give you an IQ test first day of class, hand out the grades, and then we'd go on and teach.'"

19. Dr. Jack Michael joined the faculty of Western Michigan University in 1967. According to the Western Michigan Department of Psychology website, "his research interests include behavior analysis theory, verbal behavior, and instructional technology. He received the Distinguished Teaching Award from the American Psychological Association in 1971 . . . [and] was president of the Association for Behavior Analysis in 1979 and of Division 25 of the American Psychological Association in 1983" (Western Michigan University, n.d.).

20. Michael recommended a book edited by J. Gilmour Sherman, with 41 essays by faculty who were experimenting with the Keller Plan (1974). Indeed, when Bernstein started teaching a course for his TAs called "The Teaching of College Psychology," he asked them to read another collection of essays by Keller Plan teachers, edited by Sherman and colleagues (1982).

21. At least one commentator cites other reasons for psychology's popularity. Gilgen contends that disciplines such as psychology "permit individuals who are delayed in going to college because of a war, or a false career start, or those with poor elementary and secondary school training, a chance to work toward a higher degree. It is very difficult, if a person starts late or has a poor education through high school, to do well in college physics. With adequate motivation, however, he or she will probably be able to handle psychology" (1982, p. 27).

22. The University of Nebraska–Lincoln was first classified as a Research University I in the 1994 edition of the Carnegie Classification of Institutions of Higher Education. At that time only 30 institutions met the criteria of awarding 50 or more doctoral degrees each year and, in addition, receiving $40 million or more annually in federal support.

23. At the point of the tenure decision, Bernstein had published two articles. "Reinforcement and substitution in humans: A multiple-response analysis" (Bernstein, 1978) reports findings from his laboratory experiments. "Reliability and fairness of grading in a mastery program" (Bernstein, 1979) discusses the intensive TA training required for students assisting with his Keller Plan course. During the same period, Bernstein presented his laboratory research at several experimental psychology conferences. He also had several more articles in the publication pipeline, which came out in the early 1980s.

24. A. Charles Catania received his Ph.D. in psychology at Harvard and has been a member of the faculty at The University of Maryland, Baltimore County for over three decades. He is a former editor of the *Journal of the Experimental Analysis*

of Behavior and a trustee of the Cambridge Center for Behavioral Studies. His research interests include the psychology of learning, behavior analysis, and verbal behavior. Joseph V. Brady is a professor of neuroscience and director of the Behavioral Biology Research Center at Johns Hopkins University School of Medicine. He received a Ph.D. in behavioral biology from the University of Chicago and served as the first president of the American Psychological Association's Division 25 (Experimental Analysis of Behavior). His research interests are behavioral physiology and behavioral pharmacology.

3

Recognizing Teaching as Serious Intellectual Work

. . . .

Teaching university-level courses is a form of serious intellectual work that can be as challenging and demanding as discovery research.[1]

It is not easy for people in higher education to recognize teaching as serious intellectual work, but the reason may lie less in the academy's romance with research than in its stance toward teaching itself. The resources and reputation that successful research can bring to individual faculty, their departments, and their institutions play a role, of course. So does the fact that most scholars are not prepared professionally in teaching as they are in research. Still, as Lee Shulman has argued, the most strategic difference between research and teaching lies not in the value academics place on research but in their treatment of teaching as something done not in the "community of scholars," but in the classroom behind closed doors:

> I now believe that the reason teaching is not more valued in the academy is because the way we treat teaching removes it from the community of scholars. It is not that universities diminish the importance of teaching because they devalue the act itself; it is not that research is seen as having more intrinsic value than teaching. Rather, we celebrate those aspects of our lives and work that can become . . . "community property." (1993, p. 6)

Strengthening intellectual communities that can recognize and advance college and university teaching is a second basic step in the scholarship of teaching and learning. What this means, Shulman goes on to suggest, is reconnecting teaching to the disciplines, making teaching visible through "artifacts that capture its richness and complexity," making teaching amenable to peer judgment, and, more generally, creating a climate where people talk about teaching and learning, and read, critique, and build on each other's work (1993, p. 7). Indeed, when teaching is treated *this* way, it enters the realm of scholarship, broadly construed, and can be recognized—like other kinds of scholarly work—for its qualities of thought and skill and for the significance of its results (Boyer, 1990; Glassick, Huber, & Maeroff, 1997). In this chapter, I follow Dan Bernstein as he becomes one of the leaders, first locally and then nationally, in efforts to gain recognition for teaching and learning as serious intellectual work.

This later stage in Bernstein's career took shape in the midst of a revival of interest in undergraduate teaching, which began in the mid-to-late 1980s and continues today. Higher education's "golden age" had ended by the mid 1970s, and the recessionary decade that followed was not, on the whole, very kind to teaching. Enrollments leveled off. Funding decreased.[2] While educational and pedagogical issues continued to concern faculty and institutions, the excitement, the spotlight, and the promise of the recent innovations were no longer there. Austere budgets left little room for educational experimentation, while the tightening job market also pulled air from the flames. In the heightened competition for resources, departments that could attract external funding were at a distinct advantage (Slaughter & Leslie, 1997). As competition for academic positions intensified, expectations for research productivity rose.

These were the years when the "old-boy" network in hiring receded, when "personal attributes" declined as important factors in tenure and promotion,[3] and when more formalized and complex criteria for advancement spread (McCaughey, 1994; Seldin, 1984, 1993; Whitman & Weiss, 1982). These changes helped open the professorial ranks to women, minorities, and Ph.D.s from newer graduate programs and less prestigious schools. But the attempt to make evaluation more objective also fed a system in which it made more sense for young faculty to concentrate their efforts on grantsmanship and publication than on areas that were less easily quantified: teaching, service to the institution, and outreach (Glassick, Huber, & Maeroff, 1997). While efforts to evaluate teaching more objectively also spread throughout the academy at this time, the tool of choice was student evaluations, whose methods and effects were highly controversial and did little to foster the scholarly dimension of teaching or to bring teaching the recognition it deserved (Marsh, 1987; Ory, 2000; Seldin, 1984; Theall, 2000).[4]

This lull in attention to teaching and learning did not last long. Indeed, a new arc of reform arose after public concern about the country's flagging economic prospects gained voice in *A Nation at Risk* (1983), the provocative report of the United States National Commission on Excellence in Education that outlined the weaknesses of American elementary and secondary schools. Questions soon followed about how well universities were educating undergraduates, and pressure grew from parents, legislators, and the media for higher education to do better and do more. There was new interest in general education, which had largely been dismantled in the previous 20 years (Association of American Colleges, 1985; Boyer & Levine, 1981)[5]; traditionalists and multiculturalists debated the content of the curriculum (Bloom, 1992; Searle, 1990); educators explored the ins and outs of assessing student outcomes (Ewell, 1987, 1991); and faculty and administrators across higher education began to grapple with evaluation systems that seemed to pit teaching against research (Boyer, 1990).

Like universities around the country in the 1970s and 1980s, the University of Nebraska–Lincoln suffered disappointing budgets, underfunded academic programs, student unrest, and faculty alarm. By 1979, a faculty committee calculated that "money available for operation of the University in Lincoln had declined by 22 percent over the previous ten years even as student enrollment increased by 5 percent and research activity supported by outside grants had increased by more that 100 percent. In real terms faculty salaries had decreased by some 12 percent" (Knoll, 1995, p. 175). In Nebraska, as in the nation at large, there was public concern. In 1984, a citizens committee pressed the legislature and university to support growth in the university's capacity to support economic development in the state through applied research, and this was followed by faculty action to win approval of a budget that would bring salaries in line with peer institutions. These concerns led to the largest university appropriation in 12 years in 1988, and a future that finally looked promising again (Knoll, 1995).

While overshadowed by budgetary concerns, the national renewal of interest in teaching and learning played out at the University of Nebraska–Lincoln as well. A new honors program was established at Nebraska in 1985; a Chancellor's Committee on General Education issued a report in 1987, and in 1986 a small group of campus activists, including Bernstein, began meeting to discuss ways of bringing better recognition to teaching in the university's system of faculty roles and rewards. As we saw in Chapter 2, Bernstein had turned his attention from teaching to research after realizing, with a deep sense of betrayal, that one might gain tenure for teaching, but not commensurate compensation or departmental respect. Thus, when he returned to a full teaching schedule in the mid to late 1980s, it was not only to answer the call of the classroom, but also to address policies and practices that were, he believed, still putting teaching down. When Bernstein talked with me about his later career, he spoke of his own trajectory of teaching and inquiry into learning, but also of his efforts in a succession of projects to gain recognition in the academy for teaching as intellectual work.

(RE)TURN TO TEACHING

Bernstein recalled his change of heart:

> I played out my research effort for five, six, seven years. And then in the late 1980s, I kind of looked around at the campus, and realized that systemically teaching was still undervalued, and got into a discussion group of people who were trying to find a way to bring teaching more into balance with our nominal mission.

Formed in 1986, this discussion group drew together people from a number of fields who were interested in enhancing both the quality and status of teaching at Nebraska. Among other things, these activists put together a proposal to the Fund for the Improvement of Postsecondary Education (FIPSE), for a project entitled "From Regard to Reward: Improving Teaching at a Research-Oriented University." From 1987 to 1994, this effort involved an increasingly large number of people, first as they pursued the work on their own campus and then, under a "dissemination" grant, with other campuses, as well.

A planning grant enabled the project leaders to conduct a faculty survey that showed widespread perception among faculty members that mission and rewards at Nebraska had become misaligned. The group then made an interesting move in its strategy to address this problem. Instead of assuming that the first step was for administrators to take, they proposed that the key lay with faculty themselves "working within the administrative structures closest to them—the departments" (Barrett & Narveson, 1992, p. 3). FIPSE agreed that this was an intriguing approach and awarded Nebraska a three-year grant to design and implement a process in which faculty working in departments would "define what were rewardable activities in teaching, what would constitute documentary evidence of those activities, how the evidence would be evaluated, what weight teaching would carry in determinations of retention, tenure, promotion, and merit, and what actions by administrators would demonstrate that they took seriously the departmental plans for the reward of teaching" (Barrett & Narveson, 1992, p. 3).

Overall, 27 departments in five colleges developed written plans approved by their faculties, with psychology, led by Bernstein, as one of the first to get discussions underway. Meanwhile, administrators made efforts to remove roadblocks beyond the department level, considering suggestions submitted by the faculty such as providing resources for faculty development, increasing training for graduate student teaching assistants, clarifying institutional mission, and establishing incentives for departments that develop good plans for improving teaching and report results. Like similar projects around the country, this one connected to the national scene by circulating reading lists and copies of important books

to participants, organizing presentations on the work at major conferences, and bringing national leaders to campus to speak.[6]

With Bernstein as departmental coordinator, psychology had a head
start. He had already initiated a voluntary program of peer consultation,
or "teaching circles," into the department, and encouraged the department's executive committee to make clear distinctions in merit ratings
based on teaching. As one of his colleagues explained:

> He insisted on differentiating the ratings of teaching for merit pay.
> Research and service were rated on a 1 to 6 scale, but although there
> was an implicit 6-point scale for teaching, virtually everyone got a 3
> or 4. Bernstein had argued that if you don't have variation, it won't
> affect behavior. And he had worked successfully to get that changed.

Building on these efforts for the FIPSE project, the psychology department
proposed to incorporate "teaching circles" into its formal teaching improvement efforts, strengthen support for graduate student teaching assistants, formalize the collection of information about teaching, include
sources of information beyond student course evaluations, and gain support to apply the merit ratings to this wider range of information and
effort.[7]

At the same time that he was working toward balancing mission and
rewards at his institution, Bernstein began to seek balance in his own
career. After several years of buying time away from the classroom for
research, Bernstein recalled:

> I started paying more attention to my teaching, and got back up to
> teaching a full assignment of one graduate and three undergraduate
> courses a year. I kept finding great undergraduate students and most
> of the graduate students were good, so I had a lot of people to work
> with on research. And I was getting more engaged in the fun of think-
> ing about the quality of my undergraduate teaching. It was that sense
> of balance that I was looking for. I had had a long run of putting
> research way at the top. In fact, during that time, we had a negotiated
> weighting of work in our department, and I was 60 percent research,
> officially. So I was evaluated that way. Earlier, at the times when I'd
> been teaching the introductory course, I'd been 60 percent teaching,
> when the normal load would be 45 percent research, 45 percent teach-
> ing, and 10 percent service. And so I got into balance. And I got the
> university trustees' teaching award and a Fulbright for my research.

Bernstein went up for promotion and was made full professor on a case
based more on his research record than on his teaching and teaching
activism, and took sabbatical after the decision on his Fulbright fellowship
to collaborate with a colleague at the University of Trier on a new line of
work concerning motivation in children. But when he returned, he

decided that he could finally afford to do what he wanted. He kept a conventional lab going with his graduate student research group in social psychology, but dropped his long-term lab with its expense and time commitments. Bernstein recalled this moment clearly: "I very consciously said, 'OK. I'm a full professor. I can do whatever I want now. What do I want to do?' And what I decided was that I wanted to really focus on teaching."

THE NETWORK GROWS

As far as teaching and learning were concerned, Bernstein was a cosmopolitan at his own university. He had done workshops for the people at Nebraska's teaching and learning center. He had met the people who had been involved in the older experimental projects in teaching and learning at Nebraska, and in new ones, like its honors program.[8] And through the FIPSE project, he had learned more about innovations in other departments, like English and the School of Agriculture, where people were thinking carefully about teaching and learning, and doing interesting things to represent teaching in other ways than just student evaluations. When, in 1992–1993, Nebraska got another FIPSE grant to disseminate its departmental process for the recognition and reward of teaching, Bernstein helped take Nebraska's show on the road. He started getting used to the idea of meeting faculty from other institutions and other disciplines, all of whom had the same general concern—that teaching is important, that it wasn't well-represented in personnel systems, and that their institutions needed a better way to do it.

Some of the people Bernstein met at this time were hooked into a larger network of conversation, consultation, and concern. Barbara Walvoord, former head of the Center for Teaching and Learning at Notre Dame, was one. In the early 1990s, Walvoord told me, she was directing a "Writing across the Curriculum" program at the University of Cincinnati, which was then "the university's only real faculty development program," and she was "looking for a way to address departmental change in a very decentralized major research university where departments are extraordinarily autonomous."[9] She heard about Nebraska's attempt to engage departments in their own deliberations about evaluating teaching for promotion, tenure, and merit at a national conference. When the University of Cincinnati became a participant in Nebraska's dissemination project, she visited Lincoln several times and several Nebraska people came to Cincinnati to "talk and exchange stories and information and so on." As the psychology department at Nebraska was much involved in the program, Walvoord recalled, "I got to know Dan and was very impressed with his ability to present in a vivid way to faculty what they were doing." Later, Walvoord invited Bernstein to join in an evaluation that she was doing at

Indiana University's Faculty Colloquium on Excellence in Teaching, and thus did his own network expand.

Bernstein's campus connections led to further engagements. For example, when he heard through his department chair that Nebraska was going to participate in AAHE's national Peer Review of Teaching Project, he went to see the academic affairs people right away. Why, he wanted to know, hadn't the Department of Psychology been invited? They were much more active on teaching issues than two of the three departments involved. They might have been matched by English, which, like psychology, had been in the pioneer "class" for the FIPSE project a few years before. But at that time, Bernstein thought, not much was happening in music or mathematics. The people at academic affairs explained to Bernstein that the selection had been made by AAHE, not themselves. However, they wanted Bernstein to participate as their representative, the provost's substitute. Looking back, Bernstein said, "It was a real watershed point."

With AAHE's Peer Review of Teaching Project, Bernstein entered a national world of teaching and learning virtually unknown to most of his colleagues—and indeed, to Bernstein himself. "It's surprising how insulated academic communities can be," Bernstein said. He reminded me during our interviews:

> . . . you have to understand that in the life of the normal faculty member, things like the American Association for Higher Education and the Association of American Colleges and Universities were completely off the radar. Nobody reads *The Chronicle of Higher Education*. Nobody reads *Change* magazine. The only people who knew about AAHE were the people involved with the American Association of University Professors, and they were suspicious. I wasn't an administrator, so I didn't know what the American Council on Education was. And in fact, most of my colleagues still don't. So it doesn't surprise me that I was unaware of all this at the time.

He had certainly never heard of the new project's leaders—AAHE's Pat Hutchings and Stanford University professor, Lee Shulman. Nor was he particularly sanguine about what might happen. "I didn't quite come with a chip on my shoulder, but I came with very low expectations. I was unaware that there was anybody out there thinking about college teaching who was really going to open my eyes. I mean, I was spending a lot more time thinking about college teaching than everybody else I knew."

THE NATIONAL SCENE

The Peer Review of Teaching Project was launched by AAHE in 1994 as a two-year national project designed to engage faculty as professional colleagues in teaching, as they are in research. By "peer review" the organizers did not mean just peer observations of one's classroom teaching, which is what the term most often conjured up for faculty at the time. Instead, the project experimented with a variety of methods to get colleagues talking to each other productively about specific courses, how they were planned and taught and what the students learned. Twelve universities, including the University of Nebraska–Lincoln, agreed to take part, with volunteers from at least three pilot departments: chemistry or mathematics in the sciences; English or history or music in the humanities; and for most participants, an engineering or management field (American Association for Higher Education, 1995; Hutchings, 1996).[10]

Bernstein may have started with low expectations, but when he arrived at the initial meeting of the project in Stanford in June 1994, he was already impressed by the intellectual content of the three exercises participants were asked to do beforehand, especially by "how well framed they were and the fact that they targeted student learning." "The first exercise," he explained:

> . . . was about the content of the course. What are the intellectual decisions you made? The second was about instructional practice. It largely focused on the three prepared classroom visits. It was a step forward because they were *prepared* classroom visits. You visited with the person ahead of time. You did the reading the students would do. You were not just dropping in. And it was a step forward because you were basically giving your colleague feedback on whether she or he is accomplishing his or her own stated goals. The third exercise was to pick a sample of your own students' work that's great and write about it. And then write what you think of your colleague's student's work.

In fact, all of the exercises were done in pairs, with people exchanging their work and commenting on it. They also talked about the exercises and their experiences with them at the summer institute.[11]

This last was what really caught Bernstein's attention. The first two exercises—examining the syllabus, and visiting a colleague's class—were elaborated versions of familiar, if not frequent, activities. Faculty often look over colleagues' syllabi, sometimes in order to approve a new course, sometimes in tenure and promotion reviews, and sometimes just to get ideas for a course of their own. Faculty observe each other's classes less often, and certainly with less confidence about what they're looking at or for than when they look at syllabi. Talking to each other about samples of student learning was quite rare. Suddenly, here was a project that put student learning at the center of the conversation. As the project's mission statement stated:

A first premise . . . is that the central goal of university teaching in the 21st century must be to teach for understanding. As more and more faculty are realizing, emphases on facts, and mastering information, must give way to more active forms of learning—forms that bring students to deep understandings, and engage them in making meaning. Progress on this difficult front means attention to the kinds of teaching that engage students more deeply and thoughtfully in subject-matter learning and in making connections between their lives and their academic studies. It means turning classrooms into communities of scholarly inquiry in which students can be authentic participants. (Hutchings, 1994, p. 4)

Bernstein's appreciation of the way this project saw teaching as focused on student learning was deepened by his admiration for "the magic" of its leaders. Bernstein compared the experience to the immediate affinity he felt for social psychology when taking his first seminar with Stanford psychologist Al Hastorf. "I mean," Bernstein explained, "Lee and Pat are smart people. They say interesting things. They say things that add value to my understanding. I was unprepared for that. And I came away from that week believing that this was valuable and useful intellectual work." So valuable was the project in Bernstein's eyes, that when he wrote his report for his provost, he said that Nebraska should have summer fellowships to do a similar project that faculty could apply for. That provost was Al Kilgore, an ally and mentor of Bernstein's and a strong advocate for teaching and learning at Nebraska. In this case, Bernstein said jokingly, "Al just threw across the desk at me the FIPSE RFP [request for proposals], and said, 'You want summer fellowships? Write a grant.'"

Bernstein did so, but with little expectation of being funded:

I had been part of Nebraska's earlier FIPSE projects, so I knew how FIPSE worked. I looked at the book, and it turned out that you can write a five-page proposal and the probability of even being asked to write a full proposal is only ten percent. They had 2,200 applications; 200 were asked for a full proposal; and only 60 were funded. So I figured I'd repay Kilgore by writing five pages and then I'm done. I could go back to him and say, 'OK, I tried to get money, now you find the money.'

Against the odds, Bernstein did get invited to write a full proposal, and he went at it with the grantsmanship he had learned years before from his research colleague in Baltimore. He consulted with a former FIPSE official who was working in Lincoln on Nebraska's Higher Education Commission, who gave Bernstein a great deal of useful feedback both on the proposal and on the process. At his suggestion, Bernstein called FIPSE's program officers to talk and ask questions like "What do you think of this, and what do you think of that, and what do you think is missing?" and he listened to what they said.

In the end, Bernstein got both the FIPSE grant to direct a three-year peer review project at Nebraska and matching funds from the University for the faculty fellowships that FIPSE itself wouldn't fund. The basic idea was from AAHE's Peer Review of Teaching Project, but with a special twist. As Bernstein put it: "Less than a year after I first met Lee and Pat, I had written a grant to franchise, market, and evaluate their product. I had committed to a design that would evaluate peer review as a program, by looking for changes, improvements, in student performance, because the FIPSE director and I both agreed, that was the point. He said, 'you know, I'm tired of funding faculty to sit around and talk to each other.' And I agreed with him. If this isn't going to change student learning, then it's kind of not worth the time and the trouble."[12]

Priority Crunch

From 1995 to 1998, Bernstein orchestrated three waves of peer review fellows drawn from all the colleges of his campus. Working through the university's Teaching Council, they selected a "Noah's Ark model of people in pairs." There were two from English, two from agriculture, two from law, two from business, and two from several other departments, all following the three exercises from AAHE's Peer Review of Teaching Project, reading each other's material, providing each other with feedback on the substantive issues that their students were facing, and on their decisions about what to cover. Not everyone responded well. Paul Savory, a participant from industrial engineering, recalled a colleague who was offended when he suggested that she might want to use a different book for her course. Savory himself regarded the experience of talking seriously about teaching as transformative:

> Before I even was involved in peer review, I had won department and college teaching awards. But as a result of having gone through the peer review process, Dan really challenged my way of thinking. He made me focus more on the goal to get student learning. I used to be a traditional lecturer, and now I actually don't even like standing in front of the class any more. . . . I use groups now; I use discussions; I've integrated projects into the curriculum. Thinking about students' mastering the material has completely changed my entire teaching style.

Meanwhile, Bernstein continued to meet with Pat Hutchings's and Lee Shulman's Peer Review of Teaching group at AAHE's annual conference on Faculty Roles and Rewards. He was very much influenced by the speakers at those conferences, Eugene Rice, Roy Roemer, Steven Portch, Richard Lyman, Donald Kennedy, and by the sessions.[13] Take, for example, the 1996 meeting, where Bernstein and colleagues from Nebraska organized a session on departmental implementation of peer review. According to the meeting program, they would have been able to take in numerous sessions on teaching at that conference, on topics like assessing student learning, institutional priorities and faculty rewards, teaching portfolios, and "pedagogical colloquia" in faculty hiring (American Association for Higher Education, 1996). Bernstein recalled:

> This was an amazing thing for somebody who had been almost wholly inside my field of study two years earlier. To suddenly catch on. I even bought tapes of some of the talks, because I wanted to use them to start a conversation with faculty. I felt they were talking about what I'd been talking about to myself for 20 years, but now there were other people to talk to about it, some of whom actually cared.

Moving into a new academic community can have consequences for one's participation in the old ones, and for Bernstein, the exhilaration was balanced by pain. He had not planned to get the FIPSE grant and had made other commitments. At about the same time that he launched into his own peer review project at Nebraska, he was also beginning what was supposed to be a three-year term as editor of *The Behavior Analyst*, an important scholarly journal published by the Association for Behavior Analysis—not a position one would turn down.[14] Adding to his burden, Bernstein was editing a volume of papers from The Nebraska Symposium on Motivation, his department's internationally renowned annual event. As Bernstein explained, "It's the one thing our department was known for. It puts us on the intellectual map of the field."

This was a priority crush of the first order, in which what mattered most to Bernstein became clear. The symposium proceedings came out well, if a bit late, but the journal work suffered and Bernstein resigned as editor a year early. "When push came to shove, when I had to either deal with the grant or deal with the journal, I did the teaching stuff first. . . . The thing that really survived out of it was the peer review project. And all the data on student learning we were collecting." Ross Thompson, a departmental colleague who has known Bernstein since 1981, described this moment in Bernstein's career as a:

> . . . distinct shift toward asking these kinds of questions about the scholarship of teaching—questions that weren't new for him, but what was new was focusing his scholarly activity on them as opposed to the more conventional experimental research. In a sense it was a

change of identity, but it was also maintaining Dan's penchant for doing things out of the mainstream. And it's taken a while for him to change the culture at Nebraska in such a way that those contributions can be appreciated.[15]

CHANGING THE CULTURE OF TEACHING

Changing the culture of teaching at Nebraska (and beyond), did, in fact, become an important theme of Bernstein's subsequent work. This came about, first, because approximately halfway through his FIPSE project, he invited some people from academic affairs to a meeting to hear about the data the peer review team was collecting. As Bernstein explained:

Because of the incredibly detailed evaluation component that FIPSE requires, we were gathering all kinds of information from people's classes. We were surveying students, we were gathering student work and analyzing it for Bloom's taxonomy.[16] We were describing whether they gave stages in the preparation of assignments or just one version, whether they allowed repeated testing or not, what percentage of time was on lecture, what percentage of assignments were at what levels of thinking. And we were collecting that all because this wonderful guy whom I'd hired as my evaluation consultant had helped us think through what you could possibly want to know about whether or not our work is having an impact. It might not be apparent if, for example, more people aren't getting As, but what constitutes an A is much richer. We couldn't have answered that question if we hadn't collected the data.

When the people from academic affairs saw the data from the first year or so of the project, Bernstein recalled:

They were blown away! They're under assessment pressure, they can't get anybody to tell them anything about what's going on in classes, and we have this gold mine of data about teaching. That one decision I made to invite those people made everything else possible. Instead of being a faculty-driven project over here on the corner with some academic affairs sponsorship, our work suddenly became really valuable to academic affairs.[17]

This connection made it possible for Bernstein's peer review project at Nebraska to be extended for a fourth year, with funding from the local Nebraska Foundation when the FIPSE grant ran out.

Meanwhile, Bernstein was beginning to see new possibilities in the "three interactions" about teaching and learning that formed the core of his work at Nebraska. First, came his introduction to the course portfolio, a new way of representing teaching and learning that had been introduced by psychologist Bill Cerbin from the University of Wisconsin–LaCrosse and developed by Pat Hutchings and Lee Shulman in the late stages of the AAHE's national Peer Review of Teaching Project. Unlike the older notion of a "teaching portfolio," which contains material from a variety of teaching activities, Hutchings explained, the course portfolio "focuses on the unfolding of a single course, from conception to results," enabling the scholar to document a course as they would a scholarly project, from purpose and design to enactment and outcomes (Hutchings, 1998b, p. 13; see also Cerbin, 1994; Hutchings, 1998a).

Bernstein was invited to join the course portfolio group, he believes, because Hutchings and Shulman knew they could count on him to be a "Johnny one-note" on getting, and keeping, student learning in focus. The danger Bernstein saw was that portfolios might still be all about what the teacher did. For Bernstein, the course portfolio's special value lay in its capacity to "help faculty show where the course experience contributed to student growth" (1998, p. 82). What Bernstein soon came to realize was that the course portfolio and the peer review exercises, could be easily combined. "As I say now to faculty," Bernstein told me, "the three interactions [review of syllabus, class, and student work] can be cut and pasted into a draft of a course portfolio."

Another contribution to Bernstein's thinking at this time was a preview of a new Carnegie Foundation report that he heard at the AAHE Faculty Roles and Rewards Conference in January 1997, the moment, not coincidentally, where Bernstein's path and mine first crossed. *Scholarship Assessed: Evaluation of the Professoriate*, begun by Ernest Boyer, but completed by his colleagues, Charles Glassick, Gene Maeroff, and me, was a follow-up to Boyer's *Scholarship Reconsidered*, that in essence suggested that scholarly work of all kinds, discovery, integration, application, and teaching—can be judged according to six standards: clear goals, adequate preparation, appropriate methods, significant results, effective presentation, and reflective critique. Bernstein told me that after hearing our argument, he and his academic vice president Al Kilgore came out of that meeting saying, "we just heard a revolution. And that's when I started to get some integrated sense of what these peer review exercises, and the course portfolios, could become."

Using the standards from *Scholarship Assessed* to underline the analogy between a course and other scholarly projects, Bernstein came to see the course portfolio as consisting of a presentation of and reflection on one's goals and preparation for a course (Interaction One); methods (Interaction Two); and analyzed results (Interaction Three). Putting it all together in his article for the course portfolio collection, he concluded:

> In this sense, the course portfolio model, with its focus on student learning as feedback to help instructors develop their teaching meth-

ods, is completely congruent with the framework in *Scholarship Assessed*, in which teaching is considered a form of scholarly work in which excellence is gauged in part—not exclusively—by looking at results in terms of understandings achieved by students. Excellent teaching is, by this measure, a process of ongoing, purposeful reflection on the relation between teaching practice and learner success. It is this process that the course portfolio is distinctly able to capture. (1998, p. 83)

With these ideas in place, Bernstein's next large project took shape. Funded by the Pew Charitable Trusts, Bernstein organized a consortium of universities, Nebraska, Indiana, Kansas State, Texas Tech, and Michigan, where faculty were to develop course portfolios that focused on student learning and receive written reviews from appropriate colleagues at other campuses. Conceived as a way for faculty to gain experience in articulating the intellectual work involved in teaching for an audience of peers, the consortium also aimed to give faculty experience in reading and evaluating their colleagues' efforts. Although intended at this stage as a faculty development activity, the program may eventually provide faculty with reviewed work that could be submitted as part of their teaching materials for tenure and promotion (Bernstein & Edwards, 2001).[18]

INQUIRY INTO STUDENT LEARNING

While Bernstein's faculty development projects unfolded, he was also, of course, teaching and pursuing his own line of inquiry into student learning. Invited in 1998 by Lee Shulman and Pat Hutchings to join the first class of CASTL, Bernstein found another community in which to foreground learning and develop and share his work.[19] Bernstein's project summary illustrates well his approach to teaching as serious intellectual work. Focusing on three semesters of a course that he had taught at Nebraska for 15 years, Bernstein presented data on the effects of successive changes he made in the class to get more students achieving higher levels of understanding: changing the assessment from short abstract essay questions to problems that asked students to apply concepts in new contexts; adding out-of-class questions about the readings to free up class time for discussion; and finally, adding Web-based examples of responses to test problems, so that students can learn to identify what makes some answers better than others (Bernstein, 2000). Bernstein's course still included features he had used in his teaching from his Keller Plan course days, like repeat testing. He also continued to explore ways to help more students understand more deeply and used the results from each iteration to think about what he should keep and what he should change the following semester.

Indeed, this kind of classroom inquiry has been a part of Bernstein's teaching for a long time, and one in which he makes good use of the research practices of his field. Consider, for example, some of the earlier work that he presented to his fellow Carnegie Scholars in the summer of 1999. For nine years, Bernstein explained, he had been consistently discouraged by student understanding of educational measurement, a topic in his course on conceptual issues in psychology. Convinced that students were not getting key concepts through his "well-polished lectures" alone, Bernstein hypothesized that students might do better with more opportunities to interact with the material, and asked two graduate students to help develop interactive software for his students. Then, one of his graduate students, for her master's thesis, compared results between classes that received a live lecture on the topic, a videotape of the lecture, and the electronic materials. When reviewers of the study later suggested they add further control conditions, Bernstein compared performance among groups reading irrelevant material, groups reading relevant material, groups hearing a live lecture, and groups working on the Web. "This is what you get when you enter into that community," Bernstein joked. "Additions of more conditions."[20]

Interestingly, Bernstein contrasted the more "formal scholarship of teaching" of this set of studies with the "much less formal" inquiries he next pursued in changing the level of understanding tapped by his examinations in this class. This is a somewhat surprising characterization to colleagues from other fields, who are usually impressed with Bernstein's numbers and graphs on the effects of various changes in his class. But Bernstein insisted that this work, like most inquiry that is feasible for faculty to do in their own classrooms, does not meet scientific standards of rigor, at least not those of the experimental method, which demands "high degrees of control, isolation of variables, and precise manipulation of treatments," as fellow psychologist Carnegie Scholars point out (Nummedal, Benson, & Chew, 2002, p. 174).[21] As a long-term practitioner, Bernstein values classroom inquiry highly, not as a contribution to scientific understanding, but as a contribution to teaching practice that is responsibly focused on, and responsive to, student learning.

Bernstein's attempts to advance this view among colleagues and to gain recognition for teaching as intellectual work have brought him mixed results. According to departmental colleagues, Bernstein has done more than anyone to keep teaching in sight. For example, Rick Bevins recalled that when he came to the department in the mid 1990s, "there was already a sort of very open conversation about quality teaching and really evaluating student learning." In fact, when he was interviewing for jobs, Bevins said, Nebraska's was the only department where faculty asked serious questions about teaching and Bernstein was not alone in doing so. Bevins recalled working closely with Bernstein to coordinate their first- and second-semester introductory courses, so that the fall course fed into the spring course and the latter actually built on the former. Another colleague, Ross Thompson, credited Bernstein with provoking him to use pre-tests in his Introduction to Psychology class as a way to demonstrate the kind of intellectual outcomes that would mark effective teaching.

But there are departmental downsides too. Bernstein's views of teaching and learning are not universally shared, even among his most thoughtful colleagues. Thompson, for example, objected to Bernstein's attempt to document excellence in teaching in the same way one would document excellence in research and believes that teaching needs evaluative standards of its own. "Some of the most valuable contributions of effective instruction are emotional, motivational, or even social rather than intellectual," Thompson explained. Of course, others have found Bernstein's departmental innovations irritating. Teaching circles, meaningful merit ratings for teaching, and more elaborate documentation all require too much of their attention and time. Thompson concluded:

> the changes in climate that Bernstein has sought to inaugurate produce ambivalent reactions at a departmental level. Perhaps it's because the department is where these ideas have to be tried out and developed before they're scaled up for campus or national distribution. Perhaps, too, the personal relationships that affect any department contributed to some of the more ambivalent reactions I've observed here.

At the university level—campus and system—Bernstein has achieved the highest recognition available to instructional leaders, including campus teaching awards, charter membership in the University of Nebraska–Lincoln Academy of Distinguished Teachers in 1995, and in 2001, the University of Nebraska System teaching award. But the struggle for salaries to reward those accomplished in teaching continues.[22] Bernstein credited his recent raises to his consulting, participation in national projects, the new multi-campus peer review project, and his rising reputation in the national teaching and learning community. As he said, rather sardonically:

> This hasn't changed from when I built a reputation in research. Except now what I'm doing is I'm traveling the country talking about teaching. I'm spending time at Carnegie. I'm spending time at Georgetown.[23] And the more I do that, the bigger raises I get and the more status I have. We're a designer label business. And if somebody else says we want you or we like what you do, we believe that. We would never read it ourselves or believe that we could tell that something was good.

Indeed. The fact that higher education does not have a peer review process built into the practice of teaching is one reason that Bernstein, like other advocates of the scholarship of teaching and learning, has been intrigued with finding ways to make teaching "community property" (Shulman, 1994). The idea here is not just that teaching would be better rewarded with such a system in place, but that excellence in teaching, like excellence in other kinds of scholarship, can best be assured only when there is an intellectual community of support in place. Bernstein and Richard Edwards, vice chancellor for academic affairs at the University of Nebraska–Lincoln, put it this way:

> Our vision is that, one day, many research universities will be connected through peer review of teaching just as they collaborate today in assessing research quality. If we wish to attain the same quality in teaching that we offer in research, we will need to develop a broad community of faculty members who can recognize, evaluate, and replicate excellence in teaching within the context of their individual fields of study. A system of peer exchange and review of course portfolios, focused on student learning, offers the best opportunity to create that community. (Bernstein & Edwards, 2001, p. B24)

As I write, the course portfolios for Bernstein's new peer review project are coming in. Colleagues at other institutions are writing commentary, and early feedback of what it's like to prepare a portfolio and receive formal comments on it is—as one would expect of serious intellectual work—nuanced, provocative, and good (Bernstein, Goodburn, & Robinson, 2002).

WORKING AGAINST THE GRAIN

Bernstein knows that he is working against the grain, especially in the core task of leading faculty to look student learning in the face (1998). Midway into his multi-campus peer review project, when our first conversations for this portrait took place, Bernstein noted that while they were finally coming close to producing enough course portfolios to start the external reading:

> . . . it [was] not easy to get faculty to do this writing. What seems easy and obvious to me is the opposite of what most people want to do. People don't assume it's their responsibility to show that students have learned. They don't see that their ideas about teaching should be informed by their students' performance as results. Like many others, they imagine that the impact of a college education is so big and so diverse and so ephemeral that they can't possibly measure it, that the really important things can't be measured. And at some level, I agree with it. But at some other level, you have agreed to be

responsible for a course that has some goals and you have asked people to do things over the course of that semester and you have evaluated them. No, I don't think I can tell whether my course transformed their life. But I can evaluate whether it at least gave them some new intellectual skills.

Bernstein is not discouraged. He has, after all, been working against the grain his whole career. He has focused on teaching in a university that has been ambivalent about the status of that enterprise. He has innovated "without honor" in his own department. He is committed to an embattled intellectual tradition in his field. For Bernstein, quality is more important than quantity in research; understanding is more important than speed in learning; and teaching is a form of intellectual work, which, "like any activity, can be done with varying degrees of investment of time and resources" (2001, p. 215). His goal in teaching and in faculty development is the same: to enable students and teachers to understand the intellectual issues at stake. The scholarship of teaching is not an end in itself for Bernstein, but a means to help him and other faculty design, implement, and modify courses in light of inquiry into learning so that more students will learn more deeply.

Postscript

In the late spring of 2002, Bernstein accepted an offer from the University of Kansas to join its faculty and to direct its Center for Teaching Excellence. The University of Nebraska–Lincoln suffered another loss earlier that spring while Bernstein's negotiations with Kansas were already underway. In March 2002, during the recent budget crisis, the University of Nebraska–Lincoln decided to close its 30-year-old Teaching and Learning Center in order to save costs. In its coverage of this decision, *The Chronicle of Higher Education* quoted Bernstein's colleague Ross Thompson, "When departments are targeted in this way, even if the cuts are deferred or reduced, the unit is wounded for years because the perception is they are not essential . . . what has been damaged in the process is the entire teaching climate at the University. You lose a 30-year investment in a center that is well-known and well-respected, and you have nothing to replace it" (Bartlett, 2002; see also Gumport, 2002b).

The teaching and learning communities at Nebraska, and beyond, have seen the loss of the Teaching and Learning Center there as a sign of the vulnerability of teaching initiatives in a budget crunch. Yet it may reflect something more than that. Thompson, for example, has been disappointed that in the year since the center's closing, little effort had yet been made to establish support for teaching excellence in the university's various disciplinary units (colleges and departments). He is also concerned that the administration has been slow to respond to a white paper it encouraged its Academy of Distinguished Teachers to prepare on teaching and student learning at Nebraska (2002), and that other initiatives, like the university's Preparing Future Faculty program, have ended or lost steam without a countervailing effort to keep them afloat. There is still respect for teaching at Nebraska, and a culture that allows faculty members with teaching-heavy portfolios, like Bernstein's former departmental colleague Cal Garbin, to be promoted to full professor. But Thompson fears that the university's balance, its willingness to invest in teaching and learning as well as in research, may be at least temporarily lost.[24]

In contrast, Bernstein has found that support for teaching and learning at the University of Kansas is strong. He admits that he is still new, but he has found more ceremonial attention paid to teaching than expected—for example, a Summit on Teaching that starts off the institution's academic year, twenty $5,000 teaching awards each year, and repeated statements about the importance of teaching by the chancellor and provost—and continued investment as well. While the University of Kansas, like the University of Nebraska–Lincoln, suffered serious budget cuts in the early 2000s, the University of Kansas's Center for Teaching Excellence, though only a few years old, was not sacrificed. In fact, when its founding director left to take another administrative position within the university, the university ran the national search that brought Bernstein in as the new director for the 2002–2003 academic year. Furthermore, Bernstein has found the center's advisory board and the university's faculty to be interested in his ideas about what it means to see teaching as serious intellectual work.

Of course, Bernstein's tenure has just begun, and he is just getting to know the community his center serves. He delivered the keynote at the Summit on Teaching that kicked off the university's 2002–2003 academic year; had one-on-one discussions with most of the department chairs; and has set up meetings twice a semester with the center's "ambassadors," liaisons appointed by each department to help keep him apprised of faculty interests and bring back news of the center's offerings. Bernstein has also begun to put his own stamp on the center's activities. For example, he established a faculty seminar in which he's "giving people a small stipend in return for spending time reading course portfolios and imagining how they will then teach the next version of their course as a first step toward inquiry." He invited the history department to cosponsor a historian to offer the center's spring workshop, to bring an explicit disciplinary focus to teaching and learning discussions. He is beginning to talk with faculty about how to fill the vacuum of evidence about teaching in faculty evaluation. Of course, Bernstein still teaches a couple of courses a year as a tenured full professor in the psychology department. "The message needs to be," he explained, "that the scholarship of teaching and learning is work that is done by regular academics."

NOTES

1. These lines open Daniel Bernstein's article, "Representing the Intellectual Work in Teaching Through Peer-Reviewed Course Portfolios" (2001).

2. "Since about 1975 American higher education, for the first time in its history, essentially ceased to grow. In the following twenty years, the number of full-time students increased by just one percent per year" (Geiger, 2002, p. 34; see also Geiger, 1999).

3. By "personal attributes," Seldin meant such things as a candidate's politics, dress, or friends (1984, pp. 41–42).

4. The authors of a recent report for the American Academy of Arts and Sciences note that while some authors attribute grade inflation, in part, to the widespread (and, I might add, almost exclusive) use of student evaluations as the principal measure of teaching effectiveness in retention, tenure, promotion, and merit pay decisions, there is no real consensus about cause (Rosovsky & Hartley, 2002). But see also the critique by Alfie Kohn, "The Dangerous Myth of Grade Inflation" (2002), which not only questions the AAAS report's findings but also its line of argument. In Kohn's view, "the crusade against [grade inflation] is led by conservative individuals and organizations" (p. B8) with an ax to grind. "In fact, what is most remarkable is how rarely learning even figures into the discussion. . . . The real threat to excellence isn't grade inflation at all; it's grades" (p. B9).

5. In *A Quest for Common Learning*, Boyer and Levine (1981) define general education as "the breadth component of a college education" (p. 2) and chart "a succession of revivals" (p. 5), usually occurring around times of national crisis. They date the seeds of the latest revival (at the time of their writing) to the mid 1970s, when higher education itself was facing retrenchment and loss of public confidence.

6. For example, the Carnegie Foundation's report *Scholarship Reconsidered* (Boyer, 1990) was provided to participating departments when it came out in 1990, and Eugene Rice, who had played a major role in that book's preparation, came from Antioch College to speak. Bernstein was not a particular fan of *Scholarship Reconsidered*, by the way. He was among those who read it more as an exercise in re-labeling, that might diminish the inherent value of good teaching.

7. Margaret Miller notes that, since its establishment in 1972, FIPSE "has had an effect that has been disproportionate to its relatively small size" (2002, p. 4). Indeed, its record in supporting a wide range of innovative projects is quite impressive. Virginia Smith, FIPSE's founding director, contends that the core values of the staff, in conjunction with its organizational structure, have enabled FIPSE to contribute substantially to the changing discourse and practice of higher education over three decades. With a smaller budget, yet greater autonomy from its regulatory organizations, the Office of Education and the National Institute for Education, FIPSE has attempted from its inception to make its funds widely accessible and to focus on underserved populations. Serving as testimony to FIPSE's influence is the fact that its groundbreaking projects aimed at low-income, minority, and nontraditional aged female students have re-centered reform efforts, so that mainstream educational concerns of today include these populations as a matter of course (Smith, 2002). For more information about FIPSE's history of educa-

tional improvements, see the September–October issue of *Change* (Vol. 34, No. 5), which is devoted to the topic.

8. Indiana University biologist Craig Nelson attributes his entry into a national conversation about teaching and learning to his involvement with his institution's honors program. According to Nelson, honors programs focus attention on teaching and learning issues in several ways. For instance, because the National Collegiate Honors Council is a forum for faculty and student presentations only, the emphasis remains on classroom-related issues. "And honors teaching frees people from disciplinary constraints," he said, "by giving them classes that are really permissive of experimentation. They often learn that the standard approach to material is nearly useless. So as long as an honors faculty member does something other than double the rate of delivery of material, he or she can learn a lot about teaching."

9. Writing Across the Curriculum (WAC) emerged in the mid 1970s as a reform effort that implemented theories from the developing field of composition. Fundamental tenets of the movement include: (a) an emphasis on the process of writing as means of learning ("writing to learn," rather than "learning to write"); and (b) recognition that writing practices and skills are not generic, but vary greatly across different social contexts. As a movement, WAC has been very flexible; changes to colleges' curricula range from adding increasingly varied assignments to composition courses to increasing the capacity of faculty in distinct disciplines to incorporate writing and writing instruction into their courses (Romberger, 2000; Tillotson, 1996). For more WAC information and resources, see the WAC Clearinghouse at http://wac.colostate.edu.

10. The Peer Review of Teaching Project, led by Russell Edgerton and Pat Hutchings of AAHE and Lee Shulman of Stanford University, was funded by The William and Flora Hewlett Foundation and the Pew Charitable Trusts (Miller, 1998).

11. For a full description of these exercises, see the American Association for Higher Education (1995).

12. William Buskist, a psychologist and scholar of teaching at Auburn University, considers Bernstein's major contribution in this area to be his focus on learning. "Historically, when we've looked at the nature of effective teaching, one can see in the literature that there's very little interest in student outcome," he said. "That's why Dan's research is so important."

13. R. Eugene Rice, AAHE senior scholar and former director of the Association's Forum on Faculty Roles and Rewards, was a professor of sociology and religion at the University of the Pacific for many years and helped create the first of the university's innovative cluster colleges. Since 1994, Steven Portch has been the chancellor of the University System of Georgia. Prior to that, he worked for 18 years in the University of Wisconsin system. Roy Roemer served as the governor of Colorado for three consecutive terms, from 1987 to 1998. Richard Lyman was the president of Stanford from 1970 to 1980. From 1980 to 1988, he served as the president of the Rockefeller Foundation, and then returned to Stanford as the university's first director of the Institute for International Studies until 1991. Donald Kennedy followed Lyman as the president of Stanford, from 1980 to 1992, and is currently Bing Professor of Environmental Science Emeritus at Stanford and Edi-

tor-in-Chief of *Science* magazine, the weekly journal of the American Association for the Advancement of Science.

14. According to Bernstein, *The Behavior Analyst* is the conceptual, philosophical journal. *JEAB* is the empirical basic journal and *JABA* is the empirical applied journal.

15. Bernstein's friend and fellow Carnegie Scholar, mathematician Anita Salem, sees Bernstein's engagement with the scholarship of teaching and learning in similar terms. After Bernstein's visits to consult with her institution, Rockhurst University, about improving its system of assessing faculty teaching performance, she said, "What I took away from watching him, is that you can manage to turn your passion into a scholarly pursuit if you can figure out the path that connects the two. And he had. He had figured out how to traverse that path between students and teachers. And he did it through this assessment model. But to me it was like watching someone blend two things in their lives. One that they cared about deeply and the other one that they thought was a tool that would help the first."

16. Bloom's taxonomy is one of the most commonly used heuristics for describing different kinds of learning activity and assessing their level of difficulty. Originally constructed by a committee of educational psychologists that was headed by Benjamin Bloom in the mid 1950s, the taxonomy separates learning into three basic domains: cognitive (intellectual skills), affective (attitude), and psychomotor (physical skills). Each domain is divided hierarchically, from the easiest and most fundamental tasks to the most abstract. For the cognitive domain, skill development starts with the recall or recognition of knowledge, moves through comprehension, application, analysis, and synthesis, and ends with the highest order skill of evaluation (Bloom, 1956; Krathwohl & Bloom, 1984; Krathwohl, Bloom, & Masia, 1964). This taxonomy has recently been revised by Anderson and Krathwohl (2000). See also Shulman (2002b).

17. See Bernstein, Jonson, and Smith (2000) for a description of Nebraska's Peer Review of Teaching project and a summary of its findings on student achievement, student attitudes and motivation, and faculty attitudes and practices, including in-class teaching practices and assignments and evaluation of students.

18. Bernstein's effort to create a "community of support," around the intellectual work involved in teaching is similar to that of Lorilee Sandmann and Amy Driscoll to develop networks of peers who understand outreach and public service (http://web2.canr.msu.edu/leadnet/approaches.htm; see also Huber 1999b). For examples of course portfolios in a variety of fields from the University of Nebraska–Lincoln and other institutions, see http://www.unl.edu/peerrev.

19. As fellow psychologist and Carnegie Scholar Stephen Chew remarked, "That's always the thing I can count on Dan to bring up, 'What evidence do you have of student learning?'"

20. A video of this presentation is available through the Carnegie Foundation's Knowledge Media Lab (see http://kml2.carnegiefoundation.org/html/gallery.php).

21. In taking this perspective, Bernstein is a real experimental psychologist. Stephen Chew, psychologist and scholar of teaching and learning at Samford University, explained:

It's an issue that always comes up every time we give a presentation. In some ways, experimentalists are the toughest crowd to convince of the utility of the scholarship of teaching and learning, because scholars of teaching often cannot do pure, highly controlled experiments in classroom settings. But they do the best they can under the circumstances. It's not lab research. It's more applied research. Dan will be the first one to tell you that a lot of the experimentalists will just dismiss it out of hand.

Indeed, Chew has spoken with leaders of the experimentalist group within the American Psychological Association, who have said, in essence, "My group will basically have nothing to do with this. You won't be able to get any cooperation there at all." Chew concluded, "It's kind of a tough nut to crack."

22. Bernstein's departmental colleague, Ross Thompson, suggested that there was almost no overlap between the salaries of faculty named to distinguished professorships because of their research accomplishments and the salaries of members of Nebraska's Academy of Distinguished Teachers.

23. Bernstein was invited to spend part of the 2000–2001 academic year at Randy Bass's Center for New Designs in Learning and Scholarship at Georgetown University. See Chapter 9.

24. Ross Thompson, too, has left Nebraska. In May 2003, he accepted a senior faculty position in the Department of Psychology at the University of California, Davis.

4

Thinking Like a Chemist

· ·

> Our instructional objective is to have students come to know the
> powerful conceptual unity that allows professional chemists to
> understand unfamiliar results according to a few well-refined
> principles and given enough examples from which to create
> analogies. . . . To us, conventional chemistry instruction is too
> self-referential, drawing too much from its own traditions and
> too little from the more authentic standard of what chemists
> actually do.[1]

B rian P. Coppola, associate professor of chemistry at the University of
Michigan, is in my Carnegie Foundation office in California, sitting
with me by my computer, showing me student work. He has just come
over from a neighboring think tank, where he is working with colleagues
to develop animation software with a "chemistry interface." Coppola and
I are about to start a marathon two-day interview for this case study, but
first he wants to show me how animation software is helping his second-
semester introductory students visualize a particular chemical reaction
described in a recent journal article. Coppola gets primary data from the
author(s) and then asks his students, in groups of three, to figure out the
sequence of the bonding changes that take place. Students learn to do animations in this course, they review and critique the animations of their colleagues, and the one thing they never encounter is any animation created
by the instructor. Through this exercise in "unpacking" an article from the
original literature, they are learning to think like professional chemists, to
understand how the authors moved from raw data to interpretation. From
Coppola's perspective, these students are not just learning chemistry. They
are also learning how to teach.

We watch several animations, and Coppola provides running commentary as we move from one group's animation to another and the atoms and
molecules on the screen fly hither and yon. "Now there's an interesting
pedagogical choice the students made. You can see that they can make

Case Study: Brian P. Coppola

Brian P. Coppola is Arthur F. Thurnau Professor and associate chair of chemistry at the University of Michigan. He teaches undergraduate courses in organic chemistry and graduate courses on teaching and learning in chemistry. His current research interests are in the mechanism and synthetic applications of dipolar cycloaddition reactions and in using future faculty development as a mechanism to support curriculum design, implementation, assessment, and evaluation. Coppola directs the Chemical Sciences at the Interface of Education Program at Michigan, which is devoted to creating and documenting the professional development infrastructure needed to understand and promote the scholarship of teaching and learning. Winner of the University of Michigan's Amoco Undergraduate Teaching Award and a Carnegie Scholar in CASTL, Coppola received his baccalaureate degree from the University of New Hampshire and his doctorate in chemistry from the University of Wisconsin–Madison. Visit http://www.umich.edu/~michchem/faculty/coppola for more information.

things bigger or smaller or change the color. Some students will actually think to put a text box so that not only do you get this graphical mouse-over correlation but you get a text explanation for the things that they're doing." Indeed, his students begin their animations by studying those of the previous class on a different reaction, not only for the chemistry involved, but to appreciate, as learners, what representational choices their predecessors, as teachers, had made. I recognize in Coppola's pedagogy the ancient view of Aristotle that teaching is the highest form of understanding. Coppola explained:

> If we put students into teaching situations, they must necessarily think differently, explicitly, about the fact that they're explaining

something. And if they do, they should be learning in a fundamentally better way. If we leave the impression that all you're doing in learning is generating personal knowledge, then the gap between that and success is what psychologist Elaine Coleman calls 'explanatory knowledge.' My students have to consider what it means to re-represent what they know for someone else.[2]

Teaching for understanding is what the scholarship of teaching and learning is all about. The point of viewing teaching as inquiry into learning and of making knowledge about teaching and learning public, is to clarify the kinds of "understanding" students might achieve and to elucidate the instructional choices that will help students get there. Like many thoughtful faculty, Brian Coppola hopes that his students will "take home" a kind of problem-solving or critical thinking that characterizes expert practice in his field.[3] In Coppola's case, one might call it "thinking like a chemist." But he has gone a step further, and identified "explanatory knowledge" as an integral part of chemical understanding. Like other innovators in science education, Coppola has created opportunities for his undergraduates to read real chemistry and do real chemical research. His most striking contribution, however, has been simultaneously to create opportunities for peer instruction so that students can deepen their understanding of chemistry by learning to teach. Coppola has also created an infrastructure to support a broader notion of scholarship for doctoral and postdoctoral students as well, with opportunities for future faculty to design and study a variety of settings for chemical instruction.

To understand Coppola's contributions to the scholarship of teaching and learning and the trajectory of his career, it is necessary to see his work in the context of broader developments in science education. Chemistry, like most science, technology, engineering, and mathematics (STEM) disciplines, has a long history of concern for chemical education at the postsecondary level. As Coppola and colleague Dennis Jacobs wrote, "For more than 75 years, chemistry instructors have regularly exchanged ideas about teaching chemistry at national chemistry and chemical education meetings and in refereed journals such as the *Journal of Chemical Education* and the *Journal of College Science Teaching*" (2002, p. 197). Over these years, however, chemistry and chemistry education have undergone great change.

First, in the years following World War II, the field itself moved from a "little science" to a "big science" model with an emphasis on large research teams, government and industry sponsorship, and a focus on the development and application of new techniques. The very advances in content that big science enabled, however, flooded undergraduate chemistry, which had already become quite specialized after the spread of the "elective" system earlier in the century. "As content exploded," Gene Wubbels and Joan Girgus wrote, "college instruction became more abstract, replete with quantitative models and algorithms, and filled with unconnected terms and details" (1996, p. 281). In addition, the "molecular structural revolution," beginning in the 1940s and 1950s, made it necessary for college- and university-based chemistry departments to invest in new laboratory research equipment that was expensive to purchase and operate, although some believe that newer technologies, including computers, have somewhat eased the pressures since.[4]

Immediately following Sputnik, concern over the nation's ability to compete with other nations in science and technology led to large-scale reforms in science curricula. Largely supported by NSF, these efforts aimed at attracting more of the best and brightest students into science fields. In high school chemistry, the Chemical Bond Approach and Chemical Education Material Study programs, developed by coalitions of academic scientists and high school teachers, attempted to move emphasis from "facts" to scientific principles and to help students get a better sense of the process of science, especially through improved laboratory experiences where students could "explore, discover, and understand" (Ben-Zvi, 1991, p. 936; see also Wubbels & Girgus, 1996).[5] The 1960s brought a new focus on environmental and societal problems, while the early 1970s saw experimentation with ways of engaging students through interdisciplinary approaches to chemistry. However, with the dramatic funding cutbacks of the 1970s and early 1980s, NSF retreated from support of these educational reforms (Ben-Zvi, 1991, p. 936).

The pedagogical landscape in chemistry, as in other science fields, shifted again in the early to mid 1980s, at about the time that Brian Coppola was beginning his professional career. The country had been in economic recession, and anxiety about its global competitiveness was heightened by research showing a decline in the number undergraduates choosing or staying in science majors. Concern about whether the nation would have enough scientists and engineers in the future brought back attention, and NSF funding, to the quality of postsecondary science education, as did the realization that science and technology professions were losing many good students, and that those lost were disproportionately minorities and women. More recently, the country's scientific and political leadership has broadened its focus to science and mathematics education for all students, science and nonscience majors (Seymour, 2000; see also National Research Council 1996, 1999; National Science Foundation, 1996; Tobias, 1990).

Like other science and mathematics fields, chemistry education reform has had to address a number of issues concerning student learning that arise from distinctive features of the way these fields have been organized and taught for most of the last century. Wubbels and Girgus provide a helpful list in their contribution to the *Handbook of the Undergraduate Cur-*

riculum (1996). The sequential nature of study in the sciences, the relationship of theory to experiment, the necessity for quantitative skill, the importance of research experience for understanding the investigative power of the sciences, and the "unhappy" distinction between science education for majors and nonmajors have all been foci for reform-minded educators. As a particularly strategic site for change because it is a "basic" science for students heading into many other fields, chemistry education has sported a rich array of innovative projects and attracted a good number of funders, from institutions themselves, to NSF (with several programs), the American Chemical Society, the Research Corporation, the Camille and Henry Dreyfus Foundation, the Pew Science Program in Undergraduate Education, and the Howard Hughes Medical Institute.[6]

A broad field of chemical education has been stimulated by these curricular and pedagogical reforms, including chemistry faculty writing about their teaching experiences, but now also augmented by "specialists" in chemical education and colleagues in other fields. Sociologist and program evaluator Elaine Seymour noted:

> Our collective understanding of the task at hand has clearly been widening–from an initial, narrow focus on loss or wastage among [science, mathematics, and engineering] undergraduate or graduate majors, to concern with the scientific and mathematical competence of potentially every child, student, and citizen. Those most intimately engaged with the implications of these shifts have become an interconnected nationwide community. They comprise a growing network of faculty experimenting with new modes of curriculum, pedagogy, and learning assessments in their own classrooms and departments, education researchers, program evaluators, and those public and private agencies who have promoted and funded innovation and the adaptation and dissemination of more effective SMET teaching methods. (2002, p. 85)

Coppola, of course, is very much a part of the chemistry education neighborhood of this larger reform movement in science education. Like other neighborhoods, however, this one has its tensions. There is cooperation and competition between different groups over responsibility for improving undergraduate education in chemistry. Should leadership be in the hands of chemical education specialists, some of whom are actually trained in doctoral programs in chemical education; the science education people, many of whom are housed in schools of education, but who often focus on high school science; or by regular chemistry faculty themselves? Coppola voted for the regular chemistry faculty, because you have to think like a chemist to understand how to help people learn the field. From Coppola's perspective, there is grave danger in the tendency to "marginalize the responsibility for doing this work rather than to see it as a part of a mainstream chemistry faculty member's obligation" (Coppola & Jacobs, 2002, p. 197).

Coppola is a strong advocate of the obligation of all teaching chemists to be responsible chemical educators, holding that the "design, implementation, and assessment of learning environments in higher education is a traditional faculty role" (2001a). He also believes that "chemical education" should not be seen as a refuge for those who can't *do* chemistry but as a legitimate area of specialization for a professor of chemistry to have. It was Coppola, in fact, who first proposed the idea of doing these case studies as a way of ensuring that his successful bid for a regular tenured position in the chemistry department at the University of Michigan would be seen not as an exception but a precedent for people like himself throughout higher education. In reflecting on his career, the close relationship—or as he would put it, the "inseparable interdependence"—between chemistry and chemical education was a leitmotiv running through our conversations.[7] For Coppola, who trained as a research chemist, thinking about chemistry is fundamentally the same as thinking about chemistry education, and the training one needs both for research and for teaching is similar as well. The basic requirements for professional engagement include, in his view, those characteristics necessary to carry out one's professional responsibilities. In research and in teaching, he suggested, these are "informed design, imaginative implementation, critical analysis and reflection, and honest, illustrative documentation."

APPRENTICESHIP

Apprenticeship is key to Coppola's story about how he learned to think like a chemist and a teacher. Some of his signature pedagogical plans for his students, such as peer instruction, engagement with real literature, and examinations as opportunities for students to teach, involve variations on the theme of apprenticeship. A bright student, Coppola sought opportunities to talk and work with experienced teachers and professors throughout his school, college, and graduate school years. In his childhood play as teacher, his undergraduate research and art classes, and his graduate research group and tutoring, Coppola practiced what students of apprenticeship call "legitimate peripheral participation" in the real work of experts in these various fields (Lave & Wenger, 1991).

If there is such a thing as a natural teacher, Coppola may be it. Certainly, in telling his story, he dated some of his most characteristic views about the power of explanatory knowledge to his childhood years. Neither of his parents were teachers. However, Coppola said:

I was in awe of teachers since the very beginning, and spent my time watching them, trying to emulate them, and playing out the ideas I saw. At least according to my mother, I started in first and second grade helping peers. There's a wonderful picture of me. I'm probably in second grade, standing at the chalk board in the play room of the house, with my poor brother sitting at a desk, giving him quizzes.

Coppola thought he recognized intuitively that the role of "expresser" caused him to think and learn differently:

You can find the notations in my high school yearbook. I didn't go to study hall. I found classrooms and had kids sitting in chairs and me at the board working with them. Teachers taking their breaks sitting there, watching this; and I would have conversations with them about teaching afterwards.

Coppola's interest in teaching continued at college, a period to which he dates the inspiration for some of his other pedagogical views. Coppola did his undergraduate study in his home state at the University of New Hampshire, from 1972 to 1978. In Coppola's opinion, New Hampshire had an excellent undergraduate program at that time. One of the first institutions to mandate an undergraduate chemistry thesis and to involve promising undergraduates in research,[8] talented students could feel that they were part of the scholarly community in their department. This is a quality of life that Coppola tries to create for undergraduates now at the University of Michigan, but with a twist, because unlike at New Hampshire, Coppola has created opportunities to involve undergraduates in teaching, as well as research. He dates the idea for one of his innovations in peer instruction to his experience at New Hampshire in one of the few electives his chemistry program allowed. Art was Coppola's favorite subject. He is a talented cartoonist, and he later adapted to chemistry not only his interest in visualization, but also the studio idea from these courses, in which students critique each other's work.

For the time being, however, Coppola's teaching interests were on hold. He was an undergraduate research student qualified for the top graduate chemistry programs in the country. His choice was influenced by the fact that two of his professors at the University of New Hampshire had degrees from the University of Wisconsin–Madison, but also by the advice of one of these wise professors, who knew his students as well as he knew the graduate school scene. What happened, Coppola recalled, is that he and his friend, the only two in their class going to graduate school, were choosing between the same two schools, and didn't know how to decide. So they called their professor and he said, "'Oh, that's easy. Coppola goes to Madison. The other one goes to Berkeley. I know you both and I know your characters. What you don't understand is schools also have characters, and understanding the match-up between your character and the school is something that I can see with my perspective.'" What was the thinking behind these match-ups? Coppola explained, "I like the idea of requirements and exams and prelims and a suite of courses that you take, a proposal defense, and a seminar; and Madison has this very structured program. I'm a structured person. My friend is an unstructured person, and going to Berkeley was right for him."

Supported by a research fellowship, Coppola began his doctoral study in organic/synthetic chemistry in one of the country's top-rated programs, in which there was no need, encouragement, or opportunity to teach. "Going to graduate school at Madison, and joining the research group I went into, was the beginning of at least two years of a boot camp where your mind was changed. Although it may be somewhat diminished today, in the late 1970s, the overwhelming culture there and everywhere was that anybody who is going to be anybody is going to follow in the footsteps of their research director and be a faculty member at one of 15 institutions that count." Coppola realized that he was being prepared to be a research director himself and a professor of graduate students who might never teach undergraduates. "We used to joke about that. My research director would leave small notes on our desks, saying, 'Please see me.' We would say colloquially within our group that his aspirations for us were, 'Please be me.'"

Although "dutiful" during his first year and a half of graduate school, Coppola believes that the conflict, not fully realized, with his previous values, along with the pressure he felt to "do this" and "be that," contributed toward his descent into "a fairly deep trough." He was saved, he said, by "a little green sheet of tri-folded paper" that came through the campus mail advertising the Greater University Tutorial Service (GUTS), a program that aimed to offer alternative learning environments for undergraduates on campus. This was the "brainchild" of a group of graduate students in the School of Education at Madison who, in effect, created a matchmaking service, pairing up students who needed help in a course with students who'd taken the course and wanted to revisit it by helping others.[9]

When Coppola saw the ad looking for tutors, "This thing went off like a bell in my head. And I remember walking back upstairs, going 'Oh, yeah, these are the things I'm interested in.' And it was like I'd been asleep for a while." He signed up, which was fortunate for the undergraduate study group, because organic chemistry was taught so poorly that few undergraduate juniors and seniors had the confidence or interest to volunteer as tutors. It was also fortunate for Coppola, who enjoyed the challenge of leading a group of students from different sections of organic chemistry using different texts. He also got a one-on-one education in teaching and learning when the program's leader, Harry Behrman, began using Coppola's session for fieldwork, sitting in the back, taking notes, diagramming the classroom, and the like. In the process of his weekly debriefing with Behrman, Coppola learned that there was such a thing as educational theory and methods for documenting teaching. In other words, he learned to see and talk about what he was doing as an instructor in theoretically informed terms.

This tutoring program also influenced Coppola's growing understanding of how to get things done in a university setting. Behrman had planned to use the study group program as his thesis project, but originally could not get access to rooms and the necessary agreement from departments to advertise and support the proposed activity. "So how did they manage this?" Coppola asked:

> They got what I consider to be one of the top ten ideas in higher education. When I rank the things that influenced me, this is one of the things I put near the top. They incorporated themselves as a student organization. That gave them access to the student union, a little bit of the budget, and the ability to reserve rooms. The lesson was how to use the weight of the system against itself.

Meanwhile, Coppola was pursuing his graduate work in the stimulating environment of Barry Trost's lab. Some 20 years later, Coppola and his colleague at Michigan, William Pearson, who had also been a graduate student of Trost's, wrote a tribute to their advisor, describing the pedagogical lessons they distilled from their participation in his group. They cited, for example, Trost's respect for students' conclusions, and his careful questioning to uncover the juncture where a logical flaw made the answer "wrong," their advisor's assumption that there was a "big picture" in organic chemistry that made it more fruitful to ask how something "new" was similar to something else rather than to characterize it by its differences, and the cultivation within Trost's lab of a clear and articulate style of expression. According to Coppola and Pearson (1998):

> We encountered this structured intellectual guidance in many venues: in formal courses, in weekly research group meetings, in weekly problem sessions where we were "up at the board" or simply watching one of our peers take a turn in the hot spot, and in the four-year stream of extemporaneous interactions about our research projects. (p. 417)

Like all work in Trost's lab, Coppola's work was in organic chemistry, that branch of the field that studies the properties and behavior of carbon compounds.[10] Although Coppola was working (and still does) on a chemical system that has some attractiveness to industry, it is characteristically academic, not industrial, work. Coppola explained that his research interests are in the general area of methodology, which in organic synthesis means the ability to create and understand new ways of building molecules. Although methodological inquiry ultimately provides a wider array of tools for people who need to build molecules for making new drugs and herbicides, pesticides and so forth, it is exploratory work that is difficult for people in industry to do because it is not oriented toward a commercial goal.

Trost, Coppola believed, hoped his students would pursue the classic career of an academic scientist. But by the early 1980s, Coppola had already begun to shift his sights from a research university career to a collegiate teaching environment. In part this was spurred by his experience as a tutor in intense interaction with a small group of students, but there was a push factor in his decision as well:

> There was the recoil against what appeared to be the only way one could live at the large, research institutions. And the only option that is rational at that point is to say, "Well, where can I find the position in higher education that looks more like the person I want to be?" And this still plays out in conversations that I have with my friends and colleagues. The position that I have crafted at Michigan in chemical education is in some great part motivated because the existing positions at places like Michigan do not meet the needs for what I'm interested in.

Coppola's turn to teaching in the early 1980s was a generative but costly move. Torn by conflicting desires to meet the expectations of a respected and powerful advisor (and the academic establishment that he represented) but also to meet a personal need to follow a different path, Coppola and his advisor went through a difficult period, for which Coppola took full responsibility:

> We probably had higher highs and lower lows than people generally have, and, that's reasonably attached to me. But when it became clear that I was not the person he had intended me to be, we got past that, and he supported me, as he has, from that point on.[11] He realized that I meant what I said, and so when a letter came across his desk announcing a position at the University of Wisconsin–Whitewater, he passed it on and said, "Is this the kind of thing you're interested in?"

Coppola jumped at the opportunity and, before finishing his dissertation, virtually bolted out the door.

There was a time in the expansive period of American higher education when it was not uncommon for graduate students, especially in the humanities and social sciences, to take their first academic position while still writing their dissertations. That practice greatly diminished in the tightening job market that began in the 1970s. Coppola said that in the early 1980s, it was very uncommon in science, where the normal progression for serious students included a postdoctoral fellowship after the Ph.D.[12] He admitted that leaving graduate school was a mistake. His advisor urged him to stay in Madison and complete the writing that fall, and Whitewater, too, was willing for him to start in January. "But I was belligerent. I had made my commitments, and I was going to start." He left, committed to write, although that didn't happen. "People forget to tell you what teaching is like. And the preparation that's required and so on. So there were only the normal breaks and the summer to work on it. It took two years instead of a single term, and so in 1982, I left, and in 1984, I defended the dissertation."

The last time that his advisor said anything negative about Coppola's turn toward teaching was the day of his defense. "We sat down afterwards. He was behind his desk, we were having the post-defense 'dad and lad' talk. And he folded his hands and looked across his desk, and he said, 'What you want to do with your life is a tragedy.'" Coppola now believes that his advisor was referring as much to Coppola's choice to teach at a little-known regional campus as to his interest in teaching per se, but at the time, he recalled, he just rolled his eyes, thinking "Oh that's him, that's so him," and admitted that it was the kind of remark one remembers for a long time. He sees this aspiration that research professors have for their best students as a desire for what's best for that student as well as a desire to perpetuate a legacy and perhaps even to assure a future colleague in the research enterprise. Unfortunately, the relationship between professor and graduate student is seldom egalitarian enough for the issue to be openly discussed.[13] Perhaps without realizing it, Coppola suggested, Trost, who was elected to the National Academy of Science by age 40, set a virtually unattainable model of academic success. Students looked at that and said, "That's not me. I have to go do something else." Clearly, this has been a complex and key relationship for Coppola having to do with the legitimacy of his career choice and the adequacy of the "me" that Coppola has chosen to be.

EDUCATIONAL PROBLEM SOLVING

Early during Coppola's four years at Whitewater, he realized that he had a facility for educational problem solving. Perhaps, Coppola said, it came from being one of Barry Trost's students, who have a reputation for identifying and solving chemistry problems in an especially apt way. But that first fall, when teaching organic chemistry, Coppola experienced a crisis of conscience about teaching chemistry to these students, who were probably not going to be chemistry majors. He himself was excited about the subject matter, but why was it worthwhile for them to learn? He felt his motivation slipping and was plagued with doubt about what he was doing for three or four weeks. Then, so his story goes, one cold day, he was fiddling with his 1976 Pinto, trying to change the thermostat, but the design of the engine block and location of the thermostat was bad, so none of his tools was adequate to the task. He wrestled for hours, but could not reach in with any tool he had to solve that problem. However, Coppola continued, "The minute that I thought about it in those terms, it was one of those little epiphanies, because I stepped back and just yelled at myself. Idiot! You've been trained as a problem-solver. Why don't you just treat this like any other problem that you should be thinking about." Within minutes, the bolts were off, and the epiphany provided Coppola with an answer for his students as well. By learning how to solve problems in one context (organic chemistry), they would learn techniques they could transfer. This basic insight also began to color the way Coppola thought about teaching, and in the future, was played out and elaborated in many ways.

It did not take Coppola long to realize that Whitewater was not the right place for him. Coppola, who had thrived in apprenticeships, was alone, without critical colleagues to help him build his "edifice" (as he put it) like Justus Liebig, he said, the 19th-century German chemist who was among the first to establish a teaching laboratory and who had argued that before empirical work came to be respected, theoretical chemists could create whatever airy notions they liked. He felt the effects of isolation most keenly when he went to the chemistry education sessions at a national American Chemical Society meeting in Chicago, and realized that without people "to exercise with, his muscles had atrophied." The sessions reminded him that, just coming out of his thesis, he hadn't been keeping up with the broader literature on organic chemistry or, for that matter, new developments in chemical education. In conversations at the meetings, Coppola noticed, "There were times when I heard people talk about their organic chemistry instruction in ways that conflicted with my own thinking pedagogically and also with the subject matter. I felt like Liebig. Before a system of scholarship came into research, you could have any old idea you wanted and just promote it."

Coppola realized that without the colleagues, resources, and visibility that a larger institution could provide, the odds of ever having a national effect on teaching and learning were small. Not that working at Whitewater was unimportant, but it was not the role that Coppola wanted to play. "There's a story bearing on this that Arthur Kornberg of Stanford tells," Coppola said:

A physician is trying to save people from drowning in a raging river, but every time he drags one out they crawl back in. Exhausted from his efforts, he yelled to his colleague, sitting and writing on the shore, "Come and help!" But the colleague replied, "I am helping! I'm trying to figure out why they're all trying to run into the water again." The point of the story is that without both physicians doing their jobs, the people will all die. I wanted the role of the colleague writing on the shore.[14]

Coppola revived an idea that had been in his mind before leaving graduate school—the idea of one day returning to Madison to straighten out their organic chemistry curriculum, the same course whose bewildered undergraduates he had tutored while he was in graduate school there only a few years before. It would be an unusual position, but not completely unprecedented. Coppola knew that there was a person with a Ph.D. from Madison who had stayed on in a staff position to supervise the department's laboratories. He had achieved an international reputation "as a person who develops things and writes," and Coppola began to think that they might be interested in having somebody like that in the lecture program. Thus, he developed a five-year plan, a strategy that would bring him back to Madison to teach, first in the summer to establish his "bona fides as somebody who might be able to think differently," and then "for good." While the position Coppola imagined did indeed come to pass, it was not at the University of Wisconsin, but at the University of Michigan.

INNOVATION

The University of Michigan was in an interesting situation in the early 1980s. As it was once explained to Coppola, the state's peculiar brand of Republicanism had led the University to deny the value of federal funding for scientific research in the 1950s and 1960s while university science in the rest of the country expanded spectacularly on the federal funding boom. This did not mean that the university redefined itself as a teaching institution, but rather that it hung on to an older tradition of shoestring research that could be done without a huge influx of money. Without new facilities and modern instrumentation, and without adequate start-up packages to support new faculty members' research, Michigan's science departments began losing talented scientists and graduate students to other institutions, and their reputation declined.[15] According to Coppola, the department of chemistry, which had been one of the top departments in the country in the 1930s and 1940s, sank down to the top 20 or so in the 1960s and 1970s.[16] When the university began to rebuild in the early 1980s, Michigan's chemistry department had not brought in and tenured any new organic chemists since the 1960s, and had many temporary people on staff.

The turnaround came under President Harold Shapiro in the early 1980s. As chemistry professor David Curtis, put it, "Harold took one look at the situation and said we cannot have a first-class university without world-class science." Dramatic change ensued. Curtis, who became chair in the mid 1980s, used a personal anecdote to convey the pace:

> When I was hired there in 1967, I was told that we would have a new chemistry building going up within two years. That's what the expectation was. Fifteen years later, we still didn't have a building. Then, Harold comes in and within a year, the chemistry building was the number one priority at the University of Michigan, and the state gave us the money, and we raised $14 million to endow it and so on, to get it going. And within two years, the ground was broken. The whole situation had changed.

To old school scientists, who could not accommodate the new regime of externally funded research and publication, these were unsettling times.[17] To most, it was exciting. "We've hired new senior faculty, we've hired our first choice in assistant professors. They come and they start fabulous careers," Curtis said. The excitement of the 1980s was expressed in bold new educational thinking as well.

In 1984, just as Michigan's chemistry department was on this upswing, William Pearson, one of Coppola's best friends and colleagues from graduate school, got a position there. Ann Arbor was only a five-hour drive from Whitewater, and Coppola (still aiming to end up at Madison) began to visit. It was then that Coppola met Seyhan Ege, who had received her undergraduate education in Turkey and earned her doctorate at Michigan. After several years of postdoctoral research and teaching at a number of higher education institutions, the University of Michigan agreed to sponsor her for her immigration visa and she returned as a temporary lecturer. She intended to move on to another position at another institution, but one of her mentors within the chemistry department persuaded the department to appoint her to a tenure-track position in organic chemistry that became available in 1967. She earned tenure a few years later and by the time Coppola met Ege, she was not only a full professor, but also the author of an innovative textbook in organic chemistry with a clear pedagogical philosophy, which he admired. Coppola saw immediately that she was doing exactly the kind of interesting things that he wanted to do.

At Michigan, then, Coppola found the colleagues he'd been looking for. He was a frequent visitor, and when he came, Ege said, "It was obvious that he was just starving to talk about teaching, and that he had been in a situation where there hadn't been much encouragement and support." Coppola, Pearson, and Ege did talk a lot about teaching organic chemistry. But with the chemistry curriculum open for change as result of the department's plans for the new chemistry building, their thoughts went further than the traditional undergraduate organic chemistry course. Inorganic chemistry had long been the foundation for college-level curricula, but Ege, Pearson, and Coppola came to believe that a modern organic-based course would actually be a better entry into the entire chemistry curriculum.[18] They found support. As the momentum grew over the next year or so, then-department chair Arthur Ashe called Coppola to say, "We've been talking. We know what you'd like to do in Madison. Why don't you come do it in Ann Arbor?"

Ashe was offering a two-year visiting assistant professorship, but Coppola still had enough time to consider liberal arts colleges as another route to the kind of career he had in mind. Ege recalled phone conversations with Coppola about the pros and cons of a nontenured position at the University of Michigan versus a tenure-track position at one of these smaller schools. She was sure that the Michigan job would turn into a long-term position, but whether or not it would ever have an opportunity for tenure she could not say. Could he stand that uncertainty? Could he stand the status? It was a difficult decision, but after just a few interviews, Coppola closed the door on the liberal arts colleges. He admits that he was not a good interviewee. Committed to Michigan's willingness to pursue a major revision of the curriculum that would place organic chemistry at the start, Coppola's job talk would split the organic versus inorganic faculty at the colleges. "The organic faculty would be very excited and want me to come, but everybody else would be thinking, 'Who is this weirdo? Why would we invite that kind of troublemaker to join our department?'"

Coppola's first three years at Michigan were a whirlwind of activity, in which every waking moment was devoted to having a curricular plan in place for the opening in 1989 of the department's new building. The building, which was to house teaching laboratories for general and organic chemistry, was a critical part of the rationale to rethink the curriculum. Sheila Tobias wrote, in her account of the new curriculum at Michigan, "Equipping any curriculum would most likely set the pattern for some time, so if changes were to be made, this would be a good time to make them. [The new department chair David] Curtis agreed and decided to have 'new courses to teach' in the new laboratories" (1992, p. 65). While the new building gave urgency to long-standing curriculum committee discussions, the particular shape of the new curriculum was influenced by other circumstances and rationales (Ege, Coppola, & Lawton, 1997).

In writing their story of the change, Ege, Coppola, and colleague Rich Lawton noted that they shared the "increasing uneasiness, reflected at the national level, with the direction traditional general chemistry courses have taken," citing in particular what Gold (1988) had called their "obsession with content" (p. 780). In addition, they cited a study by the Women in Science program at the Center for the Education of Women at the University of Michigan (Manis, Thomas, Sloat, & Davis, 1989) that showed that "general chemistry courses, partly because they are the science courses taken first by the largest number of first-year students, are mentioned depressingly often by both men and women students as the courses that discourage them from continuing in the sciences" (Ege, Coppola, & Lawton, 1997, p. 81). Ege and her colleagues also noted that an increasing number of students with high Advanced Placement Test scores were coming to Michigan, getting credit for a year of general chemistry, and not taking organic chemistry until their second year. "It seemed to us that many of these students might be attracted to other disciplines before they had the opportunity to experience what chemistry had to offer" (1997, p. 81).

Curtis and Ege, then, provided the leadership for curriculum change. As chair, Curtis gave backing to the effort. "In faculty meetings," Ege recalled, "he more or less put his fist down and said there will be change."[19] As associate chair for undergraduate and curriculum affairs, Ege was charged with leading the development of the new undergraduate curriculum, meeting with all the relevant constituencies, including departments whose majors took chemistry as a basic science, and bringing together whichever group of faculty within the department she thought would make an appropriate curriculum committee to make the changes.[20] As a member of the curriculum committee and self-described "foot soldier" in Ege's war, Coppola participated in the ongoing conversations about what the program would look like, was given responsibility for collaborating in the development of the new first-year organic-based program, and led the development of the new second-term, first-year course. Ege led the development of the first-term course. Later, upper-level courses were revised to follow suit.

The development and introduction of Michigan's new chemistry curriculum is well documented by Coppola and his colleagues (Coppola, Daniels, & Pontrello, 2001; Coppola, Ege, & Lawton, 1997; Ege, Coppola, & Lawton, 1997), and has even been written up by science educator Sheila Tobias as an example of a successful revitalization of a whole undergraduate program in science (1992). The centerpiece, drawing on years of innovation by Ege and her colleagues in the teaching of organic chemistry at the University of Michigan, was to offer a two-term organic chemistry course, Structure and Reactivity, as an entrée for students with a strong high school chemistry background. General chemistry, the conventional starting point in college curricula, was still available for students with a weaker high school background or for those who required it for other reasons, either as a stand-alone or as preparation for more advanced courses. The emphasis in both first-year courses is on qualitative reasoning, giving students who continue more time to take the calculus they will need for the second year focus on inorganic and quantitative chemistry. From then on, a student's path depends on the requirements for his or her particular concentration or major, but all chemistry majors, before graduation, do an undergraduate research project or participate in an "open-ended projects laboratory" (Ege, Coppola, & Lawton, 1997).

The changes this curriculum made in the usual sequence of chemistry courses were accompanied by innovative pedagogical, laboratory, and assessment practices, especially for Structure and Reactivity, the introductory organic chemistry course. To Coppola and his colleagues, these changes were necessary if chemistry were to be taught as a liberal art. They noted:

> A course content that repeatedly brings students back to the same arguments about a few principles in the context of the increasingly complex structural features found in carbon compounds fosters development of skills in qualitative reasoning typical of the liberal arts. Students begin to see how "to combine familiar elements into new forms", to engage in the kinds of "sideways" thinking that comes from learning many ways to look at things, and to experience "the fit of form with function." Any student who does not develop a tolerance for "ambiguity" and an ability to "bring order out of apparent confusion" has trouble mastering organic chemistry. (Ege, Coppola, & Lawton, 1997, p. 75)[21]

The instructional strategies developed by Ege, Coppola, and their colleagues to teach chemistry as a liberal art include an emphasis on qualitative reasoning over coverage in the two introductory lecture courses, independent and open-ended laboratory activities to engage students "in the kind of scientific thinking that chemists use in their work," and many opportunities for collaborative learning and peer instruction (Ege, Coppola, & Lawton, 1997, p. 79). Clearly, Coppola's commitment to the role of teaching as a means of student learning is threaded through many of these innovations, from the stance the group takes toward exams as an opportunity for students to "teach" their professors, to the semi-structured and structured study groups in which students develop the requisite skills of expression by presenting their work to each other. Indeed, in writing about their instructional strategies, Coppola, Ege, and Lawton (1997, p. 85) acknowledge the influence of the two models that inspired Coppola early on, his undergraduate experience with performance studios in the arts, and his graduate experience with the University of Wisconsin's Greater University Tutorial Services (GUTS).[22]

In telling the story of these structured study groups today, Coppola also acknowledged the influence of Indiana University biologist (and Carnegie scholar) Craig Nelson, whom he heard speak in 1987 and 1989 at the Critical Thinking Institute hosted by the University of Chicago. Coppola noted, "In the 1980s, Craig was part of the leading edge of 'traditional' disciplinary practitioners who dared, at some personal risk, to make interdisciplinary connections to the newly-emergent notions of progressive pedagogy arising from various parts of the academy." Among the lessons that Coppola took away: If you value group work, make it count, and remember that when things are done right, you (the teacher) are less important to students' learning than you would like to think. But this was not to say that doing it right is easy. "At those Chicago meetings," Coppola recalled, "Craig urged, cajoled, and challenged the disciplinarian to take responsibility for connecting one's deep professional understanding of a field with the design for instruction. . . . For me, less than five years out of graduate school, Craig simultaneously represented and sanctified a way of thinking. In retrospect, he opened a real trajectory toward what Boyer and his colleagues would call, a few years later, a scholarship of teaching and learning."

I will return to the chemistry department's curriculum changes in the next chapter, but for now simply make the point that this was not a case of a few dedicated innovators moving ahead in the face of indifference. Rather, as we have seen, the "organic group" had worked for years to develop and test their basic model, and had garnered strong support from the chair and from the many constituencies in other departments and programs whose students take introductory chemistry (Tobias, 1992). In our conversations, Coppola added that the climate for change was also influenced by the many new, young faculty who had been brought in to rebuild the department and who were like "a bunch of young Turks who were aggressive and wanted to think in different ways." They had walked into a department with as yet unproved ambitions for both its research and teaching programs, and in accepting Michigan's offer, showed they were willing to take a chance that the new faculty, new building, and new curriculum would succeed. "If I look at those people today," Coppola said, "they remain very sensitive to issues in education. They're what I consider sometimes to be the first wave of a generation that is a little more sympathetic to a more balanced career. Even though they knew they would have to personally pursue a very aggressive research program, these are people who took pride in and thought about the fact that they were going to take their teaching seriously too. It's really true for a lot of my colleagues."

CRAFTING A CAREER

Still, there were limits to Coppola's colleagues' imagination of what support for teaching and learning in the department might include, as Coppola discovered in his quest to craft an academic career around chemical education. Coppola started at Michigan in 1986 as a visiting assistant professor, but from the beginning it was clear that his situation was unusual. First, he had bargained when he first came for his own lab for undergraduate student research and money to buy materials. Second, unlike most visiting faculty on short appointments, it soon became clear to those who knew him that Coppola was there not just to teach but to contribute intellectually to the design of the undergraduate program. Finally, Coppola also believed that his closest colleagues were already thinking, as he was, that a faculty position might be created in the teaching and learning area.

He recalled a conversation six months after arriving at Michigan in which M. David Curtis, the new chair, presumably prompted by Ege and others, asked him what it was he really wanted to do. For the first time, Coppola articulated for both himself and the chair that he wanted to think about his position as one based on contributions to the teaching and learning area above and beyond good teaching acumen in the classroom. Coppola saw an analogy between the kind of position he hoped to craft around chemistry teaching and learning and what the rest of his colleagues were doing in their own chemistry specialties. "You have to get your grants and write your papers and get your reputation and have a contribution that's lingering and lasting and novel, because that's what you're trained to think about doing. And why not just turn your attention to this kind of problem instead of that kind of problem?" This kind of position did not yet actually exist, but Coppola had reason to believe that it might be possible at Michigan. The chair took the first step by moving Coppola out of his two-year visiting appointment and into a renewable lectureship, which began in the fall of 1987.

The place and time were right for Coppola's aspirations. A lectureship, though not a tenure-track appointment, is actually a faculty position at the University of Michigan as opposed to a staff position at other institutions, including the University of Wisconsin–Madison, where Coppola originally had hoped to go. While Coppola acknowledged that there were still a few things that a Michigan lecturer could not do (like be the sole director of a doctoral thesis or the external member of a doctoral committee), there were others that were enabled by this faculty status. In particular, a Michigan lecturer *could* be a principal investigator on grants. This was important, because by the late 1980s, NSF was showing interest in funding science education again, and Coppola began working with Michigan's development office to get grants for curriculum development.[23] His work at this time involved designing the new courses and thinking about teaching materials, assessment, and the like. He was beginning to give talks. At a meeting of the Society for Literature and Science in September 1989, he spoke on the "Languages of Organic Chemistry," and in October 1989, at the Michigan College Chemistry Association, he and Ege gave their first talks on the new undergraduate curriculum. By the end of that academic year, invitations began to come in, and by early 1990, he was on the "normal" route to making an academic reputation. However, he noted, between 1989 and 1991 he was not engaged in much new work because he was so busy getting the new program running—1989–1990 was its first year, 1990–1991 was its second year, and 1991–1992 was its third year. Each year, a new part kicked in.

By the spring term of 1991, with the new curriculum nicely unfolding, Curtis, the outgoing chair, decided to put the issue of Coppola's position as lecturer to the faculty, suggesting that there might be a new tenure track position for chemical education that Coppola might fill. Coppola believed that this was one of the few times that the department's whole faculty (about 45) had been asked to consider such an issue, most decisions being made by a small executive committee, but it is perhaps the mark of how unusual everyone considered the idea to be. Coppola said that while he was assured that the faculty had expressed unanimous support for him and his contributions as an individual, he was also told that they had rejected the idea of creating a tenure-track position for chemical education. As Curtis noted, there were too many unanswered questions and issues that hadn't been thoroughly thought through. Would this kind of position be helpful in plans to upgrade the department? Would it mean that they could hire one less research-active chemist? What would it be called—professor of chemistry, professor of chemical education, or a joint appointment as professor of chemistry and education? Could this person take graduate students? How would it be evaluated?[24]

Coppola recalled a silver lining in this black cloud that Curtis urged him to see. The kind of position Coppola wanted was new, and little would be lost by pursuing it more strategically. How, in fact, would they know that six years is enough time for starting a tenure clock for this kind of position? As Coppola recalled, "I got a lot smarter after that conversation about really thinking what it was going to take to become a faculty member in chemistry in this area. This wasn't going to be a warm, fuzzy thing that just happens, but in fact it's going to have to have the same set of standards that people use for tenure review along with other assistant professors." According to Coppola, Curtis made it clear that he thought Coppola was on the right trajectory:

> In that conversation, Dave said, "One way this may play out is, in five or six years, you'll present a tenurable vitae. By then it will be beyond the time when we could rationally create an assistant professorship. And so you'll go and be a tenured associate."

Perhaps the most important thing to come out of this conversation from Coppola's perspective was Curtis' confidence in Coppola's ability to think strategically about how to bring this about. It was not, Curtis had said, his place, or any other chair's place, to prescribe what it was Coppola needed to do. As a faculty member, Coppola had to decide that, and further, few of his colleagues could advise him competently in the area of education. Then, Coppola recalled, Curtis said three words that made all the difference: "Show us how." This, of course, was music to Coppola's ears—an invitation to teach.

In the next chapter, I will pick up Coppola's story as he began to think strategically about his own career and how his story might inspire and inform others. Let me end this chapter by returning to the theme of thinking like a chemist. When Coppola told me the story of his turning-point conversation with Dave Curtis, I asked whether he thought he began to think of his situation as a problem in the "Trostian" sense (referring to his graduate advisor, Barry Trost). Coppola said that there was:

> . . . no question by then I was treating it like that. From the perspective of a Trost-trained chemist, it's an interesting problem. It's a really interesting problem because nobody else is thinking about it. It's exactly the kind of problem you're supposed to work on. It intersected with four years of values that came from that graduate training about how one picks problems, about how one thinks about the design of strategies for approaching problems. And while I may not be able to even today articulate those strategies terribly well, I think that my instincts are good and I manage to begin to be able to train students in how to do these things, as well.

NOTES

1. This quotation is from Ege, Coppola, and Lawton (1997), p. 74.

2. For Coleman's concept of "explanatory knowledge," see Coleman, Brown, and Rivkin (1997) and Coleman (1998).

3. This is by no means an easy task, not least because what it means to think like a chemist, historian, or anthropologist is often not well articulated by members of that community themselves. Judith Langer (1992) suggests that the disciplines often leave the articulation of their ways of thinking implicit, making it harder for teachers to bring "expert" thinking into their pedagogy.

4. Coppola himself does not fully agree with this statement. In comments on an earlier draft of this chapter, he wrote:

> The difference between what one has to do to stay competitive at the state of the art and what is done everywhere else has only increased, as far as I am concerned. One of the "newer technologies" is entrepreneurial activity which, in effect, adds a differential resource stream for high-powered researchers that pushes and moves the direction of their research programs, what it takes to get them done, and so on. Some smaller schools, even with state-of-the-art 1990s equipment, are flying blind in the biolog-

ical chemistry and materials science areas because of the equipment that the few powerhouse centers have. The rich continue to get richer and the middle class grows like crazy, believing that they are being competitive when they don't even know where the playing field is—never mind a level chance to compete—in my humble opinion, that is.

5. The Chemical Bond Approach (CBA) and Chemical Education Material Study (CHEM Study) were both curricular projects that were initiated in the late 1950s with support from NSF. The CBA project, at Reed College, brought science educators together to create a thematically-oriented, introductory chemistry course for high school students. The curriculum was intended to incorporate less-regulated lab experiences and to foster logical thinking skills. CHEM Study began as a collaboration among university chemists, high-school teachers, and industry scientists. Established at Harvey Mudd and Claremont Colleges, the project developed curricular materials around the "discovery approach," using labwork as a means for high-school students to learn chemistry concepts inductively (see http://scied.gsu.edu/Hassard/mos/mos.html and http://www.usc.edu/dept/education/science-edu/glossaryA-C.html).

6. NSF has granted awards over the past two decades through several different programs in efforts to reform the undergraduate chemistry curriculum. It has allocated resources through the Course and Curriculum Development Program and the Instrumentation and Laboratory Improvement Program to various curriculum development projects. In 1994, NSF initiated a program called Systemic Changes in the Undergraduate Chemistry Curriculum. Through this program, awards were granted to four multi-institutional coalitions over a period of five years: a group led by the University of Wisconsin–Madison; a City College Consortium (led by City University of New York); and a partnership between the ChemLinks Coalition (led by Beloit College) and the ModularChem Consortium (led by the University of California, Berkeley). For an account of these kinds of reform movements in STEM education, see Seymour (2002).

7. Commenting on an earlier draft of this manuscript, Coppola argued that my term "close relationship" still does not suggest the interdependence of chemistry and chemistry education. "I would probably have used something like 'inseparable interdependence of understanding chemistry and chemical education,'" he wrote, "or a phrase that was as close to a synonym for pedagogical content knowledge as I could find." Pedagogical content knowledge, according to Lee Shulman, is one of three categories of content knowledge important in teaching. *Content knowledge* "refers to the amount and organization of knowledge per se in the mind of the teacher"; *pedagogical content knowledge* "embodies the aspects of content most germane to teachability"; and *curricular knowledge* provides "the *material medica* of pedagogy, the pharmacopeia from which the teacher draws those tools of teaching that present or exemplify particular content and remediate or evaluate the adequacy of student accomplishments" (Shulman, 1986, pp. 9–10).

8. Founded in 1866 as an A&M college, New Hampshire College established a "solid chemistry" department from the start. Even by the 1890s, writes historian Donald C. Babcock, "the pre-eminent excellence of New Hampshire's chemistry department was being noted. It was by far the best equipped department of the

college and more than one third of the students were taking courses in chemistry at all times (1941, p. 133). The thesis requirement has been a long-standing tradition at the University of New Hampshire. The first B.S. theses were completed in 1893, and by the turn of the century, completion of independent research was an established requirement for the B.S. In 1911, the requirement was modified, leaving a thesis up to the discretion of the chairs of the engineering departments, but maintaining it for all other graduates of the college (Babcock, 1941, pp. 135, 174). Additionally, according to Paul R. Jones, a former chair of the Chemistry Department, all research students, undergraduate and graduate, have worked alongside each other in the chemistry lab:

> . . . often with the latter as informal mentors for the B.S. students, although each was directed by a faculty member. . . . By the 1970s, all research students were part of the faculty member's group. They worked in labs together and attended "research meetings" together. This still holds to the present day. For example, not only do individual research groups meet, but also several research groups with somewhat common interests, convene for a weekly lunch and seminar. Every undergraduate makes a presentation on the historical background, scope of the research, and experimental results at least once each semester (P. R. Jones, personal communication, May 30, 2002).

9. GUTS originated as a service offered in residence halls in 1974, when it was called "Help at Sellery Hall." By the 1980s, the service had expanded, and the facilitators registered as an official student organization in 1982. Status as a student organization gave the program access to facilities and funding, and today GUTS plays an established role at the university, offering not just peer tutoring, but also a program in conversational English, study skills counseling, and access to a file of previously administered exams in math and statistics. The service estimates its yearly student participation at 20,000. (For information on the program's current scope, see http://guts.studentorg.wisc.edu).

10. For those uninitiated into the subtleties of chemical subfields, the *Columbia Encyclopedia* defines chemistry as that:

> branch of science concerned with the properties, composition, and structure of substances and the changes they undergo when they combine or react under specified conditions. Chemistry can be divided according to either the substances studied or the types of study conducted. The primary division of the first type is between inorganic chemistry and organic chemistry. Divisions of the second type are physical chemistry and analytical chemistry. (1993, p. 521)

In pondering his attraction to organic chemistry, British Nobelist Harry Kroto recently wrote, "Perhaps it was something to do with the innate fascination humans have for solving puzzles. Maybe I saw the same challenge in elaborating a sequence of individual synthetic chemical reactions, the stepping stones to a target compound, that others find in playing games. . . . The challenge of devising the overall synthesis of an exotic molecule . . . seemed a significantly more useful activity" (2002, p. 15).

11. Coppola and Pearson wrote, "In every circumstance dealing with students, [Trost] respected and valued any conclusion his students made regardless of its validity to him. Rather, he assumed any statement was valid within the decision-making scheme we were using" (1998, p. 417). Although their elaboration refers to students' conclusions about scientific phenomena, they suggest ("in every circumstance . . .") that it may refer to other kinds of situation as well.

12. The increased investments in university-based science research after World War II provided expanded opportunities for both undergraduate and postgraduate students in science and engineering. In 1952, the first year of NSF expenditures, NSF awarded a total of $1.53 million in fellowship money to pre- and postdoctoral students; nearly half of NSF's $3.5 million budget (Blanpied, 1999). In addition, NIH became an important source of postdoctoral support, helping the late 1950s and early 1960s become "a golden age for American science." Peter von Hippel, a young faculty member in biophysics at the time, describes it as a period when "NIH (for the first and probably only time in its history) had more research and fellowship money than reasonable applicants to spend it on!" (Blanpied, 1999, p. 10).

13. In talking about this relationship, Coppola referred me to his writing about how professors should have a "full human presence" in relation to students, so that students can better understand what drives academic life—the idea, in his own case, that "a research director would share that degree of motivation with a student so that they could understand why they might want you to have this kind of career." (For elaboration of this model of mentorship and the problems it addresses, see Coppola, 2001a, 2002.)

14. Arthur Kornberg and Severo Ochoa, biochemists, were awarded the Nobel Prize in medicine in 1959. See Kornberg (1997) for his views on the importance of basic research in science and medicine.

15. Chemistry professor David Curtis attributes the shortsightedness at Michigan to a succession of humanist deans, who just did not understand or appreciate the trend toward big science. As an example, Michael Doyle recalled that the University of Michigan rejected an NSF Centers of Excellence grant in the 1960s, saying, in effect, "we already are one. As a consequence, the physical plant declined and good students got turned off by how bad it looked." The Centers of Excellence grant program was one of several initiated by the federal government to invest in scientific research facilities within colleges and universities, including programs funded through the 1963 Higher Education Facilities Act and the 1965 Higher Education Act. NSF itself supported first-tier universities through a 1961 grant program; by 1967, it extended its financial support to second-tier institutions through the Science Development Grants, otherwise known as the Centers of Excellence program. According to historian George T. Mazuzan, "relatively large awards were made to hire new faculty, support graduate students, and construct new facilities. In 1966, the agency broadened the program to include Departmental Science Development awards and Special Science Development awards to improve those subunits at many of the nation's second tier universities" (1994, p. 13). Interestingly, new developments in the funding of academic science and technology have again left Michigan behind. Compared to other research universities, Michigan has not been very successful at "commercializing the inventions of [its] professors and graduate students" (Blumenstyk, 2002, p. A24).

16. Formal rankings of graduate departments in chemistry from the 1950s and 1960s do show a decline for Michigan. The rankings of institutions by the "quality of graduate faculty" show Michigan declining from 14th. place in 1957 to tied for 19th. and 20th. in 1964 and 1969, respectively. The 1957 rankings were part of a survey of department chairs in 25 leading universities by Hayward Keniston (1959). The 1964 and 1969 figures are from reports published by the American Council on Education. The 1964 figures are based on a survey of department chairs by Allan Cartter (1966), while the 1969 figures are from a follow-up reputational survey of faculty in leading departments (Roose & Andersen, 1970). Results of all three can be found in Roose and Anderson (1970).

17. Curtis explained that the new dean during this period of upgrading came over and said, "We'll either have a good chemistry department or we won't have a chemistry department. Of course, this was a hollow bluff. But basically, when I became chair, he instituted a new way of giving faculty raises. He'll give half the raise money and if I discriminated, I'd get the other half. If I didn't discriminate I didn't get the other half. So that made you discriminate. So I literally gave 0% raises to some faculty members who hadn't written a grant and hadn't published a paper. The ones who were really working hard and publishing got big raises. Within a few years this drove a huge disparity in salary. Where before every full professor was doddering along on $50,000, some were now making close to $100,000 and others were below $50,000. And that caused a lot of grumbling and ill will in the department between the haves and the have-nots, many of them the old guard, who for some reason never saw how chemistry was changing or what it took to be successful in the changed world."

18. According to Michael Doyle, a few other institutions have tried this, for example, Brown, Bucknell, and Hope College. But it was the first time that a very large institution had tried it. According to Coppola, however, "It's rare enough that it probably doesn't even count as an outlier. You find it in just a few places like Bucknell, but the tradition is pretty strong."

19. To illustrate the politics involved, Ege told me about a poll that she and Curtis did of the faculty to see if there was enough support for change in the department. "And we described three questions. One, there needs to be change; I'm willing to work on it. Another, there needs to be change; but I'm not wiling to work on it. And the third, no change is necessary. And the department broke down roughly one third in each of those categories. And we decided that with one third really supportive and one third feeling that something needed to be done, that we had enough support to go forward. We never expected it to be 100 percent." See also the account in Ege, Coppola, and Lawton (1997).

20. Opponents to reform in the chemistry curriculum would often argue that you can't change this or you can't change that because *other* departments need it. Yet Ege found in her negotiations with other departments that these were by and large "false restrictions." In our conversation, Ege noted:

> the biologists were delighted that we moved organic chemistry up front because that meant they could teach their modern biology as molecular biology and their students much better understood what was going on in the cell. And most engineers, when questioned closely, did not have

strong opinions on what we taught because they just had their students take chemistry because this was their requirement for certification. Of course, chemical and metallurgical engineers had opinions, but our revisions met their requirements. As it turned out, to meet the certification requirements, most engineering students were channeled into our one-term General Chemistry course, originally (intended for those students who did not make the cut on the placement exam) and the lab course that accompanied it.

As Coppola recalled, Ege's diplomacy extended to a mass letter that went out to all deans of medical schools, because they were going to change dramatically the premedical requirements for students coming out of Michigan. See also Tobias (1992).

21. The internal quotes refer to certain skills and mental processes required for business managers that Roger B. Smith, then Chairman of General Motors Corporation, identified in a 1985 speech at the University of Michigan as those that were best "acquired and sharpened in the study of the liberal arts" (see Ege, Coppola, & Lawton, 1997, p. 75).

22. Participation in the semi-structured study groups is voluntary, and pairs small groups of six to eight students with one to two facilitators drawn from undergraduate alumni of the course. They meet weekly and the students are given weekly sets of open-ended problems. Facilitators are provided with resources and suggestions for how to proceed. Students who choose to do the honors version of Structure and Reactivity take the regular lectures and labs, but participate in more formal structured study groups. In these groups, approximately 15 students work with a junior or senior undergraduate leader who follows a detailed curriculum involving exploration of molecules described in recent chemistry journal articles, student presentations, peer review, and discussion (Coppola, Daniels, & Pontrello, 2001; Coppola, Ege, & Lawton, 1997). The animation assignment with which this chapter began was from the second semester of this course.

23. Although it was not against the rules for Coppola to seek grants as a principal investigator, it was also true that lecturers did not apply as PIs very often. To give Coppola a title other than lecturer, his chair called him coordinator of the undergraduate organic chemistry curriculum. However, Coppola said, by about the third or fourth grant he submitted, the administrators finally looked beyond the title and noted he was a lecturer.

24. Curtis believed the department's discussion about this position should be seen in the context of the time. The department was still rebuilding its reputation after years of decline, and there was still a split between research active and research inactive faculty as to where resources should go and in which communities the department wanted to be known. There was also uncertainty about the new dean, and whether she would hold such a position against the department in the future, denying them another position for a person active in a more conventional field of chemistry research.

5

Pedagogical Positions

. . . .

> Contributions from faculty in the area of pedagogy continue to
> receive broader recognition and more widespread acceptance in
> universities and colleges across the United States than in the
> past. Much of this work has come from individuals in areas of
> education and psychology. Ideas that promote substantial
> progress have come less frequently from within specialized
> departments. . . . [But] nationally, the question of a chemist,
> engineer, or historian building a career track on a broadened
> understanding of scholarship has come into better focus as doc-
> umentation and discussion of successful cases has become more
> public.[1]

It is one thing to gain institutional recognition for teaching as serious intellectual work, but quite another to build careers around contributions to
teaching and learning within the academic departments themselves. To be
sure, schools and departments of education have long been home to specialists in the teaching and learning of science, math, history, and reading
(although typically at the precollege level). Elsewhere in the academy, however, pedagogical positions are still few and far between. In fields like composition, pedagogical and disciplinary scholarship often overlap (Salvatori
& Donahue, 2002).[2] In most other fields, work on teaching and learning is
only beginning to gain acceptance. Because pedagogy is not widely seen as
a legitimate focus for disciplinary scholarship, it can be a challenge to make
the case that it is worthy of departmental and institutional support.

Although there seems to be a growing willingness within the disciplines and within colleges and universities to embrace a broad definition
of "scholarship," it is still not clear how to make sure that this new work
counts. Within established disciplines, there are established cultures (with
disciplinary variations) around the scholarship of discovery, or research.
There may be disputes about particulars, but there is generally wide agreement on its genres, signs of distinction, and proportions—how much of

95

what kind is enough. However, as cultures are only beginning to form around the scholarships of teaching, integration, and engagement (to mention only the categories from *Scholarship Reconsidered*), faculty are pursuing these lines of work with much less certainty about whether they will be accepted as scholarship by colleagues and administrators, and if so, about what criteria will be used to evaluate their value, quality, and weight.

When we left Brian Coppola of the University of Michigan's Chemistry Department in the last chapter, he had just received a strong reminder of how such uncertainty can affect important decisions about faculty careers. In 1991, his department had voted against creating a tenure-track position for a chemical educator, in part because they were not ready to devote a "line" to this specialty, and in part because they were not sure how to shepherd someone whose work focused on teaching and learning through the ranks or even to evaluate such an unusual body of work. The lesson that Coppola drew from this decision was that they should not again try to make the case for the scholarship of teaching and learning in chemistry through "the language of exception." He would try to become, eventually, not a professor of chemical education, but a professor of chemistry with a specialty in "discipline-centered teaching and learning," or what Coppola later came to call "Interdisciplinary Studies at the Interface of Education."[3] He would establish a record that could be judged by the same standards that would be used to evaluate a faculty member with a more conventional specialty, like organic chemistry, physical chemistry, or the like.

Coppola's case is particularly interesting, because it has become a model, or "existence proof," within the field showing that it is indeed possible to negotiate a tenure-line pedagogical position in a highly ranked department at a major university. There are a few other examples. Coppola's career began, and could very well have continued, as do so many others in the academy today, in a nontenure-track position. In chemistry, according to The Research Corporation's Michael Doyle, this trend began with the influx of undergraduates after World War II. Fueled by rising numbers of enrollments, and perhaps, too, by the increasing opportunities for faculty to participate in externally funded research, chemistry departments began hiring nonfaculty "staff" and "lecturers" to manage and sometimes teach the laboratory and discussion sessions of their introductory chemistry courses. In the 1950s, a time of rampant gender discrimination both in academic and professional science, many such "teaching positions" were filled by women with graduate chemistry degrees.[4] Others, including an institution's own recent Ph.D.s on occasion, joined the ranks in the 1960s and 1970s. According to Doyle, "many stayed on in nontenure track positions to handle, for example, the freshman chemistry or laboratory program." Today, it is common for chemistry departments to dedicate one or more person to the teaching program in this way.

But there are, and always have been, several streams of involvement and leadership in chemical education. In our conversation, George Bodner, a prominent chemical educator from Purdue University, explained that the field today comprises three or four coexisting "generations" (Bodner & Herron, 1984). The first includes people such as Linus Pauling, "brilliant individuals who made contributions in many, many areas, including the teaching of chemistry. And they thought of themselves as chemical educators." These giants still walk the earth, lending their support, prestige, and ideas to the larger enterprise: Founding Director of the Beckman Institute at California Institute of Technology, Harry Gray, and Nobelists Dudley Herschbach of Harvard and Roald Hoffmann of Cornell. Hoffmann, for example, has not only been awarded the 1981 Nobel Prize for his research but has also received the American Chemical Society's Pimentel award in chemical education. "I have a strong general commitment to chemical education," Hoffman explained. He still teaches introductory chemistry, and he was the presenter of a television series called "The World of Chemistry," 26 half-hour programs produced in the late 1980s that are still shown to high school students on cable and educational television. Hoffmann's engagement with teaching and learning goes further, being "idiosyncratic in some ways, and having different components from other people. One is that I favor a pedagogical style in my research. And I actually think that teaching undergraduates has helped me become a researcher."

Bodner's second generation of chemical educator is the "traditional" professor, who has done some work as a research chemist, but becomes more and more engaged with teaching. "These are the people who frequently have gone into a department as normal faculty hires, gotten interested in the problems associated with teaching chemistry and spent most of their time worrying about the multitudes who take chemistry. Most of the people in chemical education are in this particular phase. They've been trained in one of the traditional branches of chemistry, often inorganic or physical chemistry; they go to a small college or sometimes to a big one, and then spend most of their time worrying about teaching students." Hoffmann agreed. The majority of the people who are "very active in the American Chemical Society's Division of Chemical Education, and at national and international conferences, are chemistry professors at small colleges," he noted.

A third generation, arriving on the scene in the late 1960s and early 1970s, were among the first to be appointed to faculty positions with the expectation that they would work on issues in chemistry education. For example, Bassam Shakhashiri, trained in inorganic chemistry, took up a tenure-track position at the University of Wisconsin–Madison in the fall of 1970 with "a clear-cut understanding that my scholarly activities would be in the area of chemistry education, which was highly unusual in a research department." This was the generation that made education in chemistry a research field and then faced the question of what kind of field it would be. Some, like Shakhashiri, who later founded a research center for chemical education at Madison,[5] believed that people who study teaching and learning in chemistry at the college level should be primarily trained as professional chemists, while also becoming familiar with the relevant work in education. Others, like Bodner, pioneered separate graduate programs in chemical education within departments of chemistry, like the program at Purdue, complete with the same kinds of research groups that characterize bench research in chemistry.[6] All, however, have had to press for the legitimacy of their work. Bodner noted that members of this generation "fought a lot of battles for recognition among chemists, and still are fighting them, to some extent."

The next generation—Coppola's—inherited the third generation's successes and continuing struggles for recognition within the field and within the colleges and universities where they are employed. There are many differences of opinion within the chemical education community (Coppola & Jacobs, 2002). Among their shared concerns is the nature of positions available to chemical educators, especially the number, status, and location of such positions. They are keen observers of developments. In particular, people in this community note with pride that more chemical educators are being offered tenure-track positions. Still, there is a sense that the most visible departments and universities have not yet made a strong commitment. For example, advocates were pleased that as energetic and creative a person as Brian Coppola was employed at the University of Michigan, but they were disappointed that he began in a nontenure track position. As I was told by Bassam Shakhashiri, who had known of Coppola's interests in graduate school, "Early on, I was a little unhappy that Michigan didn't start him out on a tenure track."

Of course, these decisions are seldom in the hands of departments alone. In particular, observers of higher education have noted with some alarm the proliferation of nontenure track "teaching" positions across the academy in recent years. To be sure, graduate students have long cut their pedagogical teeth leading the discussion sections of introductory lecture courses, and there have always been a few courses available for qualified faculty spouses and community members to teach. What is new has been the growth and elaboration of this nontenure-track sector of the academic profession since the 1970s. As more and more colleges and universities cut full-time tenured lines in favor of lower costs, flexibility, and control, introductory undergraduate instruction is increasingly provided by faculty (or "staff") working in part-time or full-time nontenure-track positions (American Association of University Professors, 1993; Finkelstein, Seal, & Schuster, 1998; Tirelli, 1998).[7]

Thus, Coppola's status as a nontenure track faculty member at the University of Michigan was, in Shakhashiri's words, "not a problem that Coppola owned." To move into a regular line position, Coppola's department would have to commit to giving him (and his specialty) a position that could not, at least while he held it, go to someone else. The dean, the College of Literature, Science, and Arts, and the university itself would also have to consider what this kind of move might mean for their institution's large and growing number of nontenure track lecturers. Clearly, this was a case that would be watched both inside and outside of Michigan's Department of Chemistry. Coppola understood that in an important way, the progress of his career at the University of Michigan would not be just about him as a scholar, but, as he put it in his promotion papers, about whether "discipline-centered teaching and learning" would be affirmed as a "legitimate area of faculty specialization." According to Coppola, "the thing that really meant the most to me was that it would be a policy decision."

Establishing a Record

Midway through the 1990–1991 academic year, after the department narrowly defeated a plan to create a tenure track position in chemical education that Coppola might fill, David Curtis completed his highly successful four-year term as chair of Michigan's Chemistry Department, and Robert Kuczkowski took over. Like Curtis, Kuczkowski believed that Coppola should eventually be on the tenured faculty, and he began talking to Coppola about how this might be done:

> As we discussed it, we came up with the idea that Brian was most comfortable with remaining in the lecturer track, but putting together a portfolio of achievements so that at some point we would go to the college and make the case, although we were a little ambiguous about how exactly we would do this. But if he had a portfolio of accomplishments—research, teaching, service, and so forth— at some point we were going to see what we could do.

Kuczkowski and other mentors would help with the politics and with strategic and substantive advice. Coppola had already learned that it was ultimately his own responsibility to do work that was "recordable" in the standard academic vernacular of teaching evaluations, research grants and publications, evidence of reputation and impact, and making the work known.

In the five years that followed, Coppola's productivity soared. There was continuing work on the department's new curriculum, of course, but Coppola also continued to build his record for pedagogical innovation. In particular, this period saw the beginnings of his vision for an infrastructure for future faculty development, a plan to create teaching opportunities for talented undergraduates, graduate students, and post-doctoral students. The fall of 1994 saw the formal debut of Coppola's "signature" work in undergraduate peer instruction—the semi- structured study groups for students in the new introductory chemistry sequence and structured study groups for honors sections, followed in 1996 by a graduate seminar in chemistry education pedagogy and a small start on the postdoctoral component of the plan. In addition, Coppola developed during these years the project- and research-based courses for second-term first-year students who envisioned themselves to be future scientists.[8] He allied with colleagues in the School of Education to develop a chemistry course, co-requisite with a science teaching methods course, for prospective elementary school teachers as well as a chemistry seminar for science education researchers. He helped design any number of smaller science outreach events and programs. He received university teaching awards, often more than one, every single year.[9]

A growing number of grants helped to support Coppola's activities, including his work with Ege in developing the department's new curriculum from 1989 to 1997. He and Ege served as co-principal investigators for four NSF grants totaling more than $700,000. Another $500,000 came from The Amoco Foundation and the Warner-Lambert Foundation, and The Hewlett-Packard Foundation awarded $100,000 to support undergraduate laboratory development in 1994. Coppola's collaboration with colleagues in the School of Education was funded by an NSF Teacher Preparation grant of more than $400,000 from 1991 to 1993 as well as by a smaller NSF Instructional Technology grant. Smaller grants came from the Dreyfus Foundation for a collaboration with Michigan's Women in Science Program, as well as from the National Aeronautical and Space Administration, the Research Corporation, and several programs at the University of Michigan, including the Office of Minority Affairs; the School of Literature, Science and Arts Computer Fund; the school's Undergraduate Initiatives, and more. Coppola was proving himself to be as entrepreneurial as any "mainstream" laboratory chemist in seeking out external and internal financial support and legitimation for projects important to his work.[10]

A tireless ambassador for the pedagogical work that he and his colleagues were doing at Michigan, and for chemical education more generally, Coppola began spending a good deal of time on the road. Between 1991 and 1996, he delivered presentations on the undergraduate curriculum to the chemistry departments of 15 colleges and universities and additionally spoke at several teaching and learning centers. There were over 50 formal presentations at events such as the Biennial Conference on Chemical Education, the national meetings of the American Chemical Society, and, to reach out to the wider science education community, at meetings of the National Association for Research in Science Teaching and, later, at meetings sponsored by AAHE. Coppola was also publishing on education topics, with some 20 pieces in print between 1992 and 1997.[11] Many of these articles, including important descriptions of Michigan's new under-graduate curriculum, laboratory activities, and other pedagogical innova-tions, came out in the field's top peer-reviewed journals: the *Journal of Chemical Education* and *Chemical Educator*, along with a string of more "philosophical" reflections on undergraduate education, including, for example, the coauthored pieces "A Case for Ethics" (Coppola & Smith, 1996), and "Mea Culpa: Formal Education and the Dis-Integrated World" (Coppola & Daniels, 1998).[12]

Not surprisingly, through all this activity, Coppola and his ideas became known. To be sure, there was ready interest in Michigan's new curriculum within the chemistry community, although as Coppola joked, it was like public interest in a "three-headed snake, which everybody wants to see, and nobody wants to take home." Still, according to Michael Doyle, there was a sense of excitement about what Michigan had done. While the idea of using organic chemistry as the entryway for freshman chemistry has not been widely adopted, the way in which it was implemented, through dis-covery-based experimentation in the undergraduate laboratory, has entered general practice in the field. "It became," Doyle said, "a topic of conversation nationwide." As chemical educator George Bodner put it:

> Brian got recognition for good reasons. First of all, he knew every-body, and second of all, he told everybody about what he was doing. He got out and he talked. He read. He wrote strange papers that sometimes people understood and sometimes they didn't. But the main thing is they realized that he was there. And he started to get recognition for being creative.

Arthur Ellis of the University of Wisconsin provided a case in point about the process of recognition in chemical education at that time. A materials chemist, Ellis became interested in chemical education:

> . . . when the high temperature superconductors came along and you could levitate magnets with them. I thought, "This would be great to get into teachers' hands." And I began to be frustrated by the way I was teaching the introductory class. It really hadn't changed in 30 years.

That is when he began to learn about the work that was going on at Michi-gan. Ellis heard about the positive effect the new curriculum and labs were having from Seyhan Ege at NSF workshops and:

> . . . was very interested to see that what Brian [and his colleagues were] writing about introducing organic chemistry as a starting

point in his *Journal of Chemical Education* articles and preprints he was sending to me, were almost similar in impact to what we were seeing by putting solids into the curriculum. Both of them were new approaches based on different content, but both were also trying to take a bigger picture view of what kind of skill you want students to come away with from these courses.

Ellis later introduced lab experiences similar to those Coppola had pioneered at Michigan and admired the "way he was bringing in some ideas from cognitive psychology." Ellis noted:

> For example, if you showed students a white compound and asked them to analyze it, he would look at how they go about it and try to map that on to how an expert would think about it. So I thought that was really creative and while I haven't used it quite like that, it sort of broadened my thinking, and I would go around and tell other people about what Brian was doing.

Consider, too, Roald Hoffmann's story about the relationship that he, a senior Nobelist, struck up with Coppola, then a mere lecturer. As Hoffmann recalled, it began when he wrote Coppola a note about one of those "philosophical, thoughtful, and reflective" papers that Coppola had published in the *Journal of Chemical Education*. Coppola replied with a draft of another paper that took a "broad cultural perspective," intriguing Hoffmann with its "admonition to learn from our students, not just to chide them for being stupid and not understanding what we tell them." Hoffmann himself had just finished reading students' responses to a very large undergraduate course that he was teaching. "Somewhat down" by their reaction to what he had been trying to do that semester, Hoffmann recalled, "I thought that Brian's viewpoint of learning from our students actually helped me recover a certain perspective." So, Hoffmann wrote the first draft of a joint paper exploring this experience, and "ten drafts later they had a very much changed paper, as much Brian's as mine about what we can learn from our students." In the process and subsequently, Hoffmann noted, "I have read all the things that he's written, and sometimes I have disagreed with him. But that doesn't take away from the fact that I found throughout that whatever Brian said was interesting to me about chemistry, our profession, and concerning questions of ethics and education."

THE POLITICS OF PROMOTION

Building a record—and reputation—contributes not only to the advancement of a field, of course, but also to the advancement of a career. In fact, many people who came to know about Coppola's work also came to know about his drive for a "real" pedagogical position. Again, the larger community's interest in Coppola's career went beyond their concern for him as a person. Creating such a position at a large and prestigious institution like the University of Michigan was in the interest of the chemical education community, and they looked after him, making sure he was on their seminar calendars. Departments, too, were supportive. During a trip to the University of Missouri–Columbia, Coppola attended the reception following his talk about the developments at Michigan. He remembered someone saying:

> "I notice you're not a professor. Tell us about that. What are the things that are planned?" And half way through the conversation, "Well, that's really interesting. You know we'd really like to have a faculty member with that specialization here too. We're very amenable and supportive of that idea, but every time we go to our administration, they want to know about the Michigans of the world that do this. So stick with it, kid, because what you're doing there becomes important to our cause."

Finally, Coppola's case was also of interest to institutional leaders for whom undergraduate education at the research university was a high priority. For example, Coppola reported that the department's external advisory board, including a university president who was a departmental alumnus, cared about the educational direction of the department and were always interested in getting an update on his case—"How's it going? Where are we at these days? Is it moving along?"

These same lines of interest among people external to the university also helped Coppola develop a presence within it. For one thing, there were Coppola's collaborations and alliances with colleagues in the College of Education, the Center for Research on Learning and Teaching, and other offices and departments of the university. There was the fact that Coppola's many teaching awards and involvement with the chemistry department's curricular experiment brought him to the attention of Edie Goldenberg, the new dean of the College of Literature, Science and the Arts in 1989. She and the university's new president, James Duderstadt, visited one of the labs to see how things were happening. Goldenberg reported:

> As I said in a number of speeches afterward, we were there, and that was fine for a few minutes. But the students were very engaged in problem-solving, and they needed to get together with one another, so we needed to step out of the way.

With the department's engagement with curricular reform held up as an example of the University's creativity and commitment to undergraduate education, Coppola became a regular speaker at the annual meeting of the university's visiting committee, a group made up of about 40 alumni and friends of the college.

The department had an external review in the early 1990s, which included three chemists from leading institutions but also Michael Doyle, then from Trinity College, who was known for his contributions to education. It was the second time that the course in organic chemistry had been offered to freshmen in large numbers, and Doyle remembered Coppola and Ege saying they thought they'd have some 170 majors the next year, and that they couldn't handle them all. Doyle reflected, "You know, that was the level of excitement. They were actually in new territory." According to Goldenberg, when the reviewers met with the College Executive Committee, the committee expected special input from Doyle, but to their surprise, the members from the large universities were also intensely interested. These chemists hadn't realized that it was possible to do this on a large scale. The chemist from the University of Texas told them that he had been skeptical about what Michigan was doing in introductory chemistry. "I quizzed those students, and I really worked them over for an hour or so; and all I can tell you is: I wish I had brought graduate applications with me." Goldenberg concluded, "It was a very powerful statement. It was a statement of unanimous praise for what we were doing from our peers."

The success of the department's new curriculum enhanced Coppola's reputation within the chemistry department itself. The department's special history—its climb back up the rankings, its new building, its strong chairs, and the creativity of Ege, Coppola, and their colleagues—had won good support for the effort.[13] "Not every single member was for it," Doyle recalled from his visit with the external review committee, "but basically you could say every division was working toward the goals that would provide for Michigan a unique curriculum." Furthermore, as Ege recalled:

> It helped that the new curriculum was as successful as it was right away, because when the faculty who were not really involved with the changes went out to give their talks on their own chemical research, they very often found that the faculty at these other institutions wanted to talk to them about our curriculum. And so they came back and quickly brushed up and asked if we had some slides or something they could take with them the next time so they would be ready for such questions.

More immediately relevant to the politics of promotion for Coppola was a structural change introduced by Robert Kuczkowski when he became chair of the department in the winter of 1991. Soon thereafter, the department began putting its lecturers through the same annual review system as other faculty, a procedure established because it was right thing to do, but which also turned out to be good for Coppola's case. First, these meetings provided useful commentary and feedback; second, they created a record of looking seriously at pedagogical work; and finally, because of their rotating membership, they made the work of the various lecturers better known within the department than it otherwise would have been.[14] These benefits, of course, accrued not only to Coppola, but to the three other lecturers in the department at that time. There was no tenure clock running, of course, because they were on three-year renewable appointments, but they all had the benefit of a formal review, with a report and a discussion afterwards, thinking ahead to the next year. In fact, then-chair Kuczkowski thinks it was through this forum that Coppola's "case" for a tenured position in the department had, "at some point," been won. Afterward, thinking ahead to next year came to mean not whether, but when to put him up for a formal tenure review.

There was a lot of other political work to be done. One piece was to clarify what kind of position the department should advocate. Another was to prepare the ground with the dean of the college, which, as Coppola's portfolio grew, the chair began to do. Would the college be supportive of creating a tenured position for Coppola, and how might they proceed? As Kuczkowski recalled, "Because he was developing quite a visible record to people outside the department, including the college and perhaps other colleges and the university at large, the dean's office knew who I was talking about, and there was encouragement to continue along the road and just bring up a tenurable file at some point. Or perhaps Coppola would get an outside offer and we'd bring it up at that point. It was not clear because there was no precedent for this in the college." Former dean Goldenberg recalled that she "was certainly interested in seeing if we could pursue this, but of course only after a recommendation from the Chemistry Department itself." In the meantime, she said:

> Conversations were necessary with the Executive Committee in advance. And I also had conversations with the provost and president. There had to be some openness at that level for receiving a recommendation that would look different. And we needed to know why we were doing it and what we were doing. The conversation in advance talked about the need in some of our large departments for having one or two such people who might be promoted primarily because of extraordinary contributions to undergraduate education. The Executive Committee then struggled with how they would think about a case like this. In evaluating such a case, we thought about various possible criteria such as national visibility, important educational contributions beyond classroom performance (which we

expect of all of our faculty), and we talked about contributions which move the educational effort in a larger field and have promise of doing so beyond the field.

With encouragement of this kind, the department, at the time of his review in 1996, told Coppola that he, and they, were ready. In the following year, the department would go forward with his promotion and tenure process exactly as they would for an assistant professor, living for the moment with the paradox that there was, as yet (as Coppola put it), "no such position to promote." During the summer his committee was formed, chaired by his mentor Seyhan Ege. Like all such committees at Michigan, this one's official function was to serve as an advocacy body for Coppola, coordinate communications with external referees, and advise the chair on how to respond to questions from the other bodies involved: a divisional committee for the sciences, the college executive committee, the dean, the provost, president and, should it come to that, the board of trustees. Coppola was given time off to ready a few last articles for publication, assemble materials, and prepare his case.

MAKING THE CASE

In making his case, Coppola and his closest mentors worked hard to avoid the "language of exception," in favor of presenting materials that could be evaluated by the same standards that might be applied to a more conventional portfolio. Coppola found strong support for this strategy in the department and in the larger community of people concerned to establish the legitimacy of chemical education as a specialty within a chemistry department. Wisconsin's Arthur Ellis, who was invited to write on Coppola's behalf, explained the basic logic of this move. "I like to tell my colleagues in the research community that all the same metrics are used [for scholarship in teaching as for scholarship in research]," he said. He continued:

> You're looking for papers published in peer-reviewed, high profile journals; you're looking for funding brought in from competitive sources like the National Science Foundation; you're looking for speaking invitations; you're looking for adoption or adaptation of the work in other people's programs. And you know by all those metrics, Coppola was doing great things. And therefore, I made the case, a very strong case, for promotion and one that I would enthusiastically support in my own institution.

Yet making such a case is more complicated than these simple metrics suggest. The fact is that the conventions by which people read an academic record do not neatly apply to "unconventional" scholarship. Coppola was pursuing a position as a "professor of chemistry, not professor of chemistry with an asterisk." In other words, he wanted discipline-centered teaching and learning to be treated in the same way as any other subject focus in the field. As Coppola well knew, not all emergent areas (even in the sciences) are warmly welcomed. Certainly, scholars in emergent fields like women's studies or ethnic studies in the 1970s and 1980s had a hard enough time convincing their colleagues that their expertise was important, their conferences and journals demanding, and their referees worthy (Gumport, 2002a). Scholars of teaching and learning could expect these problems, too.

Scholars of teaching and learning have had the additional challenge of presenting work that is not obviously, or advantageously, divisible into the institutional categories of "teaching, research, and service." To be sure, Coppola had teaching evaluations and awards that count at Michigan, as at most schools, as evidence of good teaching. He had published several articles from his laboratory work. He had done more than his share of service on departmental and university committees. What about his signature contributions—the very achievements that had convinced his department to put him forth for tenure? Where would Coppola's contributions to developing the new curriculum and laboratories be placed? What about his innovations in the area of peer instruction? Would his philosophical reflections on chemistry and education count as research? Michigan's published definitions of teaching, research, and service are reasonably broad, but because the scholarship of teaching and learning cross cuts the categories, they do not otherwise give people in Coppola's situation much help.[15]

Indeed, it is not easy to divide achievements in the scholarship of teaching and learning into the discrete categories that most universities and colleges require. To this day, Coppola believes that one of his more important contributions may have been to draft tenure and promotion documents that explain how to read the record of contributions to teaching and learning that they contained. As he said, for scholars like himself, "instructional and research activities are naturally intertwined," so that "sorting through these issues is also part of what I consider to be included in my professional and scholarly purview." Coppola's solution provides a provocative and potentially useful model for sorting pedagogical contributions. He began with three descriptive categories: (a) day-to-day teaching practices (chemistry teaching and learning), (b) the structure of an educational program (chemical education), and (c) assessment and evaluation practices (examination-related activities as well as chemical education research).

Because candidates for tenure and promotion at Michigan are required to prepare separate statements about their work in teaching and research (but not service), Coppola's second step was to decide which work he would discuss under these headings. While admitting that many of his activities "defy clear separations," he stated that he would include work within the first two categories in his teaching statement, leaving those from the last category for his statement on research. For example, the redesigned introductory chemistry curriculum and the specific features that he developed or co-developed for it (including, for example, its interactive format and peer instruction options) are elaborated under "teaching," while his publications in the area of philosophy and epistemology, teaching and learning skills, preparation and training, and assessment and evaluation are offered as "research."

Coppola's major breakthrough in preparing his papers, however, was his realization that what held most if not all of his teaching and learning activities together and gave them coherence as part of a single intellectual agenda, was their contribution to an infrastructure for future faculty development, beginning with undergraduate education, which Coppola had begun to call "CSIE" (Chemical Sciences at the Interface of Education). His vision was broader still, because "CSIE" could be considered just one site for a larger Interdisciplinary Studies at the Interface of Education (ISIE), which he saw as (potentially) an important part of all disciplinary departments. As he explained in his tenure and promotion documents, "I am suggesting that progress in science . . . depends on an infrastructure that promotes independence and welcomes creativity from informed yet novice participants. This is the lesson from the research domain that I seek to adapt to science education."

For Coppola, this was a critical articulation of a program that could be pursued further in the future—and one that also distinguished his view of the field of chemical education from that of many other chemical educators. For the basic philosophy underlying ISIE is that "the design, implementation, and assessment of learning environments in higher education" was *not* the role of a specialist, but was instead "a traditional faculty role." In his tenure documents, Coppola again evoked the culture of academic research to explain what he had in mind. "My proposition is that progress in science education is analogous to progress in all other forms of intellectual inquiry," he said. "Future researchers are well trained. However, a formal infrastructure that guides the training of the future professoriate for their teaching careers does not exist." In Coppola's view the role of specialists (like himself) was to build the infrastructure that would enable all who teach in the future to do a better job in this role.

It is impossible to know, of course, how important Coppola's written representations of his past achievements and future plans were to the successful outcome of his case. To some extent, the work had to stand for itself, without the narrative overlay that Coppola's vision might provide. Coppola's perspective could help his advocates make arguments on his behalf.

Seyhan Ege noted that she conferred with the chair on virtually every written communication about Coppola to the college administration as the process got underway, to avoid the natural tendency to represent this as a "special" case. Still, it is quite possible that those making the necessary decisions were more interested in the interpretations of those who wrote letters on Coppola's behalf—a group consisting, as far as Coppola knows, of five chemists (his advisor and four who were known for taking seriously issues in education, including two Nobelists); two with specialties in chemical education; two in chemical education research; two in science education research; one in the history and philosophy of science; and one educational psychologist. Certainly it helped to have support from the communities from which his work drew and to whom it spoke. Certainly it helped to have a scholar with the prestige of a Nobel Prize cite for praise such "standard metrics" as Coppola's grounding in organic chemistry research, his organizational abilities, and publishing record, as well as his interest in young people, broad outlook, and inspirational leadership.[16]

In the end, of course, adjustments had to be made to account for the unique nature of Coppola's case. One issue appears to have been "the standard metric," which, however convincing it may be at one level, has never been standard in its application. The fact is that in most disciplines, and especially the sciences, work in discipline-centered teaching and learning looks different than normal work to most scholars.[17] I was told that the divisional committee, composed of representatives from the science departments, said in effect, "Look, this case is just a different sort of case. And this is a decision for the Executive Committee." Even the Executive Committee, prepared ahead, sent a string of questions back to the chemistry department chair. They, too, were inclined to read Coppola's record as stronger in innovation than research. "But," said the dean (Goldenberg), "they were sufficiently impressed with the innovation in the course, and the recognition that Coppola and the department had received nationally as a consequence of Brian's and Seyhan's efforts, that in the end the vote was positive and the case went through."

Two additional issues had to be resolved at approximately the same time. Coppola might be deemed worthy of a tenured position at the University of Michigan, but what position should he fill and how should he and the position be brought together? The answer to the first was approving a new position for associate professor of chemistry, the solution Coppola had hoped for all these years. The answer to the second was a something of a surprise, because rather than promote Coppola from "lecturer" to "associate professor," they created a new position for him to fill as a new hire. In short, the university seems to have been wary of having Coppola's case interpreted as a sign that the position of "lecturer" could be seen as a regular station on the tenure track. Coppola's request that the new position be filled through a national search (in which he would be one of the candidates) was also turned down. The position would be created only if Coppola were the one to fill it. So Coppola was offered, and accepted, the position he had long sought, not as an internal promotion but as an "external hire."

PRINCIPLE OR EXCEPTION

As new associate professors are sometimes surprised to discover, tenure shifts after it is won from being an end toward which all roads converge, to a beginning, with many new paths to follow. For some or perhaps most, it leads to promotion to full professor, although the timeline is not as well defined as it is in the route toward tenure, and the stakes (at least with regard to job security) are not so high.[18] Coppola's "promotion" to his new position could rightly be taken as a validation of his work by colleagues in his department, university, and beyond. But would he continue to innovate? Could his agenda continue to generate new work of value? Would he start something new? These are questions that all associate professors face as they start the next phase of their careers.

These are also questions that Coppola's colleagues raised during interviews for this book. The Research Corporation's Michael Doyle put it in terms of the dangers of success. "It's put him into the limelight," Doyle observed:

> . . . and he has to retain some of his earlier understanding, as a facilitator. He can't be arrogant. And he's got to actually continue to be as diligent in creating new ideas and having them successful as he has in the past, because he's basically working in a venue that says, "All right, if you're good this year, what are you going to do next year?"

Another caution, from George Bodner of Purdue, questioned the potential for professional growth in Coppola's particular take on chemical education as a field for innovation and program development—in effect, using Coppola's future as a way of illustrating their friendly but ongoing disagreement about the value of specialized training in chemical education research. "Brian is a brilliant guy," Bodner said:

> He's creative as hell. And he has done the scholarship so far. But what's his age now? It's got to be 20 years to retirement. And so the next question people are going to ask is, if you're not doing research or writing textbooks, what's going to keep your scholarship going in the future?

The short answer to such questions is to note that Coppola was promoted to full professor in May 2002, five years after taking up his tenured position. A somewhat longer answer is to observe that in those five years Coppola was as energetic as ever in developing his old lines of innovation and adding new ones into the mix. Although it is well beyond the scope of this chapter to summarize all of Coppola's work in the years since (or before) tenure, the evidence is substantial that his earlier accomplishments resulted not from a short-lived spurt of energy, but from an intellectual agenda as motivating of innovation, inquiry, and institutionalization as the research agendas of more conventional scholars.

Consider, for example, Coppola's continuing efforts to provide students with opportunities for peer instruction. In his new documents, Coppola cited the institutionalization of the peer-led study groups that he first introduced in 1993. "In 1998, the PLSG was taken over by the College's Science Learning Center, given a line-item budget for hiring and training leaders, and expanded to all of the introductory science courses. This has been a nice example," Coppola concluded, "for how an individual faculty effort can be used to provide an institutional program." He also oversaw institutionalization of their system of using undergraduates to train and supervise others in the use of instruments as part of the laboratory program, published a series of papers on structured study groups (a way of using upper-level undergraduates as instructional collaborators for the Honors option in the introductory organic chemistry course), and developed four "second-generation" instructional projects modeled on this program (Coppola, 2001b).[19]

These structured study group efforts are also, Coppola pointed out, a "cornerstone activity" in his "ongoing construction of a comprehensive program for future faculty development." Although the seeds for this program (CSIE and ISIE) were sown prior to tenure, he and his colleagues substantially enlarged its scope afterwards, with U.S. Department of Education grants in 1998 and 2001 to support graduate students who blend teaching and carrying out research on teaching and learning by working with faculty in the chemistry department to implement and assess educational projects.[20] These students are regular chemistry graduate students who, in addition to working in their advisors' laboratories also "take courses in educational design and assessment, write proposals for projects, present their results, and organize symposia at national meetings." In 2001–2002, Coppola added an "externship" program to the experience, modeled on the national Preparing Future Faculty Program (PFF), for which he is also coordinator.[21] For the future, Coppola is hoping to institutionalize an ISIE certificate for graduate students who complete the CSIE work, expand the program to other science departments at Michigan, assess results, find further support for post-doctoral associates, and write a book "in order to give these ideas a tangible artifact for people to deliberate about."[22]

This brings us back to pedagogical positions in higher education, and in particular to Coppola's. "Position," of course, has two relevant meanings here: a philosophical stance and an official post. Is Coppola's take on the role of a chemical educator unusual? Clearly, there are differences of opinion within the still small group of people who consider themselves part of the chemical education community on these matters—useful differences when forcefully argued by people like Coppola and George Bodner, who care deeply about the work but on some points take opposing sides. But their disagreements do reflect a broader tension in the world of teaching and learning between those for whom "education" (discipline-centered or generic) means first a field of research and those for whom it points primarily to a world of practice.[23] With his special affinity for those who see education as the responsibility of all who teach, it is no surprise that Coppola has sought alliances with a variety of national reform and action programs oriented toward improving general practice, including those of AAHE and the Carnegie Foundation.

In addition to building an infrastructure for future faculty, Coppola's goals have long included building the emergent field of disciplinary-centered pedagogy. One of his ways of doing so has been through establishing a model through his own career. There is no question that people with an interest in the scholarship of teaching and learning consider it important to the legitimacy of the effort to have people of Coppola's stature involved. There is also no question that the position he has been able to attain at the University of Michigan is a promising sign to those who decide to make this work a major part of their academic career. Still, the broader meaning of Coppola's official post at the University of Michigan is hard, at this point, to assess. Was his case an exception or did it affirm a new principle or rule? Did it establish a precedent for parallel positions in discipline-centered pedagogy in other departments? We will not know until its meaning is negotiated through future cases at Michigan and beyond.

Coppola himself would be the first to agree that the future is what it is all about. He looks, for example, to the undergraduates who have taken advantage of the peer instruction opportunities he has designed. Some have finished college with aspirations to be college teachers of chemistry and are (already) shaking things up in graduate school. "One of my undergraduate leaders," Coppola explained, "went to [a highly ranked program at a Big 10 university] and he's got his normal TA assignment, but because he's been 'damaged' by his work with me, he can't possibly put up with a ridiculously designed educational environment. And so within the context of his TA section, he has integrated the methodologies that he learned and applied in his program." But this student is not just helping his own students. Coppola believed he has influenced his first- and second-year graduate student colleagues. "And the subset of them that are also thinking about academic careers are looking at him and saying: you know how to do something and you have information that we really think we ought to know." A cadre of faculty who care about the intellectual work in teaching and learning is the legacy that Coppola would most like to leave. "This must make you very proud," I observed. Coppola replied, "Like a dad. Like a dad."

What about Coppola's own academic "dad," the graduate school advisor who was so critical of Coppola's move to teaching, and over all this time, still embodies the road not taken? Coppola struggled hard with the choice he made as a graduate student to forego a conventional career in academic chemistry to pursue his pedagogical positions. While he has enjoyed his advisor's formal support ever since, Coppola admitted, "It is only in the past few years that I have come to know that he recognizes and respects what I do and believes that I'm making a contribution that is worthwhile." To Coppola, his advisor's praise, though genuine, still comes with a subtle edge. "Congratulations!" Coppola's advisor wrote upon Coppola's promotion to full professor, "I knew you had it in you and would not give up on you."

NOTES

1. This quotation is from Coppola (2001b), submitted as part of his dossier for promotion to full professor.

2. There is concern among composition scholars, however, that as the field matures, its theoreticians are becoming more distanced from everyday classroom concerns. According to Salvatori and Donahue (2002), "certain sectors of composition studies are now . . . situating the field away from its originating emphasis on students' writing, student writers, students' learning" (p. 83).

3. The seemingly simple term "chemical education" has become a bone of contention in the chemistry community. Coppola explained that he prefers the coined term "discipline-centered teaching and learning" or more recently ISIE (Interdisciplinary Studies at the Interface of Education. "We argued that I was not just 'chemical education,' but a bona fide *contributor* to philosophy, history, ethics of science— the 'interdisciplinary' part of ISIE, and that these involved chemistry teaching and learning as their context, hence the 'interface of education' part of ISIE."

4. In our conversation of September 14, 2000, Michael Doyle explained, "In the early 1950s, a number of women who obtained their Ph.D.s found themselves going to the liberal arts colleges on the East Coast to be instructors, to handle the laboratory, and not be part of a tenure-track stream. The institutions prospered. I'm not sure whether these women would actually describe their careers as being less advantageous than what they wanted, but in my view their institutions took advantage of them." Recollections of how the experience felt to women scientists in the 1950s and 1960s can be found in Wasserman's study (2000) of the careers of women elected to the National Academy of Sciences.

5. In 1983, Shakhashiri founded the Institute for Chemical Education (ICE) at the University of Wisconsin–Madison. The institute was intended to be a national research, development, and dissemination center to serve chemistry education at all levels. According to its current website, "All of ICE's programs emphasize hands-on science, taught interactively as a means of helping students develop powers of observation and problem solving. ICE aims to stimulate the scientific curiosity of all teachers and students, not just those traditionally well served by our educational system" (University of Wisconsin–Madison, 2003).

6. This split persists. Coppola, for example, opposes separate graduate degree programs in chemical education. He sees chemical education as an emergent inter-disciplinary area, in which practitioners need to be anchored at the highest level of education in the core field (chemistry). Joseph Krajcik, Coppola's colleague and collaborator in education at Michigan, explained:

> Brian really feels that you have to have an understanding of what chem-istry is in order to understand the learning of chemistry. And that the only way you're going to get an understanding of what chemistry is, is by doing a Ph.D. in chemistry. You really have to tackle a substantial prob-lem in chemistry in order to think like a chemist. Taking a lot of course work in chemistry is not enough.

See Bodner and Herron (1985) for an argument in favor of separate graduate degree programs in chemical education.

7. In examining the results from the 1993 National Study of Postsecondary Fac-ulty, conducted by the U.S. Department of Education, Finkelstein, Seal, and Schus-ter (1998) found a much higher proportion of new faculty (employed for seven years or less) than senior faculty employed in nontenure track positions:

> Note, too, that apart from the special case of the community colleges, the percentage of senior faculty at research, doctoral, comprehensive, and lib-eral arts colleges who hold a rank other than professor, associate profes-sor, or assistant professor ranges narrowly between 5.5 and 8.3 percent. This contrasts sharply with the comparable percentages among their new-cohort colleagues, which fall between 21.0 and 23.7 percent, except at the doctoral institutions, where the percentage is 16.7. The widespread phenomenon of these appointments throughout the new cohort of faculty suggests a resourcefulness in creating different types of ranks, very likely intended to minimize the number of tenurable appointments (p. 25).

8. The curricular and pedagogical features of these courses are articulated in Chapter 4. In summary, the courses share a set of instructional characteristics: (a) an emphasis on depth rather than breadth of coverage, (b) activities that encour-age introductory chemistry students to grapple with authentic problems, (c) a con-cern with guiding students to think and reason like chemists, and (d) opportuni-ties for students to enhance their understanding of chemistry by teaching others.

9. Actually, Coppola had won teaching awards from 1987 to 1990 as well. Between 1991 and 1996, he received the Dean's Excellence in Teaching Award from the College of Literature, Science, and the Arts every year. In addition, he won the University of Michigan Sigma Xi Teaching Award in 1990; the university's Phi

Lambda Upsilon Teacher of the Year award and "Golden Apple" Award, both in 1994; was appointed a faculty associate of the university's Center for Research on Learning and Teaching in 1995; and was an honorary inductee in the university's Golden Key Chapter in 1996, the year in which he also was awarded the United States Department of Energy Undergraduate Computational Science Education Award.

10. Or, as The Research Corporation's Michael Doyle put it, "Brian had that sweet smell of success. Veritably every proposal that he sent out was getting funded."

11. Coppola's (1999) own tally is publications: 20 (3 in lab research), 4 chapters, 1 book; external funding (as PI or co-PI): $3.5 million; internal funding (UM education): $160,000; undergraduate students: 18 research, 14 education; post-doc student: 1; awards: 1 national, 6 university, 7 college; on-campus collaborations: 5; invited talks: 15 chemistry departments, 20 symposia, 35 general; meetings with refereed papers: 9.

12. Clearly, Coppola's success in creating a record took place in the context of a field already better endowed than many others with forums and outlets for work on chemical education.

13. This history is recounted more fully in the preceeding chapter. See also Tobias (1992) and Ege, Coppola, and Lawton (1997).

14. Kuczkowski recalled, "That was normally not done, but in discussions with the executive committee of the Chemistry Department, it was agreed that we should do an annual review of the lecturers as well, to give them guidance and feedback and have everybody think about goals and progress and initiatives and the management discussion." These reviews, according to Kuczkowski, were done by a committee of two or three, but the identity of only one, a member of the executive committee, would be known to the person in question.

15. The university's "Qualifications for Appointment and Promotion in the Several Faculties of the University of Michigan" provide the following definitions:

> *Teaching*: Essential qualifications for appointment or promotion are character and the ability to teach, whether at the undergraduate or the graduate level. Some of the elements to be evaluated are experience, knowledge of subject matter, skill in presentation, interest in students, ability to stimulate youthful minds, capacity for cooperation, and enthusiastic devotion to teaching. The responsibility of the teacher as a guide and friend properly extends beyond the walls of the classroom into other phases of the life of the student as a member of the University community. It also involves the duty of initiating and improving educational methods both within and outside the departments.
>
> *Research*: All members of the faculties must be persons of scholarly ability and attainments. Their qualifications are to be evaluated on the quality of their published and other creative work, the range and variety of their intellectual interests, their success in training graduate and professional students in scholarly methods, and their participation and leadership in professional associations and in the editing of professional journals. Attainment may be in the realm of scientific investigation, in the realm of constructive contributions, or in the realm of the creative arts.

Service: The scope of the University's activities makes it appropriate for members of the staff to engage in many activities outside of the fields of teaching and research. These may include participation in committee work or other administrative tasks, counseling, clinical duties, and special training programs. The University also expects many of its staff to render extramural services to schools, to industry, to local, state, and national agencies, and to the public at large. (University of Michigan, n.d.)

16. According to Ege, the request for letters was sent with the standard wording, the only thing "special" about it being acknowledgment of Coppola's current position as "lecturer." In my phone conversations with Coppola's colleagues from outside the University of Michigan, some chose to tell me that they had served as external referees and sketched in the nature of their remarks. I was not offered nor did I ask to see these letters, which are confidential.

17. This theme is central to Sheri Sheppard's case at Stanford University and is outlined in the chapters that follow.

18. Once appointed to a full-time position, a faculty member is subject to a probationary period, after which continued employment at the college consists of permanent tenure. According to AAUP's 1940 Statement of Principles on Academic Freedom and Tenure, "the probationary period should not exceed seven years . . . subject to the proviso that when, after a term of probationary service of more than three years in one or more institutions, a teacher is called to another institution, it may be agreed in writing that the new appointment is for a probationary period of not more than four years. . . ." Policies regarding promotion, as distinct from tenure, are much more variable.

19. These include the adaptation of structured study groups in (a) Pipeline for Student Success, a "program run through the University Dental School, in which a group of 16 to18 at-risk first- and second-year college students, mostly from underrepresented populations, are brought to campus for an early intervention program in the basic sciences"; (b) Michigan Mathematics and Science Scholars, "a short-term (2-week), 60-hour chemistry program for high school juniors designed, implemented and assessed by experienced undergraduate instructors"; (c) Chem-Sense, a collaboration with SRI to promote "representational competence in visualization of chemistry" through "an environment that facilitates student–student interaction and review around the work of each other, and a set of visualization tools; and (d) Law, Ethics, and the Life Sciences, a new undergraduate course in which students "will be generating web-based documents that take topical ideas from the life sciences and then provide explanatory perspectives from basic sciences, law and from ethics in a way that makes the issues accessible to the public" (Coppola, 2001b, pp. 24–25).

20. These grants are through the Department of Education's GAANN (Graduate Assistance in Areas of National Need) program. These fellowships are awarded to individual graduate students through university departments in seven areas of "national need": biology, chemistry, computer and information science, engineering, geological science, mathematics, and physics (see http://www.ed.gov/programs/iegpsgaann/index.html).

21. The Preparing Future Faculty program, initiated in 1993 as a joint project of the Association of American Colleges and Universities and the Council of Gradu-

ate Schools, aimed to better prepare graduate students for the full range of roles they will have to fill in faculty positions at different kinds of institution. The Michigan externship program has involved students spending 10 to 14 days off campus at another college or university where they and that institution's faculty can exchange expertise on curricular and pedagogical issues.

22. For some time, Coppola thought he might call this book "Scholarship Developed," after the pattern of the Carnegie Foundation's *Scholarship Reconsidered* (Boyer, 1990) and *Scholarship Assessed* (Glassick, Huber, & Maeroff, 1997).

23. For various takes on this debate, see the articles in *Disciplinary Styles in the Scholarship of Teaching and Learning* (Huber & Morreale, 2002). Coppola and his fellow Carnegie Scholar, chemist Dennis Jacobs from the University of Notre Dame, wrote the chapter on chemistry, with a call for collaboration and reconciliation between the various segments of the chemistry education community. Of the fields represented in that collection, the closest to chemistry is probably mathematics, with its well-defined community of scholars engaged in mathematics education research (Banchoff & Salem, 2002).

6

Redesigning Engineering Education
· ·

> Our educational system has many elements that support our
> students becoming competent in both design and analysis.
> What seem to be missing are many opportunities for their use in
> an integrated manner.[1]

Design and analysis are twin poles in engineering education because they are the twin poles—the art and the science—of engineering itself. There is no simple definition of either one. As Stanford engineer Sheri Sheppard explained to me, "You can think of design as what happens when you look at a ravine and imagine what could be built to get cars safely across. And you can think of analysis as what happens when you use scientific knowledge and mathematical tools to specify and test the different elements of your design." Everyone would agree that successful engineering requires both design and analysis as part of the larger design *process*.[2] However, where the line between them is drawn and how they are valued has varied historically, internationally, and even within different communities of practicing engineers and educators (Downey & Lucena, 1995).

Sheppard, an associate professor in the Design Division of the Mechanical Engineering Department at Stanford, has long cared about how design and analysis are combined. When Sheppard returned to the academy after starting her career as a practicing engineer in Detroit, she chose her first area of research, weld fatigue and impact failures, fracture mechanics, and applied finite element analysis, because she sensed that design analysts in the auto industry could be making better decisions. Design could benefit from better analysis, she thought, and analysis could benefit from taking place in the context of design. The critical question for Sheppard was what the results of analysis mean in terms of the system they are meant to inform. What do people actually do when they design things with certain tools at hand and certain constraints in mind?

Case Study: Sheri Sheppard

Sheri Sheppard is associate professor and associate chair of graduate curriculum and admissions in Mechanical Engineering Department at Stanford University. A member of the department's Design Division, she teaches both undergraduate and graduate design-related classes and conducts research on weld fatigue and impact failures, fracture mechanics, and applied finite element analysis. Sheppard is co-principal investigator of an NSF grant to the multi-institutional Center for the Advancement of Engineering Education, directing research on students' pathways towards engineering degrees. In addition, she is a senior scholar at The Carnegie Foundation for the Advancement of Teaching, leading a major investigation of engineering education in the United States. A fellow of the American Society of Mechanical Engineering and the American Association for the Advancement of Science, Sheppard's baccalaureate degree is from the University of Wisconsin–Madison, and her doctorate in mechanical engineering is from the University of Michigan. Visit http://www-cdr.stanford.edu/CDR/faculty/sheppard.html for more information.

These same questions ground Sheppard's understanding of engineering education reform. She explained the basic problem of the typical engineering curriculum, the separation of design from analysis, using an analogy from the system she knows best:

> If you think about an educational program as if it were a car, the approach we tend to take right now is, "OK, you go off and design

the wheels, I'll go off and design the drive train, somebody else will do the engine, and the students will pick up these components as they go through their four years, and we'll expect them to form them into a car." A fundamentally different approach is saying, "We collectively are designing a car, and we also have to make sure that the components actually integrate with one another." The latter is how engineering is practiced today, but it is not how engineering education is practiced.

Sheppard is one of the small but growing number of engineering faculty who have become intrigued with the integration and redesign of engineering education. She is not alone in her view of the problem. Since the 1950s, in fact, engineering education became increasingly removed from the world of engineering practice as it made room in the curriculum for more and more science and math (Grayson, 1977, 1993; Sheppard & Jenison, 1997).[3] As one group of engineering educators describe this trajectory, "the hands-on component was reduced, and courses on mechanical drawing and design of engineering equipment were dropped and replaced with courses that emphasized scientific analysis and mathematical modeling. Engineering design . . . and operations were relegated to one or two courses in most engineering curricula" (Wankat, Felder, Smith, & Oreovicz, 2002, p. 219). Engineering practice has also changed to incorporate powerful new scientific and analytical tools, to the point where such tools are necessary for practice. Reformers argue, however, that the curriculum is giving the wrong message.[4] As Sheppard herself has pointed out, students are led to believe that engineering practice is much more analytical than in fact it is, and have difficulty applying analytical tools in the open-ended context of solving design problems (2001; see also Bucciarelli, 1994; Wankat et al., 2002).[5]

That engineering education may have thrown the baby out with the bathwater in its efforts to enhance the place of the engineering sciences in the training of future engineers has become a familiar critique. To be sure, every profession struggles with the gap between theory and practice in educating new professionals. The literature suggests that the engineering community sees "its" gap as more a matter of curricular emphasis or compartmentalization than unavoidable tension between the cultures of office and school. For example, in his well-known overview of the engineering profession, John Kemper cites an influential report by the MIT Committee on Engineering Design, from the early 1960s, which summarized interviews with industry leaders. The report noted, "Recent engineering graduates were criticized for unwillingness and inability to consider a complete problem such as a design problem. Instead they showed a desire to seek a fully specified problem which could be answered by analytical methods" (Kemper, 1990, p. 198).[6]

Over the years, critics from industry have been joined by educators in questioning the weight given to analytical approaches in engineering curricula. In the 1970s and early 1980s, many programs brought design back into the first year. This revival was short-lived. "By the middle 1980s," Sheppard and Jenison wrote, "increased pressure to include more technology in the curriculum, particularly computer-related technology, squeezed already packed curricula to the point where the freshman design courses were eliminated or scaled back significantly at most schools" (1997, p. 193). Not surprisingly, critics continued to question how well schools of engineering were preparing students for professional life, but they also began addressing new concerns.

In particular, the science-laden first year has been cited as contributing to high rates of first-year attrition from engineering programs, while the emphasis on abstract mathematical problem-solving throughout the engineering curriculum has been implicated in the low numbers of women and minority attracted to or completing a major in the field (Seymour & Hewitt, 1997; Tobias, 1990). These researchers note that students who switch out of science majors are not "dumb," (to use Sheila Tobias's phrase), "they're different." According to an ethnographic study of undergraduate engineering at the Virginia Polytechnic Institute and State University:

> Learning how to draw a boundary around a problem, abstract out the mathematical contents and solve it in mathematical terms, and then plug the solution back into the original problem is central to the fashioning of engineers and a major challenge to the bodies and minds of students. Students regularly asserted that the goal of certain courses was to "weed out" students from engineering curricula. For students who stayed, these and other courses also appeared to weed out a part of themselves as persons. . . . In engineering, students learn they must keep reactions, intuitions, or any feelings they might have about the problem out of the process of drawing a boundary around it and solving it. (Downey & Lucena, 1997, pp. 126–127)

Women and minority students, the ethnographers suggest, already burdened by under-representation in the field, can find this additional demand of engineering's educational culture particularly hard to bear (1997; see also Eisenhart & Finkel, 1998).

Given the range of outstanding issues, including better integration of analysis and design, it is not surprising that calls for renewed attention to curriculum and pedagogy continue from the highest levels of the engineering establishment. The National Research Council's science education committee has published recent reports on undergraduate engineering education (1995), the graduate education and postdoctoral experience of scientists and engineers (1995, 2000), and undergraduate education in science, mathematics, engineering, and technology (1996, 1999). Since 1990, NSF has funded a whole set of initiatives to reform engineering education, and even closer to home are the criteria for accrediting programs in engineering put forward by the Accreditation Board for Engineering and Technology (ABET).[7] Virtually all engineering programs now have senior capstone design courses and have made at least some efforts to integrate design experiences throughout the curriculum in response to ABET priorities. ABET's new "Engineering Criteria 2000," which include a requirement on "Program Outcomes and Assessment," have stimulated discussion among faculty and administrators around the country about not only how one might demonstrate that students had mastered the wide range of abilities that ABET now recommends, but in some cases how to teach so that students learn them as well (Accreditation Board for Engineering and Technology, 2000; Van Duzer, 2000).[8]

All of these developments have given curricular and pedagogical issues a higher profile in engineering than they have had before. To be sure, engineering has a long history of concern about education for the profession, reflected in a host of associations from the American Society of Engineering Education, with its conferences, journals, and awards programs, to a number of disciplinary associations representing fields within engineering, such as the Institute for Electrical and Electronics Engineers (IEEE) or the American Society of Civil Engineering (ASCE), which also provide forums for teaching-related issues. Clearly, engineering has had its full share of innovative, caring, and conscientious teachers and administrators who have developed or adapted new approaches to engineering education like co-op programs, in which students alternate between periods in school and in industry, mastery learning and the personalized system of instruction, problem-based learning, and the like (Wankat et al., 2002).

Still, the scholarship of teaching community in engineering is new and remains small. The authors of the engineering essay in *Disciplinary Styles in the Scholarship of Teaching and Learning* observe that "while research came to be considered an essential engineering faculty pursuit in the 1950s and 1960s, during those decades only one of Boyer's (1990) scholarships counted toward faculty advancement: the scholarship of discovery. . . ." (Wankat et al., 2002, p. 223). The scholarships of integration and application became better recognized in the 1970s, the authors noted, when more NSF funding became available for multidisciplinary centers focused on problems like energy production, environmental science, microelectronics, and biotechnology. It was only in the 1980s and 1990s, with the growth of NSF funding for engineering education and the new ABET standards, that the scholarship of teaching began to gain ground. Together, these developments have generated new interest in curricular integration and pedagogical innovation and, as Wankat and colleagues note, enhanced its quality by recognizing the value of educational research and appropriate assessment of results (Wankat et al., 2002).

This is the climate of excitement and possibility in which younger engineering faculty, like Sheppard, have been drawn into the scholarship of teaching and learning, whether through NSF's Engineering Education Coalitions, which aimed to stimulate the creation of comprehensive, systemic models for reform, through ABET accreditation, or through workshops and other opportunities that have appeared in recent years. With this excitement has come risk. For younger faculty and perhaps especially for younger women faculty, like Sheppard, the risks are particularly high. Individuals still find it difficult to parlay significant engagements with education innovation and reform into the normal progression of an academic career. For the larger community of engineering educators, there are risks as well. To build momentum for curricular and pedagogical change, innovators must be able to move through the tenure and promotion process with confidence that educational work will be welcomed and fairly received.

"A Bridge Person"

Sheppard aptly describes herself as a "bridge person," but she does not mean it literally. She is not a civil engineer, and she is not referring to those spans of wood, stone, or steel over which we walk, drive, or ride. She is talking instead about her penchant for "bridging" conceptual divides. She is interested in the integration of analysis and design in engineering practice as well as in engineering education; she has worked both in industry and the academy; she is a woman in a predominantly male profession (and the only woman in her academic department); and, of course, she is a "scholar of teaching and learning" in a world that usually thinks of "scholarship" as engineering science research.

Sheppard grew up in Racine, Wisconsin, the second daughter of a father who was a metallurgical engineer and a mother who taught fifth grade for many years. Sheppard's first real love as a youngster was music, taking up the violin in fourth grade and the piano in sixth. When she was in middle school and high school, she thought she would become a concert violinist, and she prepared by taking two one-hour lessons in violin a week, practicing four hours a day. Indeed, she taught violin in high school and had several students running through the house. She took a good deal of mathematics and science in high school, however, because she was good at it, and because her father had urged her to cultivate that side of her life as well.

It was in selecting a college that Sheppard's aspirations changed. She began by looking at conservatories like Julliard and Oberlin, but as she observed the intensity of these programs, she wondered if she was dedicated enough or even good enough to successfully pursue a classical music career. She did not regret the self-discipline she'd learned in her music training, but she did start to doubt if music was what she really wanted to do. As an alternative, Sheppard's father suggested she go to their state university (the University of Wisconsin–Madison) and study engineering. Sheppard agreed, but asked him to support her after that in studying law (having also enjoyed debate in high school). I asked Sheppard if it was unusual at that time—the mid 1970s—for a father to encourage his daughter to go into engineering. Sheppard said that her father wanted his two daughters to be able to make a living and do well without depending on others. Engineering might have been a strange choice because her father is a metallurgist, which is the dirtiest kind of engineering, but Sheppard had gone with him to his place of work, seen it, and had not been put off.

As an engineering student at Wisconsin in the mid 1970s, Sheppard's first year was dedicated to mathematics and science courses—offered not through engineering but through the mathematics and science departments, as was (and still is) common. Since then, most engineering programs have tried to introduce some engineering design into the freshman year, in order to give students a sense of what engineering is really about and stem attrition by helping them make better choices about their majors (Sheppard & Jenison, 1997; Tobias, 1990). For Sheppard, however, the crisis came not in the freshman year, but in her first engineering course in her second year. The course was Strength of Materials, which dealt with how loads cause stress and what happens to materials under stress. It was a small course of 35 students and she was distressed because a number of the concepts, like "torsion," were new to her. As the only woman in the class, Sheppard recalled, she feared that she was the only one confused. Surely, all the men were born knowing these concepts. Sheppard called her father and complained, "I can't do this. All the men know and I don't." His response? "Well, come home then and go back to your job as a carhop!" He knew, of course, how much his daughter had hated that job. Sheppard got the point and went to the next class. An older man in the course found the courage that day to tell the professor, "Please go back over things. I don't have the foggiest." That opened the door for Sheppard, and she soon began to enjoy the work.

Engineering programs offer their students many specialties and Sheppard joined a small program in engineering physics. With only four students graduating in her year, most of the students' junior and senior courses were graduate offerings. Another special feature of Sheppard's undergraduate career was that she won a General Motors scholarship, which gave her summer money to work at GM. Her first summer was in the industrial engineering division, helping to lay out a machine that would help make catalytic converters. For her second summer, she asked to be a foreman on an assembly line. There she worked with 17 people on the second shift on seven machines. The workers were men and women, a lot older than she, but they became allies and collaborators. Although Sheppard found out that summer that she did not like making instantaneous decisions—for example, if a machine broke, whether to call the pipe fitters, the electricians, or someone else—she gained great respect for the hourly workers and a better understanding of the manufacturing process.

When Sheppard went back to Madison for her senior year, her interest in law waned as her excitement about engineering grew. She began interviewing for jobs that would give her an opportunity to gain more engineering experience and get a master's degree at the same time. She already knew she liked cars from spending summers at GM, but she did interview more widely. Sandia and Livermore made good offers, but Sheri took an offer from Chrysler.[9] There, she was part of the prestigious Chrysler Institute, a one-and-a-half year program for a group of 30 or so new engineers, which tried to build them as a cohort and train them at the same time. They had dignitaries from around the company come and talk about what they did, and they heard lectures about cars, engines, and the like. They had rotating jobs that lasted for three months each. One job, which Sheppard especially enjoyed and which informed her later pedagogical work, was at Chrysler's Mechanics School, where the people who repair cars at dealerships are trained, and where they spent three months rebuilding engines and brakes. In addition to these rotations, the Chrysler Institute fellows got a day-and-a-half off to go to graduate school at the University of Michigan, Dearborn. This was in the late 1970s, and Sheppard entered into this program at just the right time—Chrysler soon went into crisis, asking for bailouts, and the next class of Institute fellows was laid off before their term ended.

After the Institute, Sheppard (and the other fellows) had to find a department that would hire them into a permanent position. In a time of deep trouble for the company, Sheppard found shelter in emissions development. There, they were running vehicles on chassis dynamometers, tweaking their carburetors to make sure that the pollutants coming out of the tail pipes met federal standards. It was not uninteresting work and Sheppard enjoyed it, but her real passion was for structural analysis (the applied physics of her undergraduate studies), a heavily mathematical field that is crucial to the design of "machines and structures that will not break even when subjected to extreme vibrations and other varying loads" (Petroski, 1992, p. 110). In 1981, Sheppard left Chrysler and joined a small consulting group that did structural analysis for the "big three" automobile makers. There, she was contracted to Chevrolet for about 36 months to work on the Corvette as a structural analyst. This task was made more enjoyable because the Corvette was being designed and engineered at an office outside GM's main facilities, so the team could do its work without the daily distraction of corporate issues.

During this period, Sheppard made two important discoveries. First, she realized that she loved teaching. While at Chevrolet, curious to know if she might prefer an academic career, she began teaching at the Lawrence Institute of Technology, which has an extensive night program for people working on baccalaureate degrees in engineering. As she recalled,

> I'd come home at 10 or 11 o'clock at night, up on the ceiling, so excited that it took me a long time to come down to earth. Most of the students were much older than I, but I was starting to get really intrigued with how you take a concept and make it meaningful to someone else. That started to become an intellectual challenge and like other new teachers, I spent hours and hours. I figured out my pay rate at that point—maybe ten cents an hour, but it really didn't matter.

While she was delighted to put extra time into teaching, Sheppard's other discovery during this period was that she did not like working under the regime of billable hours that the consultancy required. "You couldn't read an article," she said. "You'd get a project done, but there was no time to ask further questions."

Building on these discoveries—that she liked teaching and that she wanted a setting in which she could "ponder things," Sheppard decided to leave industry, go back to school for a Ph.D., and become an academic. Sheppard was living in Dearborn, so she chose to go to the doctoral program at the University of Michigan in Ann Arbor, which was nearby. She wasted no time. Supported by a research assistantship, Sheppard stepped into a project that was already funded and "well scoped," meaning that the problem and desired outcomes were already well defined. That, plus her own considerable expertise, enabled Sheppard to hit the ground running, and she finished her Ph.D. in just two years. At times, Sheppard says, she "regretted doing the Ph.D. so fast, because I never had to define a project myself and figure out what is a good question to ask."

Sheppard had one more flirtation with industry while applying for academic jobs and teaching a course at Michigan. After receiving her doctorate in 1985, she took a position in Ford's research labs, in the computer-aided engineering department where they were developing numerical techniques to simulate a crash test. She liked the combination of mainline engineering and lab, but again experienced the industry's intense pressure to complete the work quickly, as they wanted to use it in the design of a car then under development.[10] This was a time when corporate research labs everywhere were being challenged to show the practicality of their work, and Sheppard found no reason to abandon her plans for the different pace and pressures of the academy.[11]

Meanwhile, Sheppard's job search was going well. She had offers from Michigan (where she had done her graduate work), Georgia Tech, and Stanford, and without hesitation, she accepted Stanford, her first choice. Sheppard had arranged through her mentor at Michigan to visit both Stanford and Berkeley on a vacation trip while she was in graduate school. Berkeley was too urban for her tastes, but she had been impressed with the beauty of Stanford's campus and had enjoyed meeting several of the faculty there who would later become her colleagues. When she was offered a position at Stanford the following year, she told Ford that she would be leaving, and in January, 1986, took up her position as assistant professor in the Design Division of the Mechanical Engineering Department.

STARTING A CAREER AT STANFORD

In the mid 1980s, when Sheppard arrived, Mechanical Engineering was (and remains) one of the largest and most influential departments in Stanford's prestigious School of Engineering, and Design was a large and influential division in the department.[12] This was a unique situation. In most schools of engineering, design is a relatively small operation and has some trouble winning respect. It is generally considered to be "soft" in relation to other specialties, and in the world of engineering, prestige tends to go to the more mathematically intensive disciplines, which are spoken of as "hard." At Stanford, this is also the case, but Design there has been blessed with creative and renowned faculty, a wealth of resources, talented students, and successful alums. Former dean James Gibbons explained, "Out of that division have come some extraordinary designs that are the envy of every school in the country. Someone at MIT once said they would never be able to do this because design draws on sociology and art as well as engineering. Our Design Division is a uniquely Stanford mix of art, human factors and technology."

Like each of the divisions within Mechanical Engineering, Design has enjoyed its own budget, a lot of autonomy in deciding what to do with its money, and how its members choose to run themselves as a group. Over the years, it has developed a distinctive subculture, informal, nonhierarchical, close-knit, and tolerant of each other's interests and idiosyncrasies.[13] The division has no "head"; rather, the group meets weekly for a business meeting followed by what they call a "philosophical lunch," a brown bag affair where they talk about things that are important but not urgent. The division draws some its style from the way its people think of design itself—synthetic, creative, and original. As explained by Larry Leifer, Sheppard's colleague in the Design Division at Stanford:

> Design is an activity that requires breadth of vision to find and assimilate pieces that make sense according to a synthesis. New products, new ideas. It doesn't gain its strength by narrowing and focusing, which many lines of engineering science favor or maybe really do benefit from. Some of what we do looks like oddball stuff. An expert in microelectronics in design in Mechanical Engineering? That's for the double E department, right? Wrong. No. It was for us. We do a program with the art department. What are we doing? Engineers and the art department? We do things with the theater division. Do things with Dance. Do things with Computer Science and Ecology. And we mostly collaborate outside Mechanical Engineering and outside engineering itself.

The faculty of the Design Division have had the confidence to hire people like David Kelley, a strikingly successful designer, but not an academic.[14] And they hired people like Sheppard, who is not a designer, but whose approach to engineering is seen as compatible with design. A few members of the division, Leifer told me, "are really analytic engineers who covered technical areas we wanted to infiltrate with design thinking and who showed that they were responsive enough to the issue that they would pick it up." Sheppard's approach to structural analysis put her on the "soft" end of her own discipline—applied mechanics—but placed her on the "hard" end of design. As Leifer also noted, however, the more they've been around the division, most of these people, Sheppard included, have moved from the design–analytic toward the design–synthetic side of the equation.

There is another, explicitly gendered dimension, to Sheppard's career trajectory at Stanford beginning with her appointment itself. In the mid 1980s, Stanford was becoming concerned about the low proportion of women on the faculty, and perhaps nowhere more so than in the School of Engineering.[15] When Sheppard turned up as one of the two top candidates for the position in design, the other being a man, the department was awarded money from a special fund to hire them both. In fact, when Sheppard joined the Stanford faculty, she became the only woman in the whole Mechanical Engineering Department (not to mention its Design Division), and so she remained until 2002. It is hard to say in what ways Sheppard's career has been shaped by considerations of gender, although there is no doubt of its strong influence on the general situation of women in the sciences.[16] Still, it is important to recall that Sheppard came to Stanford already experienced in navigating a profession (engineering), industry (the automobile industry) and fields of study (applied mechanics, structural analysis, welding) dominated by men. So it is not surprising that she lost no time in establishing herself as her own person at Stanford. As her colleague and mentor Bernard Roth explained, "she was hired for her 'hard' analytic skills . . . but she did many things in her career that were identified as women's things."

Certainly, everyone with whom I spoke at Stanford agreed that Sheppard made it clear early on that she was not going to be a standard issue assistant professor of engineering. She began immediately by teaching Strength of Materials, the engineering course that had almost propelled her out of engineering her own sophomore year in college. She did not need to teach the course, and Roth actually advised her against it:

> There are some courses that are just a no man's land—no woman's land, either. They're not run by a department. They're general engineering courses controlled by committees. And there are no points for teaching them in terms of the system. They get a lot of lip service because they need people to take them on, but they are looked down on because they're so elementary and not connected with the mission of the department. For an assistant professor just starting out, it's a no-win situation. If she did poorly, they'd hold it against her. And if she did well, nobody would care.

But Sheppard insisted. The first day she walked into class and sat in the audience. When five minutes had gone by, she stood up and said, "Well, it looks like the professor isn't going to come, I might as well teach!" She had the students' attention, and while the course had a reputation for bad student ratings, it turned out well. Sheppard had taken it on as a challenge and shown that she could succeed.

Sheppard knew from her night-school teaching at the Lawrence Institute that she would enjoy teaching, and soon developed a signature style. Perhaps, as Larry Leifer suggested, she was influenced by the way many of her colleagues taught in design, not according to the standard model of lecture and individual student work, but through carefully constructed projects that students worked on in teams. Sheppard herself saw project-based teaching as entirely congruent with her own approach to analysis in the context of design:

> You can see it in the differences between my finite element analysis course and the one that's offered by the applied mechanics group in Mechanical Engineering. Even in their homework, where students are learning a fundamental formulation, there's always a problem or two which says: here's a physical situation, we're trying to find x, what kind of assumptions do you have to make to be able to analyze

it? What are the limitations of those assumptions? So the students have to look at real things and make decisions. That class culminates in a major project where they have to go out and look at a real system of their own choosing and say here's what I want to use analysis to find out about, and then use a commercial tool, a finite element code, to do it. You wouldn't see any of that—using a commercial code and looking at real systems—in the applied mechanics courses.[17]

Like most young professors, Sheppard also got advice to get her research program going well. Leveraging her work in Detroit and focusing on welding and fatigue, Sheppard started up a laboratory, as engineering faculty are expected to do, and began a program of research to develop methods for the evaluation of structural performance that were theoretically based but packaged for the use of practicing engineers and analysts. To Sheppard, these research interests exemplify her penchant to "bridge" domains. "I like having an understanding at the fundamental level," she said. "Maybe I'm helping develop that at the grass roots, but I can also walk in the shoes of people who really have to get work done in terms of designing things and I like to think about tools that these people can really use." Supported by NSF and by industry—General Motors, for example, funded her work for 14 years—Sheppard's lab (including Sheppard and her graduate and undergraduate students) produced a fundamental understanding of how spot welds fail, which is serving as a basis for the design of better simulations of impact; a method for predicting fatigue performance of spot welds that is being evaluated by two automobile makers; greater understanding of residual stresses in welded structures; and how to include consideration of these stresses in performance evaluation.

While Sheppard enjoyed the challenges of the laboratory and working with students, and while the work produced a steady stream of articles and conference papers, she soon realized that research at the university was quite lonely. "You are working with students," Sheppard said, "not colleagues as you do in Detroit. And you also start to wonder if anyone else cares about the work." To be sure, corporate funding brought with it an interesting tension of wanting quick results from a laboratory with graduate students who have different horizons of time. But this was pressure at a distance. Working in the lab at Stanford was quite unlike working in a lab in Detroit, where people in the department next door cared deeply about what you were doing and wanted to make use of your results immediately. It appeared that Sheppard was right. As we shall see in the next chapter, her closest colleagues may have considered Sheppard's bridging of rigorous analysis and creative design a contribution, but few found her specific area of application, welding, terribly exciting.

"We don't have a big tradition of studying manufacturing processes here," a colleague said.

SYNTHESIS

Sheppard was enjoying the freedom she found at Stanford to think through engineering problems in her lab, and she was finding in teaching the immediate feedback and team feeling that she missed in university research. So it may not seem surprising that she jumped at the opportunity to bring them together in a single set of activities: leading Stanford's role in a multi-institution coalition known as "Synthesis." As one of several Engineering Education Coalitions funded through NSF, Synthesis shared the common goal to "stimulate bold, innovative, and comprehensive models for systemic reform of undergraduate engineering education and increase the retention of students, especially women, underrepresented minorities, and persons with disabilities" (National Science Foundation, 1997, p. 43). The coalitions were to do this by designing models for reform, testing alternative curricula and pedagogies to bring about this reform, improving linkages to K-14 institutions, and increasing successful participation of a wider range of students (National Science Foundation, 1997, p. 43).

Synthesis was one of the eight Engineering Education Coalitions formed under the auspices of this program. These ranged from the "Academy," a collaboration of regional engineering education programs in southern New England; to "Succeed," a regional coalition formed by eight southeastern colleges of engineering; to "Synthesis," a national coalition of top research universities, state universities, and historically black colleges and universities. Headquartered first at Cornell and later at Berkeley, Synthesis included, in addition, California Polytechnic State University at San Luis Obispo, Hampton University, Iowa State University, Southern University, Stanford University, and Tuskegee. Believing that "most engineering programs are overburdened with course requirements, excessive compartmentalization, and general lack of excitement and motivation," the group planned to "design, implement, and assess new approaches . . . that emphasize multidisciplinary synthesis, teamwork and communication, hands-on and laboratory experiences, open-ended problem formulation and solving, and examples of 'best practices' from industry" (Synthesis Coalition, n.d.).

Clearly, this was an attractive project for Sheppard. When, during her third year at Stanford, engineering professor Alice Agogino at Berkeley asked if she would like to get involved with the coalition, she said yes. No senior faculty had volunteered, so Sheppard and another junior faculty member agreed to be co-principal investigators, leading Stanford's role. But however valuable the experiment, however congruent with Sheppard's approach to her subject and students, this was not the kind of move that one would expect of an assistant professor strategizing the way towards tenure. As her colleague Mark Cutkosky told me, "Even as an inexperienced contemporary of Sheri's, I could see it was a risk. I knew enough of the game to know that there was no successful precedent for it in the School of Engineering." Sheppard's colleagues in the Design Division advised her strongly against taking this on; Agogino made inquiries herself and warned Sheppard of the risks. In the late spring of 1990, Sheppard received letters from both her chair and dean advising her to withdraw from Synthesis should the grant be awarded, and to use that time instead to build a successful, high-impact research program. Sheppard resisted all this advice. In retrospect, she said she's been untraditional all along. "Being a woman in engineering is untraditional, so maybe this was just in that mold."

By the late spring, it was, at any rate, psychologically too late. Sheppard had found the process of preparing the proposal a fascinating design problem in itself. As she said,

> Synthesis was a coalition of very unlike schools, and we were talking about a pot of $3 million for each of five years. We had to look at infrastructure issues to see how to be fair and to recognize that each had strengths, without just divvying up the money in eighths and each going their own way. Hours were poured into the many meetings to design the coalition. Formulating the proposal and implementing it required diplomacy and creativity. What could we do which was significant and transportable? We had many long meetings and trips on red-eye flights to decide the whole thing.

Sheppard and her co-PI had to arrange Stanford's role in the coalition, too. This meant recruiting colleagues, and by proposal time, they had contributions from civil engineering, electrical engineering, and three projects from the Design division of Mechanical Engineering—one from a colleague and two from Sheppard, on "Interactive Case Studies" and "Mechanical Dissection: A Lab-Based Study of Design Context," to which I shall return shortly. In the end, Synthesis was funded for five years, and then continued for three more years for purposes of dissemination.

For Sheppard, the whole enterprise was intriguing. For others, like Larry Leifer, who became co-PI when the first person withdrew, it was an "exasperating" experience, because as Synthesis moved on, tensions grew. Tony Ingraffea, the Cornell-based PI coordinating the whole project, explained that what had really distinguished the Synthesis proposal from NSF's perspective was its emphasis on advanced technology. This was before the Internet, but they were very keen on developing a national library for high quality digital courseware. Unfortunately, this led to some dissatisfaction concerning the parity of the partnership among contributing institutions—was everybody innovating or some just implementing what others developed? The politics were further complicated by changes of personnel and moving targets at NSF. Ingraffea recalled, "It was just difficult to know whether we were being successful or not from their point of view. The rules kept changing—the rules of evaluation, the rules of review." Eventually Ingraffea himself resigned as PI and handed the baton to Agogino at Berkeley.

As a member of the coalition's executive committee of institutional PIs, Sheppard was not immune to the political swirl at the project's top. Yet, someone pointed out to Sheppard that while there were multiple tasks she could undertake in the coalition, the most important were her own projects, particularly "Mechanical Dissection: A Lab-Based Study of Design Context." This project was based on one of the new courses that Sheppard was developing at Stanford to address the problem of technological literacy and set the ground for integrating analysis and design.

"Students often fail to understand the context in which designs are created, or the history behind many products-designs," Sheppard wrote in her project proposal (1990). Historical understanding is essential for design. As Sheppard and June Tsai later wrote:

> Engineers design and build machines to fulfill human needs. Very few of these machines are completely new from the ground up; most are the result of engineers taking existing subassemblies and components, modifying them, then marrying them together into a complete system. Lest this task sound rote and lackluster, there is considerable creativity involved in this process. True design inspiration is often the result of seeing the novel application of a mechanism. This means being familiar with the myriad machines and mechanisms that surround us, and being able to see their use in domains far beyond their original intent. (1992, p. 1)

Clearly, a course that could familiarize students with an array of basic mechanisms would be particularly helpful to students with "limited hands-on experience" (Sheppard, 1992, p.2), including, no doubt, many of the underrepresented students that NSF and the rest of the engineering establishment were hoping to entice into the field.[18]

The core of Sheppard's course was built around a set of "dissection" exercises, in which students take a machine apart and put it back together again, preceded by discussions and activities to familiarize students with what each machine could do. These included familiar objects, such as a desktop printer, a fishing reel, a ten-speed bicycle, and something chosen by each student as an individual project. In addition, students were periodically assigned to give short class presentations on artifacts like toasters or faucets, often taking them apart to gain a better understanding of how they work. From such simple hands-on activities, presentations, and lectures with working models of mechanisms like gears and fastenings, Sheppard expected students to learn the vocabulary of mechanical systems, gain an awareness of the fact that there are many possible solutions to any single design problem, understand the power of effective communication, and develop resourcefulness and problem-solving skills. Her hope was that basic mechanical dissection would lay the groundwork for more advanced courses that would teach analysis by keying it to design. In Sheppard's experience, most current analysis courses asked only "how do you do statics, or dynamics, or strength of materials?" The analysis course Sheppard was advocating would help students develop a "tool set" to answer the question of why a particular solution to a design problem works (Sheppard, 1992, p. 6).

The problems Sheppard set out to resolve in her Synthesis project included not only developing a set of mechanical dissection exercises, but also evaluating students' experience and figuring out how to weave those exercises into a curriculum and make them available to the engineering community at large.[19] She gained an audience through a series of conference presentations and journal publications on mechanical dissection, a website, a manual, and talks all over the country. Sheppard noted that one talk, delivered by the National Technical University, was broadcast live to more than 150 sites and more than 3,000 attendees. By the end of the coalition's core funding period, mechanical dissection had not only become Sheppard's central contribution, but had also become a signature for Synthesis as well. Tony Ingraffea, the coalition's first director, told me, "Mechanical dissection was probably in the top handful of things that people within the coalition and around the country identified with us."

The Limits of Reform

Synthesis itself wound down in the mid 1990s, survived by the NEEDS digital library of courseware for engineering education, which is now a component of the national digital library in Science, Math, Engineering, and Technology Education (SMETE).[20] The impact of Synthesis, and indeed, any of its sister coalitions, on engineering education reform is hard to assess. Some innovations that have taken root in engineering schools— such as more hands-on experience and more emphasis on communication and teamwork skills—were also touted by the coalitions. More ambitious goals for systemic change have not yet been met. Sheppard herself thinks there are few schools around the country that are "really coming at education from a systems perspective and seeing the value in faculty being team players, the kind of joint ownership of the curriculum, versus the traditional model, which is each of us doing our private things with our students." There are questions, too, about how much the experience affected the coalition schools themselves. Certainly, the effort engaged only a small number of the faculty at Stanford. Former coalition head Tony Ingraffea said, "even now, 10 years after the coalition program, there are still very few people, even on the campuses in which the coalition programs have existed, who think of themselves as creators, reformers, prime movers in the curriculum." As Elaine Seymour noted, such groups as the Engineering Education Coalitions "play an important role in supporting and extending grass-roots conversations and initiatives. . . . What is not proven, however, is the theory that 'networks of such collaborations can build into a 'critical mass' in favor of reform'" (2002, pp. 91–92). [21]

It is important to note that Synthesis is survived not just by courseware and contributions to creating a wider culture of teaching and learning in the engineering community. It is also survived by individuals, like Agogino at Berkeley and Leifer and Sheppard at Stanford, whose imaginations were strengthened and commitment sharpened by participation in a community of faculty engaged in educational reform. Certainly, these three people found compelling connections between education and their own research interests—cognition, artificial intelligence, and the role of computers for Agogino; learning how design teams in industry work for Leifer; and the relation between analysis and design for Sheppard. They also learned to bring habits of mind developed from their research to problems in education. In brief, they questioned and did not just assume. In speaking of Sheppard's contribution, Agogino stressed that Sheppard made her work on mechanical dissection a "form of scholarship. She assessed it. She looked at its impact on student learning and retention." Although she set the stage for others to apply the technique and evaluate it, no one else has really evaluated it at the same level of breadth and depth, Agogino claimed. "Sheri looked at gender issues, she looked at teamwork, she looked at context. And she tried to measure it as well."

Another legacy of Synthesis, of course, has been mechanical dissection itself, which, carefully designed and assessed, entered the larger world of engineering education in the early 1990s. By Sheppard's own count (to which I will return in the next chapter), "over 26 courses or course segments at 21 universities have been created that incorporate MD activities from Stanford. . . . In addition, MD activities have been offered to K-12 teachers and students through the National Academy of Engineering's Web-based resources for teachers, and through outreach activities at, for example, the University of Virginia as part of a summer Head Start program" (2002, p. 4).[22] Sheppard has created award-winning mechanical dissection courseware that has been widely distributed through NEEDS, and she is incorporating mechanical dissection activities into the textbook she is writing on statics, to be published in 2004 by Wiley.

But the spread and especially the effect of any individual person's educational innovation or pedagogical technique, is—like the effect of the larger coalition network—difficult to trace. As in design, creative teachers invent new pedagogies by appropriating existing ideas and applying them in new ways. Unlike the products of design and, indeed, the findings of scientific research, it is hard to lay claim to a particular pedagogy. Sheppard's colleague Kristin Wood at the University of Texas noted that in the late 1970s and early 1980s, others were doing isolated instances of dissection, but no one was aware of the work. "I think that Sheri was one of the first, if not the first, to bring national and international attention to those types of activities," he said. "But you know, there's an old adage that when you see something the first time, you don't necessarily agree with it; when you see it the second time, you admit there's something there; and the third time, you claim it as your own idea. And I think Sheri has helped that tremendously." His suggestion, of course, is that Sheppard's work has helped mechanical dissection (or "reverse engineering" or whatever name it is called by) become the property not of an individual scholar but of the engineering community at large. Tony Ingraffea agreed. "The words 'mechanical dissection' have become, I think, commonplace now, and not always with proper attribution to the originator," he said. "But that's the way things are. And I don't think that would bother Sheri in the least."

Perhaps not, but this very feature of educational reform has made it particularly hard for Sheppard and others like her to make a case for the importance and effect of their work. One of the many barriers to what Seymour called "grassroots action" (2002, p. 92) is the gap between cultures of teaching in higher education and cultures of research. "A bridge person" like Sheppard has a natural affinity for the scholarship of teaching and learning, but in building her bridge, she has been subject to strong countervailing forces.

NOTES

1. This quotation is from Sheppard (2001), p. 5.

2. An influential 1961 report by the Massachusetts Institute of Technology Committee on Engineering Design defined engineering design as "the process of applying the various techniques and scientific principles for the purpose of defining a device, a process or a system in sufficient detail to permit its physical realization. . . . Design may be simple or enormously complex, easy or difficult, mathematical or nonmathematical; it may involve a trivial problem or one of great importance" (cited in Kemper, 1990, p. 197).

3. According to Bruce Seely (1999), the post-WWII transformation of engineering education had its roots in the changes effected by a number of European engineers who began working in U.S. schools of engineering after 1920. Seely noted, "In fact, these Europeans brought engineering science to the U.S. They approached engineering with a belief in the utility of applied mathematics and greater interest

in developing theoretical bases for engineering" (p. 288). However, the critical cat-
alyst for change was the huge, post-WWII influx of federal research funds. In the
context of pressure to conduct basic research on new technologies, concentrating
on the engineering science undergirding technology became more highly valued
than earlier, more immediately practical work in engineering. As engineering
schools vied for federal research grants, which were far more lucrative than the
funding from corporate sources, engineering programs concentrated on developing a scientific curriculum, preparing students for specialized engineering
research, rather than a general curriculum offering fundamental scientific training
appropriate for industry work. As a result, Seely concluded:

> . . . the final shape of the educational system based on engineering science
> that actually was developed in those years swerved away from the vision
> of its [European] founders, largely under the impetus of enormous fed-
> eral research expenditures. It created a gulf between engineering schools
> and industrial practice, and perhaps even an imbalance of theory and
> practice in the colleges. (p. 292)

The 1955 Grinter Report, published by the predecessor of the accreditation board,
illustrates the power of military research money. While an initial draft of the report
recommended that most engineering schools offer the general-professional curriculum, the final version of the report instead called for more instruction in engineering science.

4. For example, Clive Dym, professor of engineering design at Harvey Mudd
College, identified a set of problematic messages embedded in current engineering
curricula. Fundamentally, he argued that the inflexible curricular structure and
concentration on the "engineering science" component of engineering embodies
certain assumptions that do not prove true in the practice of engineering outside
of the academy. For him, part of a solution to these curricular flaws involves
rethinking the relationship between design and analysis:

> Both analysis and design are absolutely essential to the mix of good engi-
> neering learning, as they both are to engineering practice. . . . Analysis
> must unquestionably retain its centrality for formulating and modeling
> engineering problems, as well as for evaluating design results. If any-
> thing, perhaps the point is that students need to learn engineering science
> so that they can design, that is, we teach engineering science in order to
> support our students' ability to design. (1999, p. 3)

5. Kemper (1990) made a similar point. "Having been subjected to intensive
schooling during which the problems were almost always given in clearly defined
form, the new engineer is uncertain of just what to do when faced with a problem
that is vague and largely unstructured" (p. 198).

6. According to ethnographers Gary Downey and Juan Lucena (2003), today's
students are likely to begin their studies with an idea of engineering design as similar to architectural design, that is, "a deep personal expression of some distinctive
perspective. . . ." But they learn to think otherwise:

> The science-based engineering curriculum tells them . . . that engineering
> design is simply an extension of the engineering method into a messier

world. It is the timely, disciplined application of mathematical engineering problem solving to real-world problems. This shift is profound, for through it the genius of design is moved from the creator to the authoritative method, from the person to the discipline. (p. 171)

7. ABET has accredited engineering programs since 1933 and is today formally acknowledged by the Council on Higher Education Accreditation as the "recognized accreditor for college and university programs in applied science, computing, engineering, and technology" (ABET, 2003). Composed of 31 professional societies representing well over 1.5 million engineers in higher education and industry, it is recognized by faculty and administrators as having "considerable influence on engineering programs" (Van Duzer, 1999, p. 11; see also Van Duzer, 2000). For most programs, ABET accreditation is "critical to their professional reputation, funding (both internal and external) and the ability of their graduates to obtain professional licensure as engineers" (Van Duzer, 1999, p. 11).

8. These "Engineering Criteria 2000" include a new requirement on "Program Outcomes and Assessment," which lists 11 abilities that engineering programs must demonstrate their graduates have attained. These include:

a) an ability to apply knowledge of mathematics, science, and engineering; b) an ability to design and conduct experiments, as well as to analyze and interpret data; c) an ability to design a system, component, or process to meet desired needs; d) an ability to function on multi-disciplinary teams; e) an ability to identify, formulate, and solve engineering problems; f) an understanding of professional and ethical responsibility; g) an ability to communicate effectively; h) the broad education necessary to understand the impact of engineering solutions in a global and societal context; i) a recognition of the need for, and an ability to engage in life-long learning; j) a knowledge of contemporary issues; k) an ability to use the techniques, skills, and modern engineering tools necessary for engineering practice. (ABET, 2000, p. 1)

ABET also requires that "each program must have an assessment process with documented results" (ABET, 2000, p. 1).

9. Both Sandia and Lawrence Livermore Labs were founded in the 1950s to pursue research on nuclear weapons. Located in Livermore, California, they are national laboratories and explore a range of research areas. Lawrence Livermore Lab, which is operated by the University of California, summarizes its research agenda as "advanced defense technologies, energy, environment, biological sciences and basic sciences" (http://www.llnl.gov/llnl/04science/research.html). Sandia's California facility is the smaller of its two sites, with its headquarters located in Albuquerque, New Mexico. Both of Sandia's sites are managed by Lockheed Martin (http://www.sandia.gov/about/history/index.html).

10. When Sheppard was there, the work of the computer-aided engineering department involved both building software for analysis and validating that it worked in mainline engineering. The following year, these functions were separated with some engineers staying in the lab and focusing solely on software design, while others, focused solely on validation, went to mainline engineering.

11. For an account of the relationships between corporate and academic science in the early years of the start-ups in the biotechnology industry (late 1970s and

early 1980s), see chapter one of anthropologist Paul Rabinow's *Making PCR: A Story of Biotechnology* (1996).

12. The number of departments and divisions within departments in the School of Engineering has changed over time. In the mid 1980s, Computer Science joined the School of Engineering and, at least in some people's opinion, has displaced electrical engineering as the premiere department. Sheppard recalled that when she arrived, the divisions within Mechanical Engineering included Applied Mechanics, with about 5 faculty; Design, with about 11; and Thermal Science, with about 14. Today there are 5 divisions, and Design is the largest. As Sheppard explained, "Right now, design work is really in high demand by industry and it's getting lots of funding by NSF, and attracting a lot of people coming back to study."

13. Sheppard said that this particular style contrasted visibly with other divisions:

> . . . where people tended to wear white shirts and ties. There was a joke for a while that there was only one tie in the design division and we kept it in the main office so if anyone had anyone visiting, they could go borrow the tie.

Indeed, she noted that they were questioning the extent to which their identity depended on their adversarial stance, especially as they were now the largest division in the department and in a position to take a leadership role. Some were also wondering how the division's identity might be sustained as the older members retired, and stories aged.

14. An alumnus of the design division who received his master's degree in product design in 1978, David Kelley is founder of IDEO Product Development, and designer of, among other things, the lavatory sign on airplanes, the mechanical whale in the movie, *Free Willy*, and the original Apple computer mouse. The Museums of Modern Art in New York and San Francisco have Kelley designed products in their permanent collection (Levy, 2000). At Stanford, Kelley teaches in the Product Design Program (a joint program with the art department) and in the Human Computer Interface Program (a joint program with the computer science department).

15. In 1987–1988, there were a total of 125 women on the Stanford faculty, or 11 percent. In that same year, 18.9 percent of Yale's faculty were women; 18.5 percent of Brown's, 15.7 percent of Harvard's, 14.2 percent of Berkeley's, and 13 percent of Princeton's. MIT's proportion of women faculty was lower than Stanford's, at 9.8 percent, and Cal Tech's was only 4.1 percent. A breakdown by school at Stanford is available for 1992–1993; in that year, the proportion of women faculty in education was 24.8 percent; in humanities and sciences, 18.4 percent; in law, 17.9 percent; in medicine, 17.5 percent; in graduate business, 7.7 percent; in engineering, 6.8 percent; and in earth sciences, 5.3 percent (Stanford University, 1993).

16. There is a vast literature on women faculty in the sciences. Most relevant here, perhaps, is the 2002 report on "The Status of Women Faculty at MIT," which followed a 1999 study on women faculty in the School of Science. The new report examined the situation for women faculty in the Schools of Architecture and Planning; Engineering; Humanities, Arts, and Social Sciences; and the Sloan School of Management (Hopkins, Bailyn, Gibson, & Hammonds, 2002). The report consid-

ered the subtle and not-so-subtle ways in which women faculty are marginalized, their work undervalued, and their careers disadvantaged at MIT. There is no doubt, of course, that these phenomena are widespread. I return to these issues in the next chapter.

17. Finite element analysis is a mathematical method for understanding the combined effects of the different forces that can affect a structure. According to an introductory engineering textbook:

> Many work stations offer programs permitting what is called *finite element analysis*. In this mathematical analysis technique, a three-dimensional object is broken down into a network of simple elements for which stress and deflection characteristics can be easily computed. Many equations are then generated and solved. The design engineer can request the stresses and deflections occurring in various parts of the object for a variety of loading conditions. Thus the engineer can decide whether the design under consideration is sufficiently strong or too strong and heavy, or whether another type of material might produce a better part. (Craver, Schroder, & Tarquin, 1987, p. 247)

Sheppard first taught Finite Elements in Mechanical Design in 1989—the first new course that she created at Stanford. Elsewhere, she has described it as a graduate-level course where:

> . . . students learn the foundational theory of the finite element method and how this theory is implemented in a commercial software tool. In addition, they learn how to appropriately apply the tool in order to study the behavior of engineered systems. This course complements the more theory-oriented finite element course offerings at Stanford in Mechanical and Civil Engineering. (Sheppard, 2002, p. 2)

18. According to Lawrence Carlson, a professor of engineering at the University of Colorado at Boulder, this applies not only to underrepresented students, but also to a good many more. "I think the students we get now are less likely to be the tinkerers that might have been coming through school 20 years ago, so they don't have that sort of seat-of-the-pants understanding of how things work."

19. In our conversation about Sheppard's contribution, Denice Denton, dean of the College of Engineering at the University of Washington, emphasized her focus on students, as opposed to the typical focus on curriculum:

> A lot of what she is doing is trying to determine what sorts of strategies work best in the classroom. How do you get students in a team? How do you get them to perform in that team? What sort of problems might you give them to have the biggest impact on their learning? She makes videos of students working in teams and uses verbal protocols to determine what sort of things the teams are doing: it's really getting into the nitty gritty of learning. What does it take to make learning happen, to precipitate learning?

20. Conceived as a digital library for the maintenance and dissemination of innovative educational materials, NEEDS (The National Engineering Education Deliv-

ery System) was established in 1990 through the efforts of the Synthesis Coalition. In its current form, it is the distributed architecture that supports "the development, use and more importantly re-use of these instructional technologies" (Muramatsu & Agognino, 1999). These technologies consist of courseware for entire courses as well as the individual elements that compose the courseware. Thus, materials can be accessed and used as is, or specific elements can be adapted and put together in new ways. All courseware submitted to NEEDS undergoes a peer review process and is evaluated using criteria related to its pedagogical applications and outcomes. NEEDS is linked to the SMETE digital library, which provides access to educational materials from science, math, engineering and technology education communities. See http://www.needs.org/needs/public/about_needs/.

21. Seymour takes this statement of the thesis from a paper by Etzkowitz, Kemelgor, Neuschatz, Uzzi, & Alonzo (1995).

22. Sheppard has found courses using mechanical dissection activities at Arizona State University; California Polytechnic State University–San Luis Obispo; Iowa State University; Michigan Technological University; Johns Hopkins University; Mission College; Northern Arizona State University; Northwestern University; Pennsylvania State University; Queen's University; Rose–Hulman Institute of Technology; University of California, Berkeley; University of Colorado; University of Delaware; University of New Hampshire; University of Puerto Rico; University of Texas–Austin; University of Vermont; University of Washington; University of Wisconsin–Madison; Virginia Tech; Wichita State University; and Yale University.

7

The Question of Quality
· ·

> The *process* of solving this type of open-ended analytical engi-
> neering problem has been largely ignored. Traditionally, if the
> students developed a mechanism that met the stated criteria, the
> instructor was satisfied that they had learned the material. We
> have revealed that the nature of the solution process can actually
> impact the level of learning achieved by the students, just as a
> design process can determine the quality of a design.[1]

A cademic careers in the United States are profoundly shaped by expectations for scholarly accomplishment at the colleges and universities
where faculty work. From graduate school to retirement, doors open or
close depending on how well a scholar's efforts are regarded by colleagues
at their own institution and by respected disciplinary peers. This fact of
academic life underwrites the integrity and vitality of the intellectual
enterprise. However, it also underlies the dilemma of how to pursue a
career without the "careerism" of focusing on quantity rather than quality
of publications, for example, or postponing an interest in teaching until
after tenure. How, in particular, can one design a career that includes substantial work in the scholarship of teaching and learning, or indeed, in any
academic endeavor that is not in tune with colleagues' priorities or is outside their normal reading habits.[2]

While potential conflicts between academic success and intellectual
integrity date back to the establishment of the professional career path in
American universities in the late 19th century (Bledstein, 1976), the issue
has special currency in the heated world of higher education today. Since
World War II, expectations for research productivity among faculty have
increased, and it is likely that the bar for entry into academic careers and
subsequent promotion will continue to rise as competition for positions
intensifies (Altbach, 2000; Wilson, 2001). At the same time, higher education has been broadening its commitments to engage more meaningfully
in local communities, to include more women and minorities among the

faculty, and to educate a wider range of students than ever before. Bringing faculty evaluation systems into line with current realities has become a priority nationwide. As a result, there is growing recognition that higher education will not be able to meet these commitments unless what counts in faculty evaluation is both equitable and worthwhile.

Renewed attention to systems of faculty evaluation is good news for college and university faculty members who become involved in the scholarship of teaching and learning, certainly a nontraditional niche in most professional schools and academic departments. After all, most faculty members are not hired in as education specialists, nor are they expected to become so in the course of their normal duties. As scholars, they are expected to keep up with the literature in their field, to know who is doing what in their specialty, and, often, to initiate and sustain a vigorous research program of their own. As teachers, they are expected to perform responsibly in the classroom and during office hours, to receive good evaluations from undergraduates, and in institutions with advanced degree programs, to advise graduate students who go on to fine careers and do well. Finally, as academic citizens, faculty are expected to participate productively in the governance of their departments, institutions, and scholarly or professional societies.

What is not expected is that faculty will develop such strong interests in educational issues that these become a major theme or component in their work. Nor is it expected that faculty members' interests in teaching and learning will significantly engage them with colleagues beyond the campus walls. As sociologists have long argued, teaching is generally viewed as a local rather than a cosmopolitan activity (Baker & Zey-Ferrell, 1984; Gouldner, 1957, 1958; Merton, 1968), and those who actually do take their teaching interests "public" are still few and far between. Sheri Sheppard's departmental colleague and frequent collaborator on pedagogical projects, Larry Leifer, noted, "You can innovate in your own course. But to take it beyond that is not in the call of duty. If you go beyond the local, people expect it to be through research."

The movement to recognize a wider range of scholarship for tenure and promotion is beginning to provide a more welcoming environment for people like Sheppard, who get involved in one or more of the "new" kinds of scholarship at an early stage in their careers. Colleges and universities have been changing their formal guidelines in this direction (Diamond, 1999; Glassick, Huber, & Maeroff, 1997; O'Meara, 2000), scholarly societies have published reports on broader definitions of scholarly work (Diamond & Adam, 1995, 2000), and accrediting agencies are asking for more evidence of student learning (Peterson & Einarson, 1997). Presidents, provosts, deans, and even chairs are expressing support for work that furthers the full scope of university missions. It can still be a challenge for faculty to convince their colleagues that work in teaching and learning, say, or community engagement, should be seen as "scholarship" on par with more conventional research. But it is getting harder for colleagues, especially those in leadership positions, to dismiss such work *simply* because it involves education or community outreach.

A second, subtler, challenge for scholars of teaching and learning is negotiating questions about the quality of this work. Understandably, support for the legitimacy of the new kinds of scholarship goes hand in hand with insistence that it meet the same high standards expected across the board (Glassick, Huber, & Maeroff, 1997). But what exactly are these standards and how objective are they in their application to new or emergent areas of scholarly work? As we have seen in previous chapters, the "standard metrics" of grants, publication, and impact can indeed be applied to the scholarship of teaching and learning. Yet clearly there are restrictions as to the kinds of work that can be evaluated in this way. There are subtleties of application that also must be acknowledged. Are the issues that are addressed considered important and are the methods esteemed? Are the journals and conferences where this work is presented known to colleagues and well regarded? Are the external scholars who can interpret the candidate's educational work or serve as "comparison candidates" known to internal colleagues and well regarded? What constitutes evidence of "impact" when one is talking about curricular and pedagogical innovations and inquiries? How might gender fit in?

In this chapter, I follow Sheppard's experience through the tenure process and beyond, to see how she and her colleagues have been negotiating some of the special questions of quality that work in the scholarship of teaching and learning invites. I sketch in the situation for this kind of work at the School of Engineering at Stanford University, look at how the scholarship of teaching and learning appears to have played into her tenure case, examine how she developed her education activities in the years after tenure, and finally, consider issues that are coming up as she and her colleagues explore the possibilities for promotion to full professor.

RECOGNIZING THE SCHOLARSHIP OF TEACHING AND LEARNING

The recognition and reward of the scholarship of teaching and learning may be logically distinct from the recognition and reward of classroom teaching, but in practice the two are closely entwined. In part, this is because the scholarship of teaching and learning involves exploring pedagogies, curricula, and assessments that will broaden and deepen student understanding. It is also because most systems of faculty roles and rewards force work to be categorized as research, teaching, or service, and colleagues tend to think of curricular or pedagogical work as teaching (or even service to the institution or profession), no matter what its other features may be. This would not be a problem in situations where teaching is given sufficient weight in evaluating faculty performance. While teaching appears to be gaining importance in faculty evaluation in the nation's research universities, a strong record of research remains the sine qua non (Huber, 2002).[3] As education historian Larry Cuban (1999) argued, for Stanford University, "research trumps teaching," not only with regard to faculty roles and rewards but also with regard to a great many "aspects of university mission, funding, organization, student admissions, curriculum, and instruction" (p. 86).

It is true that a high level of research productivity is required for professional advancement at institutions like Stanford, and it is also true that most of the schools and departments at such institutions have developed more elaborated cultures of research than they have of teaching. This does not mean that the nation's leading universities are, in principle, unfriendly to faculty who make important contributions to educational thought and practice in their fields. On the contrary. Patti Gumport argued, "For universities, keeping pace with knowledge change is of the utmost importance . . . campuses and their faculty are expected to be at the forefront of knowledge change, to move fields forward with new discoveries or at least to stay current with new developments" (2002b, p. 47). As a result, these institutions (and their various schools and departments) are happy to house faculty who have gained a reputation for educational leadership, although traditionally, as in the case of Nobel Prize-winning scientists who become active in science education, educational leadership has been an addition to, even a consequence of, intellectual leadership in a core area of his or her field.

The School of Engineering at Stanford is a case in point. Large, self-confident, and secure, Stanford's School of Engineering is now the university's second largest school (after Arts and Sciences), enrolling approximately one in four of the university's students—2,868 graduate students and 936 undergraduates in 2000–2001. Its undergraduate programs were ranked second in the nation (after MIT) by U.S. News & World Report for 2004. Seven of its nine graduate programs were also at or near the top, according to the most recent rankings of the National Research Council (Goldenberger, Maher, & Flatteau, 1995).[4] The school's 219 faculty, together with its emeriti, have won nearly all the distinctions the profession has to offer.[5] The school's alumni are distinguished and loyal. Many of the school's facilities are now located on Stanford's spectacular new science and engineering quad, a $120 million project funded largely by the school's best-known alumni, William Hewlett and David Packard, whose company, Hewlett-Packard, is headquartered just a short distance away (Joncas, Neuman, & Turner, 1999).

A school of this size and stature can afford to support innovation, and this has enhanced the luster of the school. In particular, people often cite the close connection between Stanford engineering and the rise of Silicon Valley in its immediate neighborhood (Gibbons, 1999; Winslow & Palo Alto Historical Association, 1993). Hewlett and Packard themselves studied with Stanford engineer Frederick E. Terman, who encouraged his former students to start businesses in the area, beginning the string of Stanford start-ups that have played such an important role in establishing the Valley's character and reputation.[6] Over the years, Stanford engineering has remained closely tied to the area's high tech industries through the transfer of technology from university labs to commercial companies, industry–university partnerships in research, participation in joint events, and the pool of intellectual talent provided by Stanford's students, faculty, and staff (Gibbons, 1999; see also Brown & Duguid, 1999)

Not everyone has been directly involved in these relationships, but the spirit is pervasive. James Gibbons, dean of the school from 1984 to 1996, wrote, "The heroes in Silicon Valley are the entrepreneurs who can start and grow successful companies" (1999, p. 217). In our conversation, he assured me that the climate at Stanford has always supported entrepreneurship in a variety of forms. Some of them are almost purely academic, such as starting a lab in a new area or creating a new pedagogical approach to a subject that over time redefines the way the subject is taught. What this means for faculty, Gibbons noted, is that:

> There are lots of ways to earn tenure. The essential standard is high quality teaching and high quality scholarship. In engineering, high quality scholarship is almost always interpreted to mean high quality research, but it could also be high quality scholarship in engineering education or design or any of a number of other things. Passion for what you are doing, hard work, and impact on your profession are critical.

Another colleague explained:

> Fundamentally, I think the major research universities want faculty members who are moving towards leadership positions in their fields. And we define leadership very broadly. It's not just numbers of research publications, it's leadership in the field . . . there are lots of roads to the same result, but we want faculty to be leaders.

For examples of roads less taken, William Reynolds, who was chair of Mechanical Engineering in the 1980s and again in the mid 1990s, singled out that department's Design Division, to which Sheppard and her closest colleagues belong. Recalling faculty who helped establish the division's reputation for creativity in the 1960s, he mentioned James L. Adams, who wrote *Conceptual Blockbusting*, Douglas Wilde, who taught People Dynamics, and Robert McKim, who taught Experiences in Visual Thinking. According to Reynolds, so valuable were McKim's contributions to design that he was granted tenure at Stanford even without holding a graduate degree. A more recent example of unconventional success was cited by almost everyone I interviewed at Stanford. Designer David Kelley was tenured (and has by now been promoted) on a record not of published articles, but of award-winning product designs. This is not to say that such cases have been easy to make, but once made they have been appointments in which the school takes pride.[7]

Although the school's reputation is based primarily on innovation, research, and leadership in engineering, its educational program is also an official source of pride. For example, on the School of Engineering (SoE) website, one can find a time line extending from 1891 through 2001, which tells the school's history not only as a succession of technological breakthroughs and professional achievements by its faculty and students, but also of pedagogical landmarks, like the following:

- 1912: "A course on 'Engineering Economy' becomes the first formal class on the 'business' of engineering. It covers the engineering theory of railway location."
- 1930: "Early SoE leaders emphasize the importance of a broad—not just technical—education."
- 1953: "The SoE purchases an electronic analog computer for research and teaching."
- 1964: "Television is used for the first time to project lecture notes and drawings in an Engineering Drawing course."
- 1969: "The Stanford Instructional Television Network begins broadcasting classes to Silicon Valley companies, using a microwave talkback link for questions and answers." (Stanford University, "History of Stanford and the School of Engineering," n.d.)

Naturally, the school's pedagogical life extends beyond the introduction of new subject matter, the use of new technology in teaching, and outreach to new students. For starters, everyday teaching is taken quite seriously with regard to tenure decisions and in setting salary increases. Former dean James Gibbons told me that the school has long been measuring student response to courses,[8] and that under his leadership one half of one's salary increase was dependent on evaluations of one's teaching.

He said to advance to tenure, one's teaching as measured by students must be better than the departmental average.[9] Curriculum is another area of concern, and recent changes to make engineering a more attractive major have included the establishment of freshman seminars, design experiences for freshmen and sophomores, and a research experience for juniors.

Stanford engineers have made contributions to engineering education beyond the local as well. Textbooks are the most familiar way to do so in engineering, and several Stanford faculty members—including Frederick Terman—have published successfully in this genre. William Reynolds recalled that Terman, as dean, encouraged faculty members to publish textbooks, although he thinks this was more common in the 1950s and 1960s, when the emphasis on research was less encompassing than it is today. Of course, people are still writing textbooks at Stanford, including Sheppard. But as we have seen, Sheppard is also a pioneer of new and less familiar ways of contributing to engineering education. Over the years, this body of work has included prototyping classroom approaches (as in the mechanical dissection exercises discussed in the preceeding chapter), directing summer workshops on pedagogy for new engineering faculty from across the country, leading a national study of engineering education, and exploring the very process of learning engineering—how teams work, the ways in which students solve problems, the interplay between "hands-on" and simulation activities—all with an eye towards bringing the learning of engineering into closer touch with doing engineering itself.

Sheppard herself would be the first to say that Stanford has provided a favorable climate and excellent platform for pursuing this work, and others in the engineering education community saw her achievement of tenure there as "existence proof" that it is possible to be recognized and rewarded at a major research university as both an engineer and a scholar of teaching and learning. While Sheppard's education work ended up playing a positive role in her tenure case, it also (in some colleagues' eyes) made her seem less focused in her research interests, making her position more precarious than it might otherwise have been. Sheppard's story also suggests that even in the best of circumstances, the scholarship of teaching and learning may not be well served by the "standard metrics" that the academy uses to indicate leadership in a field.

TENURE QUANDARIES

By the time Sheppard came up for tenure at Stanford in the 1992–1993 academic year, she knew that her combination of research in engineering science and educational work gave her an unusual profile, but she went into the process with confidence. In addition to her classroom teaching, she was doing work in her specialties of spot welding and numerical analysis;

she had graduate students; she was a leader in the Synthesis Coalition, one of NSF's Engineering Education Coalitions; and she was developing mechanical dissection activities in which students participate in hands-on investigations of the relationship between the form and function of various mechanical devices. We saw in the last chapter that Sheppard's mentors, chair, and dean had warned her to forego the education work and focus her energy on research, but Sheppard believed in the importance of her education work and knew that she had the support of her colleagues in design. In fact, Larry Leifer, her senior colleague and co-PI of Stanford's portion of Synthesis, was serving as her official mentor, helping prepare the papers for her tenure case.[10]

The question for Sheppard and her supporters, of course, was whether her education work would count for or against her tenure bid. They soon had reason to fear it might be the latter because, as Sheppard said, "flags started going up" early on. Approval at the department level seemed likely, but Sheppard's chair let her know that a happy ending at the school level was by no means assured. Sheppard recalled, "they kept adding more and more external reviewers, and I didn't know if it was to make my case or find a flaw." There was also a disconcerting string of requests for clarification and elaboration as the final papers were compiled. What was the exact status of this grant, that honor, that paper still in press? Could they supply further information on the extra comparison candidates volunteered by external reviewers? Could they get more letters from former students? What exactly had Sheppard done to adapt mechanical dissection for middle and high school students? With growing concern, Sheppard and her colleagues began to suspect that the chair was planning to argue to the school's committee that what *really* distinguished Sheppard's record at Stanford was not her welding research (however solid) nor even mechanical dissection as a college-level pedagogy (however promising), but rather mechanical dissection's potential to transform science education in grades K-12!

The denouement, though favorable, was tortuous. As expected, support for Sheppard was strong in her own department, but inconclusive among the school's executive committee of all department chairs. A meeting of the school's senior leaders, the Appointments and Promotion Committee (A&P), was called and a great deal of strategizing ensued. The dean, seeking a solution, asked Sheppard to consider a nontenured position as professor (teaching), which she said she "vigorously declined." A delegation of Design Division faculty met with the dean to discuss the situation, and one accompanied their chair to make the strongest possible case to the A&P. Finally, after Sheppard won that committee's support and (at some point) received an offer for a tenured position at a competitive institution, the dean decided to let the case proceed. Sheppard's papers were sent to the provost, who approved them and sent them on to the faculty advisory committee, which also approved them. It had been a white-knuckle tenure process—a "debacle," as Sheppard jokingly called it—but it ended well, with commendations to Sheppard from the advisory committee on both her engineering research and the mechanical dissection part of her education work.

I do not know what happened in the confidential deliberations of that winter and spring of 1993. Looking back, Sheppard's closest colleagues seemed to agree that her education work complicated her case, although exactly how was hard to pin down. One view was that things might have gone more smoothly had her tenure and promotion papers made more of her welding research and numerical analysis and less of her work in education, that is, if she had presented a more conventional profile. Another view was that the education work was important because having done both, she might not have made it on the size or strength of her engineering research alone.[11] Perhaps the most interesting, albeit minority, view was that that her education work itself wasn't sufficiently visible, particularly that she had not followed through on mechanical dissection in the entrepreneurial, "Stanford" way. I will return to this issue.

From the perspective of people in the engineering education community, the principal issue in Sheppard's case was whether scholarly status had been accorded to Sheppard's education work. For example, Tony Ingraffea of Cornell, first head of Synthesis, said:

> The affair of Sheri's tenure was a major enterprise. It was a historical landmark, I think. It was touch and go and all the other things you could think of. It really shook the people in the coalition, because we were all relatively young, idealistic, true believers. We had been going around saying things like, "Wow, there really is scholarship in curriculum development." And we would hear deans boasting that their schools were members of the coalition. And then there was the case of Sheri's tenure, where what I began hearing directly and indirectly was that she still has to show that she's a world-class researcher. And if she doesn't do that, she's not going to get tenure at Stanford, regardless of whether she is a world-class curriculum developer. But we thought curriculum development was scholarship! "It's a different kind of scholarship," they'd reply. "Well, how so?" And we never did get closure on that. No one has ever gotten closure on that.

It is easy to see why the community was convinced that education work could be considered "scholarship." NSF had funded Synthesis, and Sheppard had presented papers on mechanical dissection at conferences and published about it in professional journals. Yet, as Wankat and colleagues note in their essay on the scholarship of teaching and learning in engineering:

> Activities that characterize the formal study of teaching and learning in engineering are basically the same as those usually associated with disciplinary scholarship in the field—seeking and securing grant support for research, presenting research results at professional conferences, and publishing them in refereed journals. Certain differences between engineering research and educational research, however, pose significant challenges to engineering faculty intending to engage in the latter (Wankat et al., 2002, p. 226).

Among the challenges these authors noted is the fact that education research is oriented towards goals, such as "learning" and "understanding," which are much less precisely defined than those in other kinds of engineering research, such as "tensile strength, efficiency, and profit." Furthermore, education research almost always involves "confounding factors" that cannot be "clearly identified and their influence eliminated." Finally, "appropriate metrics and valid and reliable instruments to measure them are much easier to identify in science and engineering than in education, an obstacle that has limited engineering education research until fairly recently" (Wankat et al., 2002, pp. 227–228).

While issues like these contribute to many academic engineers' sense that the scholarship of teaching and learning should not be considered "research," the classification of such work as "teaching" brings to the fore its own set of quandaries. A very significant one concerns its visibility in the external evaluations that so many institutions rely on to triangulate the nature and level of a candidate's achievements. Stanford is like many other institutions in this respect. As a senior colleague explained:

> We normally ask referees about the impact that the faculty member has had in his or her field. What's your prognosis for future success for this person? Is this person developing into a leader in his or her field? We don't say, "Is this happening in this specific technical field?" We simply ask the broad question. So if a person has had a major national impact in developing new curriculum or new teaching methodologies, or a textbook, we would expect that these external referees would know about that. These are all engineering educators, after all, so if no one mentions it, then one can draw one's own conclusions about the impact the person really had.

Certainly, there is merit to this practice for faculty who are not using the scholarship of teaching and learning to make their case. An alternative for those who are would be to invite additional letters from people who are acknowledged leaders within the engineering education community. But this brings with it further problems, because they may not be as well known to committee members as the leaders in more conventional engineering fields. As another colleague said, anticipating a strategy they might pro-pose for Sheppard's upcoming case for promotion to full professor:

> You can go ahead and get letters from important people around the country, but the committee members don't know these people. If somebody's in fluid mechanics or thermal systems, you can go and get a letter from some crusty old character at MIT, and somebody will say, "Oh, I know him, he's tough. If he says this person really is the best among these three people, you can believe it." As soon as some-body makes a comment like that, you know the case will probably go through. But in engineering education, there wouldn't be anything like that, because the committee doesn't know how to measure it.

The selection of comparison of candidates is equally fraught. Many leading institutions ask external reviewers to rank the candidate in ques-tion with others of roughly similar age and experience in the same area of specialization. There are only a few engineers who have distinguished themselves both in engineering science and in educational scholarship beyond the classrooms and curricula of their own institution, and some of these are also people who should be writing letters as referees themselves. Should one arrange for two sets of referees or comparison candidates, one for science and one for education? Would you average the response?

A similar range of issues arises with regard to questions of the produc-tivity, style, and impact of education work. The conferences and journals in which engineering education is made public, as well as the awards and distinctions that engineering education has to offer, may not be well known to colleagues who think of pedagogical and curricular reform as "teaching" rather than "scholarship" (in the rigorous sense that engineer-ing science is seen to be). Educational work that involves participation in major projects like Synthesis can strike engineers as "politics." One of Sheppard's colleagues said, "people in engineering don't like anything political, anything that involves using others to create a reputation." A new teaching method, he explained, is a different matter, especially if it changes things. This colleague said Sheppard's mechanical dissection was seen as a method that had *promise* of changing things, and that was critical to the case.

What about gender? When Sheppard was tenured and promoted to associate professor, she was the first and only woman to receive such an appointment in the Department of Mechanical Engineering at Stanford and until 2002 remained the only tenured woman among the department's 36 faculty members.[12] While Sheppard did benefit from affirmative action in being hired, no one suggested in the course of my discussions that this was a factor in her tenure and promotion.[13] However, as Alice Agogino of Berkeley emphasized in our discussion, the effects of gender on women's professional lives are subtle and pervasive, affecting choices that in turn affect how they are perceived. When those choices include spending time in non-elite pursuits like education, their work may be doubly discounted. The tendency to discount women's work in core areas of the field is exacerbated by the tendency to discount *anyone's* work in areas perceived as marginal.[14]

Certainly, Sheppard's colleagues felt that her tenure case had been a very close call, and were watching to see how her work would develop in her post-tenure years. Would she be blocked for promotion to full professor if she continued her work in education, as some feared? Or would she win academic advancement for the scholarship of teaching and learning and engineering education reform?

INQUIRY, LEARNING MATERIALS, AND LEADERSHIP ROLES

After receiving tenure and promotion to associate professor in August 1993, Sheppard found that the politics of the Synthesis Coalition were in full swing. Sheppard and Leifer, co-PIs of the coalition at Stanford, began work that identified them (in Leifer's words) "much more with evaluation and assessment than with technical development or even pedagogic framing." Sheppard and Leifer argued that more assessment was needed and urged that it be built in to the activity (through pre- and post-tests) rather than just done post facto. This view apparently prevailed, according to coalition colleagues at Tuskegee University. They noted, "the Synthesis Coalition emphasizes assessment of the effectiveness of any curricular innovation" (Aglan & Ali, 1996, p. 329).

For Sheppard, this line of work involved a series of assessments of learning materials and teaching methods. In an account of her activities prepared in 2002, Sheppard described several projects that examined how students go about learning engineering. In exploring how interactive multimedia courseware might enhance hands-on learning, Sheppard and a graduate student developed multimedia courseware to accompany a version of Sheppard's bicycle dissection exercises and videotaped three groups of students engaging in the work (Regan & Sheppard, 1996). They assembled a multidisciplinary group of reviewers to analyze the videos with a technique called video interaction analysis and concluded with "a set of design principles for creating effective courseware more generally" (Sheppard, 2002, p. 7). Another project explored whether educational interactive multimedia software effectively teaches engineering concepts. This involved a statistical analysis of pre- and post-tests of students' work in a curriculum module on direct current motors and motorized systems, which utilized interactive software created by Sheppard and another graduate student. Among other things, their findings indicated that students with different learning preferences "responded differently to the various learning techniques employed in the curriculum" (Reamon & Sheppard, 1997, 1998). Sheppard also did research while writing her textbook on statics, developing a method called "Text Learning Capture" to enable any textbook's "readability, comprehensibility, and usability to be assessed" (Sheppard, Jones, & Jeremijenko, 1998).

Clearly for Sheppard, these inquiries and assessment tools have gone hand in hand with the development of teaching methods and learning materials to promote active learning in undergraduate engineering, from multimedia materials to accompany mechanical dissection activities to the preparation of a textbook on mechanics that makes use of the ideas from dissection and what her inquiries have taught her about how students learn. The book, due out in summer 2004, begins by presenting the physical principles and concepts that describe systems in equilibrium through activities that ground understanding in the reader's own experience of bicycles and bridges, and then moves to an analytical problem-solving methodology that the reader can apply in evaluating structural systems. Students revisit real engineering examples throughout the book, and there are a variety of graphical representations, because many engineering students are visual learners, and because of the importance of graphical information and communication in engineering practice.[15]

As Sheppard's reputation grew, so did opportunities for leadership in engineering education. For example, in the academic years 1994–1995 and 1995–1996, she and Leifer co-organized Stanford engineering's participation in AAHE's Peer Review of Teaching Project, directed by Lee Shulman and Pat Hutchings.[16] Seeing it as a way to engage mechanical engineers in activities around teaching and learning, Sheppard and Leifer invited the participation of Michelle Marincovich, director of Stanford's Center for Teaching and Learning, and organized mentorship pairs of senior and junior faculty, as well as other faculty and graduate students who wanted to learn more about teaching. In weekly meetings of 7 to 10 people, the group (ME-Peer) explored different ways of assessing teaching and engaging peers, and they eventually decided on a process of formative evaluation in which peers interviewed students. The focus was on the course (not the faculty member) and the teacher prepared a reflective document that the reviewer read before interviewing students following a series of prearranged questions. The group reviewed at least nine classes this way and asked a graduate student to do an assessment of the process, including how much time it took. They made the work available through a number of publications, one of which won an IEEE/ASEE Frontiers in Education "Best Paper Award" (Sheppard, Johnson, & Leifer, 1998).[17]

Like many scholars of teaching and learning, Sheppard has found that it can be a long and slow process to engage one's own departmental colleagues in activities designed to improve pedagogy and curriculum. For example, Synthesis and ME-Peer had involved only a few colleagues. Sheppard had urged her department to continue the Peer Review of Teaching Project after its two-year run, on the grounds that it would help the department prepare for ABET's new outcomes-oriented review process, but the argument did not, as she put it, "carry the day."[18] Beyond the department, however, Sheppard found more interest in serious efforts to advance discussion and innovation in teaching and learning. She was appointed to the Presidential Committee on the Role of Technology in Learning, which recommended the establishment of what became the Stanford Learning Lab, and joined Leifer and another colleague as its co-directors when it opened after the end of Synthesis, in 1997.[19]

Sheppard's educational activities have extended beyond Stanford, for example, through the New Century Scholars Workshop, an NSF teaching initiative for junior engineering faculty from around the country. According to Sheppard, the peer group idea originated with NSF. The first workshops were sponsored by Georgia Tech, Carnegie Mellon, and the University of Wisconsin and were designed for people who were plus or minus one year of getting their engineering Ph.D.s. However, with Sheppard as principal investigator, the Stanford summer workshops (begun in 1998) have served faculty who have been in tenure line positions for one to three years, giving preference to pairs from the same school. Participants focus their energies on a work product for the end of the first week. Each person writes a reflective memo about a course they wish to work on, delivers a lecture that is videotaped and discussed in small groups, and engages in several other hands-on activities. Workshop faculty usually include Sheppard; Michelle Marincovich of Stanford's Center for Teaching and Learning; Richard Reis of the Stanford Learning Lab; Richard Felder and Rebecca Brent from North Carolina State University, who teach about learning styles; and other guests invited to teach segments of the program.[20]

This network grew when Sheppard was invited by Lee Shulman to direct the Carnegie Foundation's national study on engineering education as part of a series of studies on Preparation for the Professions. Shulman had come to know Sheppard's work during her tenure case, when he, then a professor in the school of education, chaired the university's Faculty Advisory Committee—the committee that advised the president on all hiring, tenure, and promotion decisions. Later, of course, he worked with her on AAHE's Peer Review of Teaching Project, of which Sheppard's ME-Peer project was a part.[21] After consulting colleagues in the engineering education community, Sheppard agreed to work with Shulman again, making a three-year commitment to investigate teaching and learning practices in engineering programs across the country and abroad, to discover how engineers are being educated for professional practice. This study is one of a set that is looking at how preparation for the various professions deals with cross-cutting educational dilemmas, such as tensions between theory and practice, tensions between technical and ethical dimensions of professional learning, and whether and how student assessment supports desired goals for professional learning.[22]

As the Carnegie study approaches completion, Sheppard's education agenda remains full, with departmental responsibilities as associate chair for graduate studies, another large NSF project, numerous positions and commitments within the larger engineering education community, and continuing evaluation and revision of her textbook. When I asked Sheppard if her work on teaching and learning in her years after tenure had taken over her professional life, she said no—she keeps up her research on structural behavior, in part because it is fun and she likes staying engaged in traditional engineering work with Ph.D. students, but also because she has learned that to have a voice in teaching and learning, you need to stay active in your disciplinary area. In fact, Sheppard continues to publish in welding, but she has begun to focus on lead-free soldering, which is particularly important now in computers where the load is thermal.[23] Her funding is now from new economy rather than old economy industry, but it has the same advantages and disadvantages as all corporate funding, including being oriented to solving a problem rather than to long-term understanding. Still, understanding how engineering science plays out in this world of practice, with all its pressures and pitfalls, is central to Sheppard's view of what preparation for engineering professionals should be about.

THE IMPACT OF PEDAGOGICAL SCHOLARSHIP

In our interviews, Sheppard noted that she had actually considered not pursuing promotion to full professor, because it would very likely involve a replay of the issues she faced at the time of tenure and become a major distraction from her actual work. In the end, after discussing the situation with colleagues and advisors, Sheppard decided that it would be more honorable to make the argument for promotion than to simply avoid the fray. She knew she needed to be aware of where the arguments against her might come from and work with critical people in the department accordingly. She also knew that she would have to figure out who her reviewers would be and update them on what she's been doing. By now, some of the same people who could recommend her on welding were better prepared to recommend her on education. For example, one of her welding colleagues at MIT was asked to lead a major curriculum committee and brought in as one of his consultants Sheppard's former supervisor from Ford, and both are reading her education articles. However, others who would be well qualified to comment on the education work may not have the respect of some of the chairs. For example, one colleague who is at a top university and was named to the prestigious National Academy of Engineering for accomplishments in education is criticized for not being engaged in engineering research, while another is criticized for taking time off from traditional research to help lead programs at NSF.

Sheppard, of course, understands that the same critique could be leveled at her, because she too has chosen to spend time on engineering education. Still, this is Stanford engineering, which takes pride in being open to innovation. The question, then, is whether her department, school, and university will advance her to the position of full professor, recognizing her achievements in this unusual area of work. Eight years out from her appointment to associate professor, Sheppard realized that promotion does not happen without a scholar's own personal advocacy. Her advisors concurred and said, in effect, tomorrow won't be any better than today. Working with the department's associate chair for faculty development,[24] one of her Design Division colleagues, Sheppard began putting her materials together and testing the waters to see if the time was right to argue the case.

As I write, it is still not known whether Sheppard's case for promotion will go forward. Regardless, the question at the heart of the case is a critical one for the scholarship of teaching and learning. What has been the effect of her work? One of her colleagues told me that he believed that to get promotion, she would have to write an influential textbook and possibly be elected to the National Academy of Engineering (NAE); another said, somewhat hypothetically, that if she could get her mechanical dissection activities into the science curriculum for California secondary schools, he himself would propose her for membership in the NAE. I heard these remarks to mean that the school might be willing to promote a person whose achievements were primarily in engineering education, but that the level of that achievement was likely to be judged by conventional signs of impact and leadership in this field.

This is fine as far as it goes, but the scholarship of teaching and learning often includes unconventional work. Consider the situation of a pedagogical innovation like mechanical dissection (or, for that matter, Brian Coppola's peer instruction for honors students in introductory chemistry at the University of Michigan, or even Dan Bernstein's version of the Keller Plan in introductory psychology at the University of Nebraska in the 1970s). Sheppard introduced mechanical dissection into a course she designed and taught regularly at Stanford, presented descriptions of these activities in conferences; published articles on them in journals; created multimedia materials to accompany mechanical dissection, assessed their effectiveness, and published the findings; made the multimedia materials available to the community through a well-publicized Web-based library for course materials; experimented with the applicability of mechanical dissection for younger students and published about it; disseminated her approach through the Synthesis schools and through a talk delivered by the National Technical University broadcast live to over 150 sites with 3,000 attendees. Yet what is its impact? Who owns a teaching innovation? These are timely questions, but not only because they affect the careers of Sheppard and other scholars of teaching and learning.

Let's begin with the first question. What might be evidence for the kind of impact a teaching innovation can make? One answer is within reach of most scholars of teaching and learning, and that is evidence of students' learning from a variety of artifacts and assessments of students in one's own courses or in the courses of others. Sheppard, for example, could also cite evidence that she's presented and analyzed in conferences and journals. Another kind of evidence, familiar as a "standard metric" in published research, might be citations of one's work, although in Sheppard's case, most of the leading journals on engineering education are not scanned for the science citation index.[25] What about awards? Sheppard can show awards for publication and for innovative course development, and she was recently named a fellow of the American Association for the Advancement of Science, but these are not the honors that are most esteemed in her department.

Another approach to impact concerns an innovation's spread, an approach with clear affinity to textbook adoption. However, tracing the "travel" of a pedagogical innovation can be a difficult task. Sheppard has done Web searches, telephoned colleagues, and followed up references to mechanical dissection to see who is using it and how and to see whether she or Stanford are referenced as a source. Yet while cultures of research in virtually all academic fields have elaborate modes of citation and reference for the ideas and works upon which scholars draw, this is not true for cultures of teaching and learning. Here, the ethic and practice is to take freely what you find promising or helpful in your classroom. Indeed, most faculty do not learn about new ideas in pedagogy from the conferences or journals in education in their fields, in large part because they do not attend or read them (Wankat et al., 2002, p. 234). Syllabi specify course readings, but not sources for the pedagogy of a class.

In fact, like any pedagogy from peer instruction to problem-based learning or service-learning, mechanical dissection has features drawn from a web of tradition and innovation. For example, in an article on mechanical dissection, Sheppard's colleagues from Tuskegee University credit her "efforts . . . for spearheading the work on mechanical dissection within the Synthesis Coalition (Aglan & Ali, 1996, p. 330), while also writing:

> Mechanical Dissection as an art or science is not new; probably as old as ancient Egypt. In the middle of the third millennium BC, a dissected boat was buried south of the Great Pyramid of Giza. . . . The question why the ancient Egyptians buried the boat in a dissected fashion has not so far been answered. It appears that the ancient Egyptians realized the importance of dissection to the understanding of stored, complicated artifacts. (p. 327)

They do this not to belittle Sheppard's (or anyone else's) contribution, but to suggest that the procedure of dismantling a system in order to understand it—a process sometimes called "reverse engineering"—whether for reassembly in the afterlife, to design a better mousetrap, or as pedagogy in a university course, simply makes common sense.

Ways of thinking about teaching and learning that make it hard to credit individual contributions complicate the discernment of distinction in educational work and contribute greatly to the challenge of legitimizing the scholarship of teaching and learning in the faculty reward system. The challenge goes beyond faculty rewards, especially in the current historical context where the traditional commons of postsecondary teaching is under challenge by such forces of commodification as for-profit providers of distance education (Knight Higher Education Collaborative, 2002; Levine, 2000). It may be acceptable, as MIT engineer Woody Flowers (2001) suggested, for certain kinds of instruction to be "delivered" in this way, but it also poses a challenge to colleges and universities to take teaching and learning more seriously. Improvements in teaching and learning should not simply be left to the for-profit sector, willing to pay instructional developers to sell their wares. As a recent policy statement from the Knight Higher Education Collaborative on "Who Owns Teaching?" (2002) concluded:

> A central question to be resolved in the years ahead is the extent to which postsecondary teaching is an entrepreneurial activity carried out by individuals in search of personal gain, or a community activity carried out by people with shared commitments who are in conversation with one another. (p. 8)

If higher education is to improve this "commons" and make the promise of access meaningful in the sciences as well as in other fields, it should be encouraging faculty to engage in pedagogical and curricular innovation with its own forms of reward and recognition.

The importance of tenure and promotion as recognition for the scholarship of teaching and learning cannot be overstated. Engineering educator

Alice Agogino at Berkeley, who knows well the ins and outs of Sheppard's career, told me "if it hadn't been for Sheri I think I would have advised my Ph.D. students much more conservatively than now." Then there's Cornell's Tony Ingraffea, who explained:

> I am now mentoring two of our younger faculty, and I think the best thing I've done in both cases was to recount history. Tell them stories about Synthesis, and tell them stories about Sheri and others. And tell them to be what they are, be courageous, be brave. Follow their ideas and do the right thing. I have not advised them to just do research and then later, when they're successful, then they can start doing teaching. No, not at all. What I've advised is that there has to be balance.

Sheppard may or may not succeed in her case for promotion to full professor at this time. Perhaps she will have to wait until her portfolio includes such traditional signs of success in teaching and learning as adoptions of her new textbook and testimonials about its success. Perhaps too, like many women in engineering, she will find other pursuits more rewarding—move on to administrative roles, move back into industry, or move into other efforts entirely. In the meantime, she is serving as associate chair of graduate curriculum and admissions in her department and is leading Stanford's role in a new NSF initiative, the Center for the Advancement of Engineering Education, which began work in January 2003. Sheppard remains fully engaged in engineering education research and reform.

NOTES

1. This quotation is from Reamon and Sheppard (1997), p. 6.

2. This paragraph and the next are adapted from my earlier article on "Faculty Evaluation and the Development of Academic Careers" (Huber, 2002, pp. 73–74).

3. As I reported in my earlier article (Huber, 2002), ". . . the Carnegie Foundation's 1997 national survey of college and university faculty suggests that a greater emphasis is being given to teaching in research universities nationwide: nearly half (45 percent) of faculty at these institutions said that teaching counted more for purposes of faculty advancement than it did five years ago. On the other hand . . . [a] sizable proportion of research university faculty said that while teaching counted more, the demands for research and creative work had not diminished (25 percent) or had risen at the same time (11 percent). Some even reported that although the importance of teaching remains the same, the importance of research has risen (11 percent). Faculty at other types of institutions tell a similar story" (pp. 77–78).

4. Of the nine graduate-level programs within Stanford's School of Engineering, Mechanical Engineering, Electrical Engineering, Computer Science, Aeronautics, and Civil Engineering were all ranked in the top three. Chemical Engineering and

Materials Science were ranked in the top seven. The National Research Council did not have rankings for Management Science and Scientific Computing.

5. Among the School of Engineering's current and emeritus faculty, there were 68 members of the National Academy of Engineering, 42 Presidential/NSF Young Investigators, 29 members of the American Academy of Arts and Sciences, 18 members of the National Academy of Sciences, 12 NSF Faculty Early Career Development Program Awardees, 9 winners of the National Medal of Science, 4 winners of the National Medal of Technology, 3 members of the National Institute of Medicine, 2 winners of the Kyoto Prize, and 1 Nobel Laureate.

6. Terman served as dean of the School of Engineering from 1944 to 1955 and as provost of Stanford University from 1955 to 1965, the period when Stanford was pursuing "national distinction" through a "strategy of securing federal and industrial-strength research dollars and bringing star-quality faculty" to the University (Cuban, 1999, p. 29). Terman was appointed dean of the School of Engineering by Stanford's then new president Donald Tressider, who, according to historian Larry Cuban, was "deeply committed to making the university managerially efficient, [and] also sought closer ties to industry. He created the Stanford Research Institute and appointed . . . Terman dean of the School of Engineering to forge those linkages" (1999, p. 27). Tressider died, but plans for the Stanford Research Park became reality under his successor J.E. Wallace Sterling, who appointed Terman as provost in 1955 "to upgrade the faculty and make the sciences the envy of sister institutions" (Cuban, 1999, p. 28). According to a Web-based history of Stanford and the School of Engineering, it was under Terman's leadership that the School of Engineering experienced "some of its greatest development, including new liaisons with industry, the first significant government research contracts, and aggressive recruiting of faculty and graduate students. Terman implement[ed] his theory of "steeples of excellence" in faculty recruiting. The steeples are small groups of experts who demonstrate leadership in their professions" (Stanford University, "History of Stanford and the School of Engineering," n.d.).

7. In making the case for Kelley, Reynolds (as chair) recalled taking the dean to see Ideo, the product design firm founded by Kelley and his brother. In addition to the question of whether Stanford would accept designs and patents rather than articles and research grants as the basis for a scholarly record, cases like Kelley's have raised such issues as whether creating a company should be recognized for purposes of faculty advancement and whether an individual should be credited with patents owned by his company.

8. See Cuban (1999, pp. 69–70) on the introduction of student evaluation of faculty teaching at Stanford University. Though first proposed in two reports, one in the mid 1950s and the other in the late 1960s, it was not until 1973 that the Faculty Senate first required it, and not until 1979 that the senate required use of a particular form.

9. Gibbons acknowledged "this means that the average will keep pushing up and some have complained that it is not statistically a good idea." However, he went on to say, "it's unfair only if everyone is an excellent teacher and this is just not the case."

10. A tenure file at Stanford's School of Engineering normally includes a candidate's curriculum vitae, summaries written by an expert of the candidate's major

publications, and a statement by the candidate on the significance of his or her work in terms of teaching and research. But the real meat of a tenure case are the external letters asking about the impact a candidate's work has had on his or her field. So important are these letters that a preliminary set of papers with the candidate's curriculum vitae and the names of those who will be asked to write them (and the names of "comparison candidates" they will be asked to rank) are sent first for approval to the executive committee of the candidate's department and then to the school's executive committee of all the department chairs. Once the lists are approved, letters are solicited and the final papers prepared. When the papers are assembled, the department's executive committee votes on the case. If successful, the chair presents the case to the committee of chairs. The committee of chairs advises the dean, who may also decide to get the opinion of the department's appointments and promotions committee, comprised of senior statesmen believed to have the long-term interests of the school at heart. Based on advice from these committees, the dean decides whether to forward the papers to the provost, and the provost decides whether to forward them to the advisory committee of faculty representatives from all schools in the university. This committee, finally, makes a recommendation to the president and board of trustees.

11. This suggestion did not refer to the quality of the work, which all agreed was first rate. Rather, the suggestion was first, that Sheppard's research was more applied than theoretical; second, that welding research was something of an old economy outlier at a new economy school like Stanford; and third, that she hadn't built the operation to the full extent expected of a research operation at Stanford. One colleague said:

> Welding is seen at Stanford more as a problem in industry than as an academic problem. Sheri had an unusual approach that combined mechanics and thermodynamics, but it was funded more by industry than the National Science Foundation. The color of your money matters in how people view your research.

Another colleague agreed that Stanford was not a big manufacturing school and that welding therefore did not have much of a "wow factor here," but thought "she might have made it on welding alone if she had built it up into a fairly good-sized operation, because a busy, vibrant lab that is clearly having impact is even more important than money at Stanford." Perhaps, he said, her numerical analysis might have been an "easier go" than welding because it had more cachet, but "she may not have done enough of that, either, because of the education work."

12. Sheppard was actually the only woman at all in this department until the appointment of a new female junior faculty member for fall 2002.

13. Interestingly, Sheppard's case took shape at the same time that outgoing provost Gerald Lieberman appointed the Committee on the Recruitment and Retention of Women Faculty in October 1992. While the report recommended that "Stanford develop and maintain a culture of mutual respect, care, trust and support among faculty members" and recommended steps that the provost, deans, department chairs, and individual faculty could do to better support junior faculty, in particular, it did not recommend affirmative action with regard to tenure and promotion for women. This was in tune with the views of former committee mem-

ber Condoleeza Rice, who became the new provost to whom the report was submitted (Stanford University, 1993). In an account of "two hours of often heated discussion about the status of women faculty" in the faculty senate in May 1998, the weekly *Stanford Report* quotes provost Rice as saying that she was "'completely opposed to the introduction of affirmative action criteria at time of tenure,'" but goes on to report that she "strongly supports it at the time of hiring" (Manuel, 1998).

14. It is often noted that women scholars are more likely than men to work in new or marginal areas of their fields. See Eisenhart and Finkel (1998) for an account of how women scientists and engineers experience better success in non-elite subfields and institutions. Stanford engineering, of course, is an elite institution, but as the comments on Sheppard's work indicate, neither her welding research nor her education work were perceived as elite areas. Interestingly, the 2002 Reports on the Committees of the Status of Women Faculty at MIT noted, "Entire fields can be undervalued in the male-dominated culture of science and engineering" (Hopkins, Bailyn, Gibson, & Hammonds, 2002, p. 5). Thus, faculty in the School of Humanities, Arts, and Social Sciences feel marginalized relative to science and engineering, faculty in the humanities relative to those in the social sciences, faculty in qualitative fields in the School of Management relative to those in quantitative fields, faculty in interdisciplinary areas and nontraditional niches in engineering relative to the more conventional engineering fields. Women often work in these lower status areas, contributing to their sense of marginalization. The report noted, "This choice may contribute to their isolation and make it easier for men to undervalue their work since there may be no colleagues to collaborate with and few who can comprehensively evaluate them" (2002, p. 5).

15. This description of the textbook is taken in part from Sheppard's (2002) account of her activities at Stanford and in part from our interview.

16. For further information on the AAHE Peer Review of Teaching Program, see Hutchings (1996).

17. Frontiers in Engineering (FIE) is one of two big engineering education conferences sponsored by the IEEE and ASEE. FIE is held in the fall, and the ASEE conference is held in June. I asked if these conferences attract people who do other things but get temporarily interested in educational issues or if they are primarily for a specialist community. Sheppard's guess was that over half of the people who attend have put a major stake in engineering education and that there is a community there. In fact, there is tension between these two general crosscutting conferences and the professional societies that also have a stake in engineering education, like the American Society for Mechanical Engineering (ASME).

18. The chair of Mechanical Engineering later established a position of associate chair for undergraduate education and a curriculum committee under the associate chair's direction. Sheppard thinks that the accreditation process finally "lit the fire that got this going."

19. Created in 1996 to increase Stanford's use of technology in teaching and learning, the Stanford Learning Lab pursued 18 distinct projects until the spring of 2002, when it merged with the newly established Stanford Center for Innovation in Learning (SCIL). SCIL is a larger, multi-university collaboration and is pursuing a larger range of technology-related studies.

20. Additional information can be found at http://www.ncs.Stanford.edu

21. It was at Shulman's suggestion that I invited Sheppard to participate in these case studies of faculty who have made the scholarship of teaching and learning a part of their careers.

22. For further information about Carnegie's engineering education study, see http://www.carnegiefoundation.org/PPP/TakingStock/index.htm.

23. Sheri has undertaken work on lead-free soldering in a climate of international concern over the hazards involved in dumping lead, especially its potential to poison ground water supplies. Although the electronics industry is only responsible for a fraction of total lead consumption, it is trying to reduce its use of lead because its products are rarely recycled and usually end up in landfills (Richards et al., 1999). A series of practical issues, for the most part related to the higher temperatures needed for lead-free soldering, require more research before lead-free soldering can be implemented. A consortium of organizations from Japan, Europe, and the United States have agreed to phase out lead solders within the next several years (JEITA, 2002). With that deadline in mind, U.S. companies are experiencing the pressure of competition, and developments in soldering technology by the Japanese manufacturing sector are propelling action both in Europe and the U.S. (Richards & Nimmo, 2000). Not surprisingly, Sheppard's interest in soldering research reflects her predilection for "bridging." In this case, she is familiar with the highly theoretical models being developed at Sandia National Labs, but she is working to realize more practical applications.

24. This position was created in the 1999–2000 academic year. Until then, Sheppard said, there was "no one in charge."

25. *SciSearch: A Cited Reference Science Database* includes the contents from approximately 4,500 journals, and covers a range of scientific and technological subjects, including the broad field of engineering, and subspecialties such as mechanical engineering. SciSearch is distinguished from other journal databases, such as INSPEC and El/Compendex: Engineering Index, by its "cited search" tool.

8

New Media Pedagogy

The changing landscape of higher education that spawned the calls for a more expansive and flexible notion of scholarship to begin with is being given fuller realization in the expansive, integrative and collaborative spaces of digital culture.[1]

To scholars like Randy Bass, associate professor of English and executive director of CNDLS at Georgetown University, information technology has opened a new chapter on how knowledge in the humanities is discovered, integrated, and used, and on how these fields are taught and learned. Scholars (and, indeed, the public at large) now have access to materials that were previously available only to those with the time, money, and expertise to consult the holdings of distant archives. Furthermore, these new, "virtual" archives are not limited to words. With an Internet connection, one can examine not only electronic versions and facsimiles of books, newspapers, letters, diaries, and official records, but also maps, photographs, movies, and recordings of speech, music, and other sounds. New materials are digitized daily. Scores of scholarly projects with evocative names, like The Perseus Digital Library (classics) and the Valley of the Shadow (civil war), are assembling multimedia resources on hundreds of persons, places, times, works, and events.[2]

These new technologies and materials are changing the ways in which scholars in the humanities do their research; influencing debates about such key terms as *narrative*, *image*, and *text*; providing new media for creative artists in music, film, and photography; spawning experiments in poetry, drama, and prose; and generating new genres of their own. In college classrooms around the country, pioneering teachers are exploring ways to engage undergraduates with these materials, to help students participate in the creative process where appropriate, and to learn about literary, historical, and cultural subjects by doing real literary, historical, and cultural research.

Case Study: Randy Bass

Randy Bass is an associate professor of English and a member of the American Studies Committee at Georgetown University. He teaches courses in American literature, American studies, and the electronic representation of culture and knowledge. Bass has worked with educational technology since 1986 and has directed or co-designed a number of electronic projects and publications on the use of technology in teaching culture and history. He is also executive director of Georgetown's Center for New Designs in Learning and Scholarship (CNDLS), a university-wide center supporting faculty work in new learning and research environments, and he directs the Visible Knowledge Project, a five-year scholarship of teaching project that is exploring the effect of technology on learning in the humanities. Winner of the EDUCAUSE medal for outstanding achievement in information technology and undergraduate education and a Carnegie Scholar in CASTL, Bass received his baccalaureate degree from the University of the Pacific and his doctorate in English from Brown University. Visit http://www.georgetown.edu/bassr for more information.

Information technology is on everyone's agenda in higher education these days, not just visionary professors of the humanities. Recent statistics on the use of telecommunications in higher education indicate that by now, over half of all instructional faculty and staff and nearly as many students make daily use of the Internet.[3] The use of email and the Web is ubiquitous in academic life. Participation rates in distance education courses increased rapidly in the 1990s, involving 8 percent of undergraduates and 10 percent of graduate and first professional-degree students by the end of the decade (Sikora, 2002). Over the same period of time, the use of telecommunications in the conduct of regular college courses also became much more widespread. In the fall of 1998, according to the National Center for Education Statistics, "about 69 percent of full-time faculty and 46 percent of part-time faculty used email to communicate with students in their classes, and 40 percent of full-time faculty and 34 percent of part-time faculty used course-specific web-sites" (Warburton, Chen, & Bradbum, 2002, p. 47).

Statistics like these don't begin to chart the different ways that these tools are being used, nor do they touch on the classroom use of electronic archives, technical computing software, computer-aided design, simulation systems, and the like. They do, however, suggest that the material culture of teaching and learning is rapidly changing. This means that beyond the pioneers and early adopters, mainstream faculty members are having to rethink classroom practice with new tools in mind. How does one manage and make good use of email communication with students? How does one manage and make good use of course specific websites, with the opportunities afforded for collaborative learning via asynchronous discussion boards and live chat by widely adopted "learning systems" such as Blackboard and WebCT?[4] What do the new technologies mean for assignments and assessment? How are new media changing the nature of expert practice in one's field? Do these changes in how mathematicians, scientists, social scientists, humanists, or management professionals conduct their work change what and how students should learn about these fields and what and how their teachers teach?

These are leading questions. Sometimes the path leads down the hall to the office of a colleague who has been there and done it. Sometimes the path leads to technical support staff or to the campus center for teaching and learning. The path might also lead to a workshop or conference session, or to books, articles, or online resources in one's field. For some, the challenge of technology in the classroom might lead only to teaching tips or other "low threshold activities" that help "faculty make better instructional use of technology that is already almost ubiquitously available and familiar to them" (Gilbert, 2002). For those who keep asking, like Randy Bass, the challenge can lead to recasting teaching questions as scholarly "problems," which have both practical import and intellectual weight. As Bass noted, in a much-cited source in the scholarship of teaching and learning:

> One telling measure of how differently teaching is regarded from traditional scholarship or research within the academy is what a difference it makes to have a "problem" in one versus the other. In . . . research, having a "problem" is at the heart of the investigative process; it is the compound of the generative questions around which all creative and productive activity revolves. But in one's teaching, a "problem" is something you don't want to have, and if you have one, you probably want to fix it. Asking a colleague about a problem in his or her research is an invitation; asking about a *problem* in one's teaching would probably seem like an accusation. Changing the status of the *problem* in teaching from terminal remediation to ongoing investigation is precisely what the movement for a scholarship of teaching is all about. How might we make the prob-

lematization of teaching a matter of regular communal discourse? How might we think of teaching practice, and the evidence of student learning, as problems to be investigated, analyzed, represented, and debated?" (1999c, Introductory Section, paragraph 1)

Certainly, new technologies invite such "problematization." That's the good news. They also invite a great deal of controversy and concern. For every article, book, speech, or conference session that thoughtfully considers what *can* be done with technology in teaching, there must be 10 that extol its cost-saving and income-producing potential and 20 that respond with alarm at the prospect of further commodifying higher education. This debate has complicated the lives of new media pioneers, particularly in the humanities. Citing David Noble's widely read "case against the online onslaught" in the 1997 essay "Digital Diploma Mills: The Automation of Higher Education," Gregory Jay, a leader in teaching with technology in English and American studies, wrote:

> Noble sees the battle in manichean terms: "On the one side university administrators and their myriad commercial partners, on the other those who constitute the core relation of education: students and teachers. "This important critique deserves a wide audience, though I think it overstates the case and misrepresents what many teachers are doing in their classrooms. It also romanticizes traditional pedagogy, which is often nothing more than a low-tech version of clicking and downloading. Noble's account conflates all uses of information technology with the drive to commercialization of online courses, and thus ironically mirrors the administrator's dream." (Jay, 1999, paragraph 6)

Despite the challenges—and there are many, in addition to colleagues who may be suspicious of the politics and uncertain about the scholarly nature of work in teaching and new media—the field of humanities technology can be hugely attractive, even seductive, to those who stay the course. Entering this world as a graduate student in the mid 1980s, when the technology was young and the hopes (and hype) were boundless, Randy Bass has devoted much of his career to developing its promise for strengthening "learning culture," a phrase he uses in both senses of the term.[5] On the one hand, Bass has fostered a "learning culture" among faculty through major projects to develop Web-based resources for scholarly communication about teaching and learning among faculty in his field and at his university. On the other, he has designed and developed pedagogies and materials for students "learning [about] culture" through new media. Along the way, Bass has puzzled and delighted his colleagues by attaining international stature for his work in technology and the humanities and, not coincidentally, challenging just about every convention by which scholarship in the humanities is normally judged.

Humanities, Media, and Academic Reform

This was not what Bass intended or what his mentors expected when he began his academic career, although it was by no means an accidental path. Indeed, Bass's interests in the humanities and the media had formed during his undergraduate years in Stockton, California, at the University of the Pacific, a teaching-centered institution whose website today describes it as a "university where professors know students by name." The University of the Pacific became well known in the 1960s and 1970s for its experimental "cluster colleges" where undergraduates could take their courses in Spanish (Covell College), or focus on international relations with a year abroad in Asia (Callison College), or study the arts and sciences in an interdisciplinary program with written faculty evaluations but no grades (Raymond College). When Bass enrolled in 1977, the cluster colleges were nearing their end, but arriving as a pre-law/economics major with a strong interest in the humanities, he signed up for one of the multidisciplinary course linkages that was a vestige of the university's old general education program, called Investigation and Inquiry. It was a turning point.

The course Bass took, "The Ascent of Man," was built around Jacob Bronowski's 13-episode film series surveying the sciences, which was produced by BBC and Time-Life Films in 1972.[6] Taught by three core faculty from different disciplines, and a dozen or so guest lecturers, students watched a different episode each week. This course was linked to a literature course and history course, so that 9 of his 12 credits the first semester comprised this one block of integrated humanities study. "I was taking history, I was reading masterpieces of world literature, we were talking about science," Bass recalled, "and from that moment, I fell quite in love with the concept of the humanities, and of multimedia, which at this point meant videotapes of this television series." At the end of that first semester, he changed his majors to literature and history and continued to pair courses whenever possible, so that the semester he took medieval literature, he also took medieval history, and when he took Shakespeare courses, he signed up for Renaissance history as well. "I was very interested in interdisciplinary connections," Bass remembered, "and before I decided I wanted to get a Ph.D., when people asked what I wanted to do when I graduated, I would say I wanted to get a master's degree in the humanities and make multimedia documentaries for PBS."

Bass regards two other experiences he had as an undergraduate to be formative. One began in the short inter-semester of his first year when he took an independent study in the School of Education and wrote a review of the freshman orientation program at his San Francisco Bay area high school. When he was looking for a job at the University of the Pacific shortly thereafter, Bass drew confidence from his study and went to the dean's office to see if they needed an intern to do research on educational issues on campus. They didn't have a job for him, but they did appoint him as student representative on a committee to reform the general education program at the university. This also involved participation with a set of schools doing similar work through the Project on General Education Models (Project GEM), sponsored by the Society for Values in Higher Education (Gaff, 1980). As Bass recalled:

> It took all of the rest of my college career for general education at [the university] to be reformed, so basically I was on this committee from the middle of my freshman year to the end of my senior year. . . . I went to conferences and got to know everybody going to the Society for Values in Higher Education, where we had the national meetings for Project GEM. That was my introduction to the world of academic reform.

In fact, Bass's first published article was a short piece he wrote as a senior for *Liberal Education*, published by the Association of American Colleges and Universities. In a special issue devoted to general education reform, Bass wrote about what it was like to have watched and participated as a student in this process (Bass, 1981). He explained, "We'd gotten intensely involved with each other. I was very close to all the faculty who were on this committee, and I was very close to the academic vice president who ran it. And then my senior year became the coming out party for the program and it got attacked, demolished, watered down, and by the time we were done after four years of work, we had ended up with a program that looked vaguely rationalized, but was really just a standard distribution model of general education. So, while the entire arc wasn't really embittering, it was certainly eye opening. Given that I've ended up as an academic and an administrator involved in academic reform, that was as important as anything in my undergraduate education."

The other formative experience Bass recalled was his relationship with the University of the Pacific's academic vice president, Clifford Hand, who chaired the general education committee and with whom Randy completed two semesters of independent study during his junior year. This was, in fact, another remarkable instance of "pairing," because while working with Hand to reform the curriculum on campus, Bass chose as his independent study topic the history of the liberal arts. Meeting every couple of weeks, Hand led Bass all the way from the Sophists through John Dewey. Bass read important books on the topic, such as Bolgar's *The Classical Heritage and its Beneficiaries*, and wrote two or three papers each semester on topics such as Greek philosophy of education, Renaissance humanism, and the emergence of the liberal arts in the 11th, 12th, and 13th centuries. This powerful academic experience was intensified for Bass when, working for the university's admissions office after graduation, he watched Hand develop cancer, weaken, and die. Hand had wanted to go back to teaching after a decade of administrative work but never got the chance, a lesson that Bass, whose time is now split between administration and teaching, "harbors in the back of my mind."

Bass's four years in admissions after graduation provided other lessons as well. At that time, the University of the Pacific was still a provincial place, and Bass was "quite intimidated" at first by the idea of going off to graduate school. The admissions job gave him time to think. So, while he worked on admissions office tasks, including publications and slide shows, he entertained various options, including a career in public relations, before deciding he really wanted to live an academic life and perhaps even become a president or provost. However, it was also a political time on campus, with faculty rising up against the president, and Bass realized that "one of the things people held against our president was that he wasn't an academic. So that convinced me that if I wanted to stay in a university setting and higher administration, I had to get a Ph.D. in a discipline."

By the time Bass got into graduate school, he realized how much he had gained from his experience at the University of the Pacific. Unlike other graduate students, most of whom went through a crisis of purpose at some point in their graduate school careers, Bass had gone through that before and had no question as to what he wanted to do. Furthermore, Bass left Stockton with a highly "eclectic, integrative view of what it meant to be an academic." He concluded:

> I think that this is relevant, for when I got to graduate school, I was very different from my peers who wanted to get a Ph.D. in English because, to quote one of my colleagues in graduate school who I'm still very close to, she used to read Jane Austen under the covers at night with a flashlight. So her interest in graduate school, like many others', was that they just loved literature and reading. It wasn't that I didn't love literature and reading, but my orientation was much broader. I was already very interested in teaching and educational reform. So by the time I got to my fourth and fifth year and started getting involved in technology projects that were highly integrative, this was less a detour from where I'd been than tapping into who really I was, picking up on interests that had been latent while I went through the reading, writing, and socialization of the first few years of graduate school.

PRESENT AT THE CREATION

In 1985, Bass enrolled as a graduate student in English at Brown University, a newly prestigious program at that time. Brown's undergraduate programs had exploded in the 1970s and 1980s and, Bass believed, the graduate programs experienced a halo effect. Bass was placed on the waiting list and probably would have gone to another school if one of his mentors from the University of the Pacific had not written Robert Scholes, chair of the English department at Brown, and told him not to miss out on Bass. Admitted in a very competitive environment to a class of about 12, Bass felt that he was the least well-read in his class, and certainly that he had been to the least prestigious undergraduate school. Of course, he distinguished himself while there and after as well. For years, in fact, Bass was one of only a couple of graduates from his class in the dismal humanities job market to get a full-time academic job.[7]

The English Department at Brown in the mid 1980s was split between a "theory" and "anti-theory" (or "traditional") faction, the latter of which included many of the faculty in Bass's specialty, American literature. It was a stimulating time and place to be a student, but a number of professors, both young and senior, were turning away from the department to get involved with more compatible colleagues in departments and interdisciplinary programs elsewhere on campus. Some of these problems were reflected in Bass's committee, whose internal members were from opposite sides of the department's intellectual divide and who found working together a delicate task. All were gracious to Bass, but it was a fine line for a graduate student to tread.

Bass's dissertation on documentary narratives of social crisis in the late 19th century looked at portrayals of social problems that contemporaries considered real or true. "It ran the gamut," Bass said, "from literary treatments of realistic narrative with Mark Twain as the main canonical figure [to] some recently rediscovered women novelists who were important feminist figures in the 19th century, to journalism, early muckraking, evangelical tracts, economic tracts, utopian literature, and things like that." While his dissertation did not really have a cultural studies focus on discourses and boundaries, he was interested in the fact that while the realists were always attacking sentimental and sensational accounts, they were at the same time using highly sensational, highly interpretive Christian millennial rhetoric as part of the strategy of documentary narrative. In other words, a rhetoric that we see today as religious was invisible then as anything but realistic. He called their approach "millennial realism."

The key thing that happened to Bass in graduate school, about a year before he finished his dissertation, was his almost accidental introduction to a technology project housed at Brown University's famed Institute for Research in Information and Scholarship (IRIS), a think tank where some of the early experiments in hypertext and hypermedia in the humanities took place. Bass likened IRIS to "an early dot com in the sense that it had this great software at first, and then all the money ran out. But it was what helped catapult Brown to leadership in the field." George Landow, a well-known Victorianist in the English Department and hypertext pioneer, gave Bass and other graduate students a tour of the lab and an introduction to Intermedia, IRIS's pathbreaking software, which was being used to create linked resources on Brown's computer system for students in world literature and other courses.[8]

Many months later, Landow remembered Bass. IRIS was then collaborating with The Center for Children and Technology, then at Bank Street College in New York City, on part of a massive federal project. Their piece was to create a multimedia hypertext database on Mark Twain and the Mississippi for middle school students.[9] They didn't have quite enough money for a real scholar, but they could afford a graduate student as content advisor on the project. According to Bass, Landow said (in essence), "Perfect. Here's this guy . . . he's writing his dissertation on Twain and he's using Intermedia to study for his comprehensives." Although based on a partial misunderstanding, as Bass was not in fact using Intermedia for exam preparation, Landow's invitation netted him the opportunity to create materials for Intermedia and gave new direction to his career.

For about a year before Bass graduated, then, he was very involved in creating this database of more than 100 documents on Mark Twain and the trans-Mississippi West. Bass was able to do almost all of the actual database creation, because Intermedia was very simple software to use. "The Intermedia software allowed you to do very complex linkages and juxtapositions," Bass explained, "so I could trade texts. I would do careful readings and because we were working on big 24-inch Macintosh monitors, I could create really powerful juxtapositions." For example, he would juxtapose a piece of Twain text, a piece of a historical document, an image scanned in from a 19th-century document, and a piece of analysis from a scholar. The idea was to create these interdisciplinary juxtapositions and try to get young people to think across texts. Bass noted:

> It was everything that had been so interesting to me before, but in this kind of concrete form, and it also felt like it was marshaling so much out of my dissertation. It was truly a blend of a kind of scholarship and pedagogy for me. And it was challenging. Here I was, reading all this material about the great railroad strikes of 1877, but how do I put that together with millennialism, and how do I make that clear to a seventh-grader?

Bass soon realized that his work at IRIS was introducing him to a whole new world of pioneers in educational program design for children and technology. He was working with a team of people from the Center for Children and Technology, which was on the cutting edge of experiments on hypermedia and children's learning. Largely educators with backgrounds in instructional technology and interest in the interdisciplinary potential of early hypermedia, this group had created a public television

series called *The Voyage of the Mimi* and worked on a pioneering hypermedia project on laserdisc about Palenque, the Mayan ruins.[10] Their expertise
in thinking about how to use technology in a pedagogical context gave
Bass his introduction to learning theory and his best lessons about
onscreen pedagogy. "Working through IRIS and Landow and early hypermedia, and with the Center for Children and Technology was like a second
graduate education," Bass said.

The connection with George Landow and Intermedia was critical in
other ways as well. Although IRIS and Intermedia ended shortly thereafter, its late 1980s experiments remained famous. Bass had had the incred-
ible good fortune to be in the right place at the right time:

> In the early part of my career when I traveled around and met peo-
> ple famous and otherwise in humanities computing. I would say that
> I was at Brown with Landow, working on Intermedia. It was like
> being present at the Creation. And it gave me a kind of pedigree that
> was very important.

Landow, later one of Bass's external reviewers for tenure, had stature even
among scholars who had little contact with the world of technology. Bass
said, "He certainly fits the category of somebody with a long traditional
vitae in literature that no one could quarrel with, along with being one of
the best known people in hypertext."

Perhaps most important was the excitement Bass experienced at IRIS,
the sense of being on the cutting edge of hypertext and humanities pedagogy, the pace of the work, the team dynamics, and the recognition and
reward. "I was working on a team," Randy recalled. "I was flying to New
York every week. I was paid $25 an hour as a consultant. We were bring-
ing something together, sitting in front of a screen and brainstorming and
it was just incredibly stimulating." This world was remote from that of the
typical graduate student in English, and it was clear to Bass even then that
it was not a world from which he could easily walk away.

Yet it was also clear to Bass that his work at IRIS was ancillary to the academic preparation, dissertation, and teaching that would be the keys to his
career. He was ahead of the curve with regard to teaching, because while
the English department at Brown had little going on with technology or
pedagogy, it provided good teaching opportunities to its graduate students. By the time Bass was on the job market he had also taken (as all
English graduate students did), a course on methods of teaching writing.
He had taught 12 courses, 10 of which were his own courses with syllabi
of his own design, and he had won a university teaching award. During
the same year that he worked at IRIS, he was one of three graduate student
fellows at Brown's Center for the Advancement of College Teaching,

where he designed workshops for graduate students across the university. "You know, now that I'm narrating this work," Bass commented:

> . . . it's just amazing to see how inevitable it was that I became the scholar I am. In retrospect, I'm sure that all the elements—dissertation, teaching, and technology—were pivotal in my getting from Brown to Georgetown. Although the job at Georgetown was in no way defined as having anything to do with technology, I know that those dimensions helped make me the person whom they ended up hiring.

GETTING STARTED AT GEORGETOWN

In 1990–1991, the English department at Georgetown University was advertising one of the most attractive jobs available to newly minted English Ph.D.s. It was a tenure-track position, and Georgetown was a prestigious institution in a beautiful section of Washington, DC with a growing reputation for research alongside its continuing commitment to undergraduate education in the Jesuit tradition. Like other English departments, Georgetown's department had a familiar mix of theorists and traditionalists, and Bass believed he was a bridging candidate:

> I think I looked traditional enough to the traditionalists—"Oh, you're the Twain scholar." And I think I looked current enough to others because I was doing relatively interdisciplinary work, looking theoretically at gender across documentary discourse, and exploring millennial realism as a theme. I probably also sounded thoughtful and sophisticated about teaching, at least in comparison to other candidates, because of my work at IRIS and my teaching experience.

Whatever the reasons—and Bass suspected some happy combination of committee fatigue and his own virtues—the interview was an outstanding success. Bass had had another offer from a small school in New York for over three weeks, which he would have taken if necessary, and Georgetown was his last alternative. The pressures of such a situation are enormous, and candidates often wait weeks if not more to hear whether or not they've been chosen. Bass's presentation and interviews lasted all day, and he was supposed to go to dinner with some of the English faculty that night. But that very evening, when he went back to his hotel to change for dinner, the committee called and offered him the job. "It was just fabulous," Bass recalled. It was the best possible way to start.

The department that Bass joined in the fall of 1991 had the largest number of majors on campus, 35 to 40 tenure-line faculty members, and a small army of adjuncts, and it was still growing at the time. While disagreements about the discipline's direction among the tenure-line faculty may have complicated the search that brought in Bass, they did not poison departmental life. From Bass's perspective, "Coming from Brown, it felt almost perfect!" While Bass later came to believe that the department had "polite surfaces for deeper schisms," he also thinks that in comparison with other departments, it had adopted a "'big tent' theory pretty well." Brown, he noted, was centrifugal, with every new interest turning into a separate program, while at Georgetown, people just accepted the diversity that English studies nationally had become.[11] At Brown, alienated Americanists spent most of their time in the programs in which they had joint appointments, while at Georgetown, where almost half the faculty had joint appointments, everyone still felt like a citizen of the English department. It was and is an eclectic and tolerant place.

It was also somewhat unusual with regard to its expectations for junior faculty. For one thing, Georgetown is more teaching-oriented than many peer institutions. As English professor John Glavin explained, "Georgetown was then essentially a Jesuit liberal arts college that had grown big feet. It had a medical school, a hospital, a law school, and graduate programs. But at its core, it remained what it was up until this expansion began around 1970: an elite liberal arts college with a special Jesuit spin. And the people who ran it conserved those values." In the case of Georgetown, this has meant a commitment to philosophy and theology as a required part of a liberal education, to interdisciplinary initiatives in support of social justice, and to educating the whole person. Georgetown's goal is to "educate leaders who serve." The Jesuit phrase is "men and women for others," Dorothy Brown, former provost, explained. For students, she continued, this meant being "engaged, active, a participant in," and for faculty, it meant "caring about students and teaching. Nobody gets tenure at Georgetown unless they're a good teacher."[12]

This teaching orientation is reflected in the English department, according to Leona Fisher, a recent chair, through a culture that welcomes discussion about teaching and learning, an elaborate program of classroom visitation for junior people, including adjuncts, and a lot of serious evaluation of what people are trying to do. Glavin explained:

> We ask candidates to write a statement about their teaching, and then we send two tenured faculty members in to watch people teach as they're moving towards tenure. We have all the student evaluations with the numerical values and the written portions available to everybody. So there are a lot of people who have seen the teaching; there's a lot of written evidence about the teaching—including syllabi for all courses and all the other supplementary material you give out in a course. We spend more than half of the time in every tenure evaluation talking about teaching.

While this does not mean that faculty there are more attuned to pedagogical theory and experimentation than faculty elsewhere, teaching itself is obviously important.

Yet Georgetown is not only a teaching-focused liberal arts college. It is also a research university. The university has departments with no graduate programs at all, and some, like English, with only a masters program, and there are others that award the Ph.D. While the English Department had still not changed its official guidelines to require a book for tenure in the early 1990s, no one was unaware—and least of all assistant professors—that their careers at Georgetown would depend on establishing a successful record of research and publication. Leona Fisher said that the same was true at the university level:

> Departments like theology, classics, and art, music, and theatre have had no graduate programs whatsoever. But I can promise you that at the university-wide level Rank and Tenure Committee, they're held to exactly the same standards as departments that give masters and doctoral degrees.

Fisher noted that this made equity a real challenge because of differences in teaching loads. She also noted that pressures to excel in research, and the accompanying tendency to hire "hotshots out of graduate school," were placing pressure on Georgetown's ability to keep its teaching mission alive and well.

During his first few years at Georgetown, Bass did what most assistant professors at Georgetown and other research universities do. He spent a lot of time getting his courses up and running and, with the aid of a couple summer grants, chipped away on further research for articles and a book. He began to write. But he did not give up on humanities technology. While at IRIS during his final year at Brown, Bass had had the idea of creating a hypertext database of teaching materials to accompany a textbook, and he had talked to different publishers about it. He eventually signed a contract with D. C. Heath to create electronic resources to accompany the *Heath Anthology of American Literature*, which Randy describes as "a ground-breaking multicultural literature anthology that was sort of the anti-Norton" (referring to the more traditional selections in the *Norton Anthology of American Literature*).[13] It was an entrepreneurial coup for a graduate student in English, fully in keeping with the temper of the technology world, but not of the academic world that faced most young humanists at that time.

Perhaps nothing underlined the gap between these worlds more than the state of the English department's computer system in the early 1990s, at the time Bass arrived at Georgetown. Glavin recalled, "We had individual word processors supplied by the university that were plugged into our offices and had programs, but we didn't have a network, so [we] had nothing more than these kind of glorified typewriters." Bass, Glavin said, was personally instrumental in making both the department and the university aware that much more was possible. He spent a summer going into offices with technicians to put in a network, and became very helpful to the university in doing things like wiring classrooms:

> Everybody was enormously grateful to him for doing that. Everybody's work capacity changed. And now we have wonderful classrooms in which I sometimes teach, in which each student has a computer and all kinds of capability. It's terrific because I often teach classes in which I show films.

It wasn't that the university had been opposed to technology, Glavin explained. It was just that it hadn't mattered until Bass came with his vision of how technology could serve humanities scholarship and teaching.

A Change in Direction

Bass had gotten off to a good start at Georgetown, working on his teaching and his research and placing his skills and interest in technology at the service of the department and the university. His project with Heath, however, was becoming a seductive distraction from the lonely labors that humanities research and writing usually entails. There was the pleasure of working with others, of course, and the excitement of the anthology's controversial project to provide a multicultural alternative to the conventional canon in American literature. Moreover, as Bass knew, this project went together perfectly with the innovative ideas about knowledge, text, and pedagogy circulating in the hypertext community at that time. He later wrote, "American literature is enhanced and transformed with the use of electronic tools and technology resources" (1997c, p. 1).

First, Bass pointed out, electronic environments meant an end to the sense one gets from a book that there is a single story to tell about American culture. With the additional texts and materials that electronic resources can provide, an anthology like the Heath becomes a "front end" to a "broader archive," and not a definitive collection of texts in and of itself. Second, not only can a wealth of electronic resources be made accessible, but these materials can also be searched, manipulated, annotated, made into hypertext, and connected. Indeed, with open tasks and appropriate guidance, students themselves can *make knowledge* by "learning to read closely" and connecting texts to their broader contexts. Third, they can *represent that knowledge* through hypertext projects of their own. These ideas about "story and archive," "novice in the archive," and "visible knowledge" became the hallmarks of Bass's later work.

However, the *Heath Anthology* was not the only experimental project that Bass took on. In Bass's second year at Georgetown, the general editor of the anthology, Paul Lauter, was elected president of the American Studies Association (ASA). According to Bass, Lauter had been involved in some syllabus collection projects, which led to the Project on Reconstructing American Literature in 1982, and then to the *Heath Anthology* in the early 1990s. Now, Lauter wanted to create something like a curriculum archive for the ASA, and, having worked with Bass on electronic resources for Heath, knew exactly whom to ask. Bass consulted with:

> . . . cutting-edge friends, started conceiving of it as a work project or a virtual university, named it Crossroads, and then pitched this larger idea. Let's not just think about syllabi, but create an online institute that would become an online home to American studies scholars and teachers all over the world.[14]

With this larger concept in place, Bass began the work needed to make it happen. He wrote a proposal to FIPSE, which awarded them a grant of more than $170,000 ("pretty big money for an English department"), and they received another grant for $170,000 from the Annenberg Foundation later that year. Together with smaller grants from Georgetown and other sources, Bass and the ASA had $400,000 over three years to launch Crossroads. "When those grants came through was when I knew that I was at a crossroads myself with my scholarly career," Randy noted. "I think I knew that I was never going to do all this and also write the dissertation-based articles and book."

The Crossroads Project was an ambitious attempt to create an electronic environment for American studies scholars. "From the beginning," Bass wrote, "Crossroads' mission has been three-fold: to create a comprehensive online resource for the global study of American culture; to help faculty and students make the best use of new technologies in the study of culture, history, and the humanities; and to assist in charting the future of American culture studies in an era of electronic resources and collaboration" (1995, p. 2).

Over the years, Crossroads has hosted a number of projects, including a guide to American studies programs, electronic mailing lists on particular topics, electronic resources for teaching American studies, workshops at regional and national meetings, and important efforts to link and make visible the work of faculty who are experimenting with the use of technology in the classroom (Bass & Eynon, 1998). In short, Crossroads was hugely productive as well as a huge sink for Randy's time. As he described recent advances in the September 1995 ASA newsletter, "This summer's achievements are the culmination of two years activity that at times has teetered on the brink of overload."

Bass's work with the ASA was also making him very well known. For one thing, public interest in the Web was growing and the Crossroads Project became the subject of stories in the *Wall Street Journal*, *The Chronicle of Higher Education*, and the *Internet Scout Reporter*, a widely circulated guide to new developments on the Web. For another, interest in Crossroads among Americanists was widespread. "Crossroads was an international project," Bass emphasized, "with six test sites across the United States, several international test sites, publications, and a Website with 100,000 hits a month. It had something for everybody." Understandably, Bass was now an insider in ASA circles. He was on close terms with the officers of the organization, he was recruiting participants for Crossroads forums and projects of various kinds, and his "dance card" at the annual meeting was filled with sessions, staffing a Crossroads booth, meeting with potential collaborators, and the like.[15] Furthermore, both his work on Crossroads and as founder and moderator of an electronic mailing list for teachers of American literature (T-AmLit) was making him much appreciated among the large and growing numbers of American studies scholars abroad as well as at home. Bass's obligations grew along with his network, of course, and he was often on the road. There were invited keynotes, plenary presentations, conference presentations, and panels, but also what his online vitae calls "the digital chicken circuit," an impressive round of campus-based faculty development workshops about teaching with technology in higher education.

Bass did not completely give up on writing during these years, but what energy he had left for it went into a textbook project he had undertaken—also that second year at Georgetown—when he was approached by Houghton Mifflin about developing his multicultural American literature course into a book. Bass had accepted, and the result was his well-regarded thematic reader called *Border Texts: Cultural Readings for Contemporary Writers*, now in its second edition.[16] With selections arranged into chapters on self and home; belonging and community; otherness and difference; the dynamics of difference; imagined and virtual communities; and the world's new borders, globalism and tribalism; the text defined "border" as:

> . . . *any place where differences come together,* whether these are national differences, cultural and social differences, differences in values or language, differences in gender, or differences in family heritage or economic status. Therefore, this book focuses on all of the many borders that shape individual identity as well as American cultural identity itself. (1999, chap. 1, p. 1)

Some 700 pages long, with a substantial apparatus of material that he wrote himself along with (of course) online resources, Bass believed in hindsight that it was probably a mistake to take on the book project without a co-editor when he did. "I think I just figured I could do it all, but it took five years, while I was working on tons of other things." Indeed, as his engagement with the challenges of Crossroads intensified, *Border Texts* "became a huge albatross around my neck."

Bass's new direction did not go unnoticed by his departmental colleagues. There was no formal third year review at the time, but he met with the chair every year.[17] His colleagues were very supportive of the length and breadth of the things that he was doing and indeed, for the first two or three years, it looked like he was on the right track. Bass was developing interesting courses and writing a textbook, his teaching evaluations were high, he was getting summer grants and doing library research on millennial literature in 19th-century America, *and* he was doing all these innovative electronic projects as well. Then, when the grants came through and intensive work on the Crossroads Project began, the tone of his conversations was transposed to a more anxious key. Bass's senior mentor, Lucy Maddox (who had been chair when Bass was hired), was worried. "My concern," she recalled, "was not about the importance of the work he would be doing [on Crossroads and his other new media projects] or how good he was going to be at it. My concern was getting him through all those hoops you have to go through. My concern was that we'd lose him."

Everywhere Bass turned, the advice was the same. No one in the department said not to pursue the new media work, but to couple it with a base of scholarly publication. Bass recalled that Maddox compared his situation to that of an abstract painter. If that person can draw really well, could paint a conventional painting, then people are willing to accept the artist's abstract work. Otherwise there's always doubt. Outside advisors agreed. For example, Bass talked to John Carlos Rowe, a leading scholar in American studies and American literature, who was particularly appreciative of Crossroads' service to the international community of American studies scholars. As Rowe remembered it:

> We talked a little about his plans for publishing his work on American literary naturalism and it sounded like an interesting, but traditional kind of research project. And I encouraged him to go ahead with it and to go ahead with his more innovative electronic ones too. So my advice was to do both. My reasons were that the traditional project sounded very interesting, but also that our field is composed of a lot of people who are very traditional and who are going to look askance at the work that he was doing in the electronic area, which I thought was the most exciting work.

Yet Bass resisted, even when Maddox suggested that with his growing portfolio of achievements in new media and pedagogy, he could meet expectations with a couple of good articles and not worry about the book. She remembered:

> ... many conversations in which I said just do the things you have to do right now to get tenure, and he would say, "Yes," "OK," "You're right. I have to do that." And a couple of days later he'd come in and say, "No, that's not what I want to do. The world doesn't need another academic article of the kind I would write. I know what I want to do and I'm going to do it."

In fact, Bass remembered it very much the same way, "I wanted to, and I tried and I had plans, but I just couldn't."

Part of the problem, Bass recalled, was that traditional scholarship required a different rhythm than life in the technology lane. Also, the further one moved from the discourse of the principal journals in one's field, the harder it was to get back in. The denouement? According to Bass:

> All these things inhibited my writing, and time went by, the next deadline came up and the next Beta version of the software, and the next posting on T-AmLit, and the next report to FIPSE. It started to feel like I would be producing those articles only for certification. It was hard. And the other very deeply inhibiting thing was that if I produced two articles that were ok and they were just two of several articles and a book, there wouldn't be an issue. But if those are the only two traditional things on the table then they're just going to get sliced and diced. Do I want to be an above-average Twain scholar with a couple of articles that are fine, but not part of a larger body of scholarly work? I just felt like I couldn't do that. As much as I wanted to, I felt that it was really a trap to try to do both the traditional and nontraditional work.[18]

Conclusion

Bass "chose" the road less traveled, although perhaps it would be better to say that this road chose him. This choice entailed loss as well as gain. His mentor, Lucy Maddox, said, "It was difficult for him to make a place in the department once he decided that what he really wanted to do was work with technology and pedagogy rather than following a more traditional path." Bass's success in his new ventures increased the distance between himself and the world of his colleagues, few of whom even at the peak of their careers would receive or accept as many invitations as come to players in the education and technology field. John Glavin captured the contrast is in a striking image. "You would go to the front gates of the campus and there was Randy with a suitcase waiting for a cab," he said. "It wasn't a daily occurrence but felt like one. There was a kind of lurking sense in the department that what he was doing he wasn't doing for us." I will turn in the next chapter to how these issues about traditional and nontraditional scholarship played out in Bass's tenure case.

But let us end this chapter with assurance that the scholarship of teaching and learning in the strict sense of the term will make an appearance there as well. Clearly Bass's engagement with technology was also an engagement with teaching and learning, from its earliest beginnings in that undergraduate course at the University of the Pacific built around Jacob Bronowski's television series, *The Ascent of Man*, to his apprenticeship in the production of experimental, interdisciplinary computer-based educational materials at Brown, to his work on the Heath Anthology, the Teaching American Literature electronic mailing list, and the American Studies Crossroads Project at Georgetown. While these efforts all included important elements of the scholarship of teaching and learning, Bass only put the pieces together in the process of examining one of his own courses in the year before his tenure case was due to be heard. It was a synthesis that was to take Bass down a road even less traveled than the one he had earlier chosen and generate a whole new dimension to an already extraordinary career.

NOTES

1. This quotation is from Batson and Bass (1996), p. 47.

2. See McGann (2001) for a provocative discussion on "hyperediting," in particular on differences that make a difference between critical editions of literary works in book form and on the Web. The Perseus Digital Library, located in the Classics Department of Tufts University, "is an evolving digital library, engineering interactions through time, space, and language," and now contains primary and secondary sources not only in Greek and Latin classics, but also in early modern English literature, nonliterary papyri from the Ptolemaic and early Roman period, a collection relating to the history of London from its founding to the 19th century, and more (Crane, 2002). The Valley of the Shadow project, according to its website, "takes two communities, one Northern and one Southern, through the experience of the American Civil War. The project is a hypermedia archive of thousands of sources for the period before, during, and after the Civil War for Augusta County, Virginia, and Franklin County, Pennsylvania. Those sources include newspapers, letters, diaries, photographs, maps, church records, population census, agricultural census, and military records. Students can explore every dimension of the conflict and write their own histories, reconstructing the life stories of women, African Americans, farmers, politicians, soldiers, and families" (Ayers, 2001).

3. According to the NCES report, *Teaching with Technology*, "In fall 1998, 97 percent of full-time instructional faculty and staff who taught classes for credit at degree-granting institutions had access to the Internet . . . [and] a large majority of part-time instructional faculty and staff had access to the Internet (88 percent) . . ."

(2002a, p. iii). The 1998 Campus Computing Survey showed that 51.6 percent of college faculty used the Internet at least once a day. At research universities, the percentage reached well over 50 percent, while the estimate of daily use for community college faculty was approximately 40 percent. The same survey indicated that 45.1 percent of undergraduates used the Internet daily, again with a range that was higher at research universities (over 50 percent) and considerably lower at community colleges (29.1 percent). See Green (1998).

4. According to its website, Blackboard counts "more than 2,000 clients in more than 70 countries, including colleges and universities, corporations and associations, K-12 (district-level and state-wide) [and] leading commercial education providers." It includes course management features for content management, communication, assessment, and instructor control. The communication features, for example, include discussion boards, real-time virtual classroom interaction, and group communication tools (Yaskin & Gilfus, 2002). This and other course management systems, such as WebCT, provide the means for instructors to develop and conduct online courses without much programming knowledge. Despite differences among them, they offer fundamentally similar tools, which structure the substance of the course and assist with administrative functions, such as enrollment, grading, and testing.

5. The provisional title of Bass's new book is *Hyper Activity and Under Construction: Learning Culture in the 21st Century*.

6. The film series, first aired on television in 1972 and rebroadcast many times, was accompanied by a book of the same title (Bronowski, 1974).

7. Bass was told "third-hand" that Scholes had given a talk about how hard it is to choose the right people for graduate school, citing Bass and his position at Georgetown as a case in point. The empirical evidence provides another view of the challenge for English Ph.Ds. Since 1977, the Modern Language Association (MLA) has conducted surveys of Ph.D.-granting departments of English, foreign languages, linguistics, classics, and comparative literature. The surveys request information about the departments' recent doctoral program graduates and their job placements. The results of these surveys indicate that the job placement of English Ph.D.s in the early 1990s was in decline. Fifty-one percent of respondents to the 1991–1992 survey took tenure-track positions, 32 percent took non-tenure track positions (more often full-time than part-time ones), and 6 percent were unemployed. In the 1993–1994 survey of a smaller number of respondents, 46 percent reported finding tenure-track positions, while the percentage of unemployed graduates reached 11 percent. Findings from the 1996–1997 survey revealed even lower proportions of tenure-track employment, an increasing percent of non tenure-track placement, and a steady rate of unemployment (Modern Language Association, n.d., Table 3).

8. Intermedia was a hypermedia system, created at IRIS for educational uses. Employing object-oriented programming on a Unix-based system, its tools included editors for text, scanned or graphic images, video, and animation. It also enabled students to engage in collaborative work, incorporating tools for group writing and decision-making. (See http://www.scholars.nus.edu.sg/landow/cpace/ht/HTatBrown/Intermedia.html.) Landow himself used Intermedia in teaching literature courses at Brown University and assembled the projects created

by his students into a vast collection of networked documents. Some of the projects created in Intermedia now exist independently on the Web, in the form of The Victorian Web (http://www.scholars.nus.edu.sg/victorian/) and the Perseus Project (http://www.perseus.tufts.edu/). In an online-only update to his book, *Hypertext*, Landow described the "death" of Intermedia in 1990 and its move to a different system (1995).

9. Bass was consultant and content coordinator of the Mississippi-West Project in 1990–1991.

10. Bass continues to work with the same people at the Center for Children and Technology (now a division of the Education Development Center). According to Bank Street Corner, a website that advertises educational materials produced by Bank Street College's Publications and Media group, *The Voyage of the Mimi* and *The Second Voyage of the Mimi* are groundbreaking programs created by The Bank Street College of Education. They were among the first multimedia materials to use interactive technologies in an inquiry-based, integrated approach to teaching and learning for the middle grades, with an emphasis on science and mathematics. They consist of video, software, and print materials, including lesson plans, hands-on activities, and student-directed and collaborative projects. The 13 video episodes of *The Voyage of the Mimi* take students and teachers on a scientific expedition to study whales. The 12 video episodes of *The Second Voyage* tell the story of archaeologists in search of a lost Mayan city. See http://www.bankstreetcorner.com/voyages_of_mimi.shtml.

11. There is a large and spirited literature on the tumultuous history of literary studies since the 1960s (see, for example, Graff, 1987; Herman, 2000; North, 2000). For views on the transformation of traditional literary research and the broadening scope of the subject matter treated by scholars in departments of English, see Abrams (1997); Epstein (2003); Gallagher (1997); and Saldivar (1997). Bass actually doubted that a traditional Americanist can get a job. So, even though he doesn't consider himself a cultural studies person in the strict sense of the term ("I'm not that theorized"), his dissertation's focus on noncanonical literature, and indeed not even "literary" literature, was more an American studies project than one a traditional Americanist in a traditional English department would have been likely to undertake.

12. Georgetown's educational program continues to reflect the principles of its Jesuit heritage—principles that can be traced back to Ignatius Loyola's vision, recorded in the Constitutions of the Society (part 4) (Ganss, 1989). Several key features of Jesuit higher education documented in Loyola's writing include commitment to education in the humanities, an orderly integration of both secular and spiritual subject matter, and fostering students' involvement in the larger civic community (Boston College, 1994; Ganss, 1989). On its website, Georgetown highlights several aspects of its Jesuit identity, including "educating the whole person," opportunities for engaging in "service and social justice," and acceptance of diverse faiths in connection with "spirituality and ministries." Additionally, this page suggests Georgetown's global involvement, describing its international presence with the keywords "diversity, global experience, international reputation" (http://www.georgetown.edu/home/about.html). These principles also appear in Georgetown's mission statement:

> Established in 1789 in the spirit of the new republic, the University was founded on the principle that serious and sustained discourse among people of different faiths, cultures, and beliefs promotes intellectual, ethical, and spiritual understanding ... Georgetown educates women and men to be reflective lifelong learners, to be responsible and active participants in civic life, and to live generously in service to others. (http://www.georgetown.edu/president/mission_statement.html)

13. Bass remains one of the electronic resources editor of the *Heath Anthology of American Literature* and is on its editorial board. *The Heath Anthology's* multicultural and feminist collection helped fuel the debates of the 1980s and 1990s about the canon—the literary works that educated citizens should know. According to *The Chronicle of Higher Education*, the *Heath Anthology* "has displaced the more traditional *Norton Anthology* in many college classrooms" (McLemee, 2001, p. A12). For more on the electronic resources, see Bass's own introduction (Bass, 1997c).

14. Actually, at that time, Bass noted "people experienced the Internet through 'Gopher' (an all-text hypertext system), and 'listservs' were already popular, but it was still a couple of years before the full emergence of the World Wide Web." In a 1995 newsletter article on "the release version" of Crossroads, Bass wrote, "When we first conceived of the Crossroads Project, the World Wide Web was so new that we weren't even sure it would be the wisest environment for development."

15. For example, see a description of the pace of activities at the 1996 ASA meetings and the issues this raised for the future in Bass's essay in the December 1996 *ASA Newsletter*.

16. The second edition, published in 2003 by Houghton Mifflin, is titled *Beyond Borders: A Cultural Reader*. It is edited by Randall Bass and Joy Young.

17. Actually, because of rotation, that meant three different people served as chair over the four years (his second through fifth) before the year in which his tenure case was due to come up.

18. Bass has spoken and written about this issue himself (Bass, 1999a), and was retelling the story to me in our conversation.

9

Making Teaching Visible

....

> ... there is a real affinity and indeed connection between the
> public and hybrid nature of new media, and the principles of the
> movement for a scholarship of teaching.[1]

"Visibility" is a key value and challenge for the scholarship of teaching and learning. Somehow, teaching must be made visible to colleagues if it is to enter a community of scholars who can provide con-
structive critique and evaluation and build upon it in their own
pedagogical work (Shulman, 1993). As I noted in the last chapter, research
in the humanities is being transformed by the capacities of new media to
provide access to cultural and historical records, and by tools for working
both with these materials and with colleagues engaged in the same quest.
That the new media can do the same for undergraduate teaching and
learning in the humanities has been the touchstone of Randy Bass's career.
Along the way, he has come to regard building "visible knowledge" about
teaching and learning through the new technologies as a necessary step in
reaching that goal. Just as print technology made possible the Renaissance
humanists' "republic of letters" (Grafton, 2002), today's new media, Bass
believed, are critical to the formation of intellectual communities around
the scholarship of teaching and learning.

Print media and face-to-face forums have their place, of course. But as
access to new media and the Internet widens, and as experience deepens,
the limits of our conventional scholarly media become more apparent. As
is true with the broader society, the academy is now largely accustomed to
doing important business on the Web, through email, and with computer
applications of many kinds. It seems that the share of business done electronically will continue to grow. With the rising price of academic journals
and the economic pressures on publishers of scholarly books, educators in
all fields are looking to alternative genres as outlets for research (Knight
Higher Education Collaborative, 2001; Phillips, 2002). For example, in May

2002, Stephen Greenblatt, president of the Modern Language Association, circulated a letter to the association's members about the publishing crisis in the humanities, which would likely prevent a whole generation of young scholars from publishing the traditional first book that tenure, promotion, and academic mobility have come to require (Greenblatt, 2002; Ruark & Montell, 2002).[2]

In addition to the general pressures on print media, there are other, special limits on the use of conventional outlets for the scholarship of teaching and learning. Certainly there are a growing number of journals, both disciplinary and cross-disciplinary, that are interested in publishing this kind of work, and several publishers house sizeable lists of pedagogical books and series (Huber & Morreale, 2002; Weimer, 1993).[3] However, it is still a struggle for scholars of teaching to find appropriate print venues for their work and, as Sheppard's case attests, those outlets that do exist are not necessarily given the respect they deserve. It is also the case, of course, that the scholarship of teaching and learning is not always best shared through or created for print.[4] For example, Dan Bernstein's colleagues are preparing course portfolios to share initially with a small set of peers in order to further reflection and improvement. But Bernstein has found that preparing portfolios *electronically* is far more time-efficient, as that is now the way in which most course materials and much student work are prepared and shared.[5]

One of the most compelling arguments for a role for the new media in the scholarship of teaching and learning concerns the fact that there are aspects of teaching and learning that are simply hard to represent well in print.[6] A number of genres are now emerging that make visible a larger swath of what Shulman called "the extended act of teaching," from vision, through design, to interactions, outcomes, and analysis (1998, p. 6). Some efforts, like MIT's massive OpenCourseWare initiative, make teaching materials available without much about pedagogy or student learning (Hatch, Bass, Iiyoshi, & Pointer, 2003).[7] But others are exploring designs that provide depth by looking at the unfolding of a single course, like the electronic course portfolio developed by Bass himself, or the experiments of his fellow Carnegie Scholars in conjunction with the Carnegie Foundation's Knowledge Media Lab (Bass, 1997a; Hatch, Pointer, & Iiyoshi, 2001).

New media also offer unprecedented opportunities to interact around issues in teaching and learning and to form communities of varying spread. For example, Bass's T-AmLit electronic mailing list and the American Studies Crossroads Project gained an international following. The site, with its links to curricular materials, exchanges, and discussion forums, brought together for perhaps the first time the growing community of scholars in Europe, Asia, and elsewhere around the world who study American history, literature, and cultural subjects and teach them to college and university students. In our discussion, Bass's colleague, John Carlos Rowe of the

University of California, Irvine, credited Crossroads with changing the structure of the field. "As soon as there was a flood of exchange on the . . . Crossroads Project from all over the world," Rowe said, "most intelligent people had to acknowledge that all sorts of work was being done outside the U.S. and that we in the U.S. could learn from it."

The potential of new media to change the way people think about and interact around teaching and learning more generally is surely just as great. For example, Tom Hatch, Desiree Pointer, and Toru Iiyoshi (2001), of the Carnegie Foundation's Knowledge Media Lab, mention the following as audiences who might want to learn from electronic course portfolios: veteran and new teachers interested in trying out a new teaching method, teaching assistants and section leaders seeking activities for their students in the same or similar course, students interested in selecting a college or university, and students interested in choosing a field. The authors also point to the opportunities for feedback that electronic portfolios make possible—they can be shown to individuals or groups and discussed in person or online, and of course, discussion or comment forums can be built into the site itself. Finally, Hatch, Pointer, and Iiyoshi suggest that when enough examples are available they may also be of value for collective use—for example, for a department considering the cumulative effects of its program on student achievement and growth or for an institution trying to figure out which initiatives to improve student learning show promise for further investment (2001).

But the challenges are many and real. Design problems have not yet been resolved and access remains uneven, especially with regard to poorer institutions and to the technical support most faculty still need to represent teaching and learning in sophisticated ways. There are intellectual property issues with regard to reproducing others' materials in a course portfolio, for example, and ethical issues with regard to making student work public (Hatch, Pointer, & Iiyoshi, 2001; Hutchings, 2002). As Hatch, Pointer, and Iiyoshi also noted, making teaching visible raises thorny dilemmas about control and credit. Faculty (and institutions!) may worry about who controls the rights to a course represented through materials or a portfolio on the Web. Their concern must be balanced by the opportunity the Web provides for "faculty to demonstrate what they have accomplished and [for] others to recognize and acknowledge those accomplishments by linking directly to them" (2001, p. 8).

Perhaps the least tractable challenge to realizing the full potential of the Web for the scholarship of teaching and learning is the often justifiable anxiety faculty feel about the value of "visibility" in teaching itself. Bass himself noted:

> . . . visibility in one's scholarship, one's professional repute, or the capacity of a faculty member to raise the visibility of his or her insti-

tution, is all something to be desired. In scholarship, the "field of visibility" is the engine behind faculty productivity. . . . But with teaching, this has worked a completely different way. With teaching, visibility has generally been closely tied to accountability, and often in negative ways. . . . [This] close tie between visibility and accountability narrows and inhibits faculty innovation and the way it is regarded as an intellectual enterprise. (1999b, section 2, paragraph 10)

That teaching has been visible to peers primarily at the time of tenure and promotion and through such limited vehicles as student evaluations and one-shot classroom visits by colleagues has contributed further to faculty concern.

Skepticism about the value of visibility goes beyond concern about one's own tenure and promotion to concern about academic freedom and the potential consequences of accountability writ large. For example, the historians writing in *Disciplinary Styles in the Scholarship of Teaching and Learning* argue that while their colleagues may talk a lot to each other about teaching, "they do not care for . . . the idea that classrooms, traditionally considered a private domain for professors, should be made accountable to larger publics by opening up what goes on inside them" (Calder, Cutler, & Kelly, 2002, p. 53). They cite as a case in point former vice president Al Gore's course in journalism at Columbia University, where the dean barred students from talking with reporters, explaining "normal classes are off the record" (2002, p. 53). To be sure, the authors acknowledged, there is concern about preserving both freedom of expression and a space where one can be "playful," "adventuresome," and "*not* perfectly perspicacious" (2002, p. 54). The darker side, however, is that historians quietly enjoy the freedom they have in class to offer historical opinion and interpretation that would not fly at professional meetings. "The greatest challenge ahead will be to convince skeptical history teachers that they have an intellectual opportunity as well as a moral responsibility to bring the scholar's playfulness and piety into their classrooms" (2002, p. 54).

It must be noted, too, that educational practices that are not only invisible but also largely unarticulated can have powerful socializing effects. In commenting on the nature of graduate training in social anthropology in Britain, for example, Jonathan Spencer credits the research seminar as the principal vehicle through which through the field created and sustained a coherent style from the 1920s through perhaps the 1970s and in diminished form today. Spencer goes on to suggest that this kind of apprenticeship, once described by Adam Kuper (1992) as "education without instruction" (p. 60), has been endangered by the United Kingdom's strong accountability regime:

[T]he institutional environment in British education is now especially hostile to the endurance of the implicit and the unstated. In her

Cambridge inaugural in 1994, Marilyn Strathern concluded with a meditation on the recent mania in higher education for rendering explicit what often works best by being left implicit: To put it more crudely than she ever would, the translation of Kuper's "education without instruction" into a set of aims and objectives at the head of a reading list, with appropriate cross references to the institutional mission statement [Strathern, 1995]. A classic example would be fieldwork itself, which, in [1940s–1960s] Oxford, simply could not be taught, it could only be learned by doing. (Spencer, 2002, p. 19)

Although made with specific reference to graduate training in a specific discipline at a specific time, the concern voiced here is more general: when teaching is made visible, education may be made trivial. The suggestion that the lessons to be learned can be adequately characterized by a set of aims and objectives on paper is, in fact, a hazard that many U.S. faculty fear in the formalizations of education specialists and school bureaucracies.[8]

This focus on what might be lost when teaching becomes visible (rather than what might be gained) reflects the fact that on both sides of the Atlantic—and in the Pacific as well—faculty work is being more closely examined than ever before, a trend that will likely intensify as demands for social and financial accountability increase (Altbach, 2000). A Canadian contribution to a collection of essays on the emergence of an "audit culture" in higher education compares the situation of faculty to that of inmates in Jeremy Bentham's Panopticon—a prison design in which the incarcerated are always potentially visible to authorities—which Michel Foucault made a central figure in his well-known study about the creation of the modern penal system in the west and its techniques of behavioral control (Amit, 2000).[9] From the perspective of faculty concerned about the diminishment of faculty autonomy and control, the increasing use of technology in and for teaching and learning seems only to render them ever more vulnerable.

Yet technology is Janus-faced. Randy Bass is among a growing group of educators who believe that its use in a *scholarship of teaching and learning* can be liberating—helping to counter (rather than promote) simplistic views of teaching, reclaim technology in teaching from those who would use it unwisely, encourage what Pat Hutchings (2000) has called "an ethic of inquiry" in the classroom, facilitate intellectual exchange about teaching and learning, and improve practice through knowledge-building. Indeed, the desire (or need) to incorporate new technologies into one's courses has prompted many thoughtful faculty to rethink their goals and ask questions about student learning that they hadn't asked before.

Bass cited his own experience to make the point. Like many other faculty who have redesigned courses to incorporate new pedagogies, Bass's first attempt to intensify the use of technology in his own teaching was not very successful, and his student ratings fell. But Bass's whole tenure case revolved around new media pedagogy, so he could not afford to retreat:

> What saved me both personally and professionally was the process of reflection and redesign I went through as I resolved to make every course component intentional. That is, I tried to articulate for myself the reasoning behind every aspect of my courses, especially the connections between technology and discipline-based pedagogy. In doing so, I found myself asking questions about student learning I had never asked before. (1999b, section 3, paragraph 1)

Putting this lesson together with new ideas about documentation that he was learning elsewhere, Bass used his skills with the new media to create a prototype hypertext course portfolio. He also began speaking and writing about his redesigned course as a case that other people could consult for themselves on the Web.

As Bass's tenure experience will make clear, however, new media scholarship, especially new media scholarship with a focus on teaching and learning, faces hurdles that have affected other "pathfinders" working at the edge (Gumport, 2002a). This is the dilemma that Bass called the "double bind," in which new work is done simultaneous honor and disservice by being judged as both different than but similar to the old. As we have seen in this book, the scholarship of teaching and learning is especially vulnerable to discounting on grounds that it doesn't measure up to the standards of "real" scholarship in the field. When the work involves new media, as Bass's did, one gets further caught up in "arguing on the one hand that new kinds of work are just like other more traditional kinds of work, they just happen to be in a different medium; and on the other hand, the idea and often the fact that new kinds of work, because they are in a different medium, are different kinds of work" (1999b, section 2, paragraph 26). In cases like this, can—should—the "same metric" for assessment apply?

Since gaining tenure, Bass has continued his career-long effort to further humanities pedagogy through the use of technology, but now with the scholarship of teaching and learning going hand in hand. In the process, he has enriched the scholarship of teaching and learning by exploring how the new media can help faculty reclaim accountability for their work with students. Can new media help make teaching visible in ways that can be put in service of improving student learning without stifling innovation? Can technology help faculty build pedagogical knowledge through creating scholarly communities around teaching and learning rather than isolating teachers in their own classrooms, with little choice but to follow tradition or reinvent the wheel? This is not to say that Bass has followed these lines of work at no cost to his own career. As usual, he has found himself in new territory, on a course ever more divergent from the one he initially thought he would follow.

REFLECTION AND REDESIGN

We left Randy Bass in the last chapter as he was coming to terms with the fact that the scholarly projects he had chosen to pursue—the textbook anthology *Border Texts: Cultural Readings for Contemporary Writers*; the electronic resources for the *Heath Anthology of American Literature*; the American Studies Crossroads Project—simply did not leave time or space to also write the book and articles on 19th-century documentary narrative that he and his colleagues had initially expected he would publish. Bass felt a sense of loss in this realization. But he did not doubt himself as a scholar, "in part because there was a kind of breathless cutting-edge quality about everything else. And I didn't feel like I was failing." Quite the contrary. As we have seen, his reputation in new media scholarship and pedagogy had soared beyond what more traditional scholars would ever achieve.

Then, in the fall of 1995, disaster struck, or so it seemed. After deciding to base his whole tenure case on new media scholarship and pedagogy, Bass intensified the role of technology in his teaching, including his own and Georgetown's first-ever freshman writing course in a networked classroom (Bass, 1999b). Despite his savvy and experience, the software was creaky and the course design involving collaborative work among students failed. Unfortunately, classroom innovation that takes students by surprise is often rewarded with low student evaluations—in this instance with grave effect. According to Bass's English department colleague John Glavin, "His students at that time were used to a certain set of classroom instructions for success and became baffled and angry. . . . Being told that you have to have elaborate conversations with fellow students, and that you're going to have to know things and discover others on your own was bewildering."

Bass recalled the moment when he received the results in February 1996. "I knew in the first 15 seconds that I had just deconstructed my entire portfolio," he said. It did not get better. When Bass met with his committee later that spring to talk about his tenure case scheduled for the following year, he realized just how problematic his situation now appeared. James Slevin, chair at the time, counseled Bass to take this as an:

> . . . interpretive, not a judgment, moment. With someone who I know is doing a good job and is serious about it, I often feel that bad evaluations signal something about the culture. The hardware and the students were not ready for his course. And the course description could have done more to clarify just how much was going to be computer-based in order to find the right audience for the course. The

combination meant for me that it just would need a little more time to get the hardware and the software together and to be sure the course description was clear about how much computer-based work would be involved.

After agonized sessions, Bass and his chair negotiated the necessary time by postponing his tenure decision for a year. "And so then it became, 'What can I do over the next year?'"

What he could do, Bass decided, was redesign his course. Beginning that summer, Bass completely recast his American literature course, reflecting not just on how he would use technology, but on every component, from the reading list to the assignments to the exams. In the process, he discovered that it was not a simple matter to be intentional about these choices—not just because the new media are so new, but also because so little is known about how college students learn in humanities fields. Take, for example, the question of "coverage" versus "depth"—an issue with deep roots in the humanities, where the tension between general education and close reading has engaged humanists since at least the 16th century.[10] Bass's decision to cut the number of books in his course from 10 or 12 to 5 and "to work with these fewer texts in new and different ways and more deeply" involved a studied departure from the ways he'd been taught and therefore had taught until that time.

Clearly, Bass was not working on a blank slate. In redesigning his course, and in thinking about how to work differently with fewer texts, he drew on and contributed to ideas that he and colleagues in the hypertext and hypermedia communities had been developing for years.[11] Gregory Jay, director of the Cultures and Communities Program at the University of Wisconsin–Milwaukee, said that he would narrate Bass's contributions to new media pedagogy through a series of stages, each characterized by synthesizing new insights. First, Bass "married the composition approach towards writing-to-learn with the benefits of writing on the Internet and writing on computers. Then he helped bring that into the larger sphere of research with his 'novice in the archive' approach. He began to emphasize how student-centered learning didn't have to be just about writing to learn. It could be about researching to learn too." Bass's new design for American Literary Traditions, taught for the first time in spring 1997, focused on only five texts and required "extensive" electronic student writing and research (Bass, 1997a).

But Bass did not stop at redesign. Along with Dan Bernstein, Bass was working with Pat Hutchings and Lee Shulman in the course portfolio group of AAHE's Peer Review of Teaching Project, and he took the opportunity to document his course on American Literary Traditions in a hypertext portfolio.[12] In recalling this move, Bass stressed that he had not started out with documentation in mind. His reasoning had been, "I'll postpone tenure for a year and fix my teaching of the course, but . . . then the ideas converged." Gregory Jay counted this synthesis with the scholarship of teaching and learning as Bass's third major contribution to teaching and technology in the humanities. Indeed, Bass has been developing its implications ever since.

In short, this was a highly creative period in Bass's life, but one that he experienced as "trauma" from the "fall" (as he refers to the moment when he received those low evaluations) until official word of his tenure and promotion came through. "Beginning with the evaluations, I was distraught through that entire next year, feeling like I was on eggshells trying to fix my teaching and [feeling] that everything was at stake." He was also teaching a graduate course, and while his evaluations there were not great, they were strong enough, and at any rate not counted as highly as undergraduate courses. Fortunately, Bass's focus on the American literature course paid off. "My spring semester evaluations came back and they were well into the comfort zone," he said. "And I felt a little bit of a sigh of relief, and then very concerned that the same thing happen in the fall and it more or less did."

By the fall of 1997, Bass began putting his materials together for tenure. With his teaching evaluations up, his documentation online, and *Border Texts* finally completed, he was feeling reasonably confident, and he believed he had support from some of the deans and even the president on account of his work in technology. Indeed, the fall before, the president had asked Bass to help with his convocation address about how a Jesuit University can be shaped by technology, a talk that received favorable comment from technology-savvy members of Georgetown's Board. The real challenge, Bass suspected, would be to get through the departmental level of review. He was no longer "walking around with a dagger over my head," but he was still not through his "extraordinarily long period of defensiveness about who I was."

THE TENURE CASE

When I first heard Bass speak about his tenure case, he was standing at a podium in the Grande Ballroom of the Sheraton San Diego Hotel, keynoting a plenary session at the seventh AAHE Conference on Faculty Roles and Rewards. It was January 1999, and he was telling a crowd of nearly 1,000 academics about the tribulations of going through the tenure process "without a traditional record of scholarship . . . at an institution that requires such things" (1999b, Section 1, paragraph 1). Bass's talk was only partly about the problems that arose when his colleagues tried to evaluate work that lived on the Web rather than on the conventional printed page.

He also spoke about his "fall" from student evaluation grace, his being "saved" through the scholarship of teaching and learning, and the potential benefits of the intersection of the scholarship of teaching and learning with new digital media (Bass, 1999b, section 1, paragraph 6; section 3, paragraph 1; see also Bass, 1999c).

There was something for just about everyone in Bass's tenure story. It was already circulating in the new media community as welcome relief from bad news concerning the academic fate of technology pioneers.[13] It was also making rounds among teaching and learning activists, who were equally anxious about recognition and reward. *The Chronicle of Higher Education* covered Bass's talk as a story about faculty development in technology and pedagogy, titling the article "With Web Skills—and Now Tenure—a Professor Promotes Improved Teaching" (Guernsey, 1999). Certainly, his case spoke to AAHE's agenda of promoting a broadened vision of academic scholarship and, indeed, to the Carnegie Foundation's own efforts to develop leaders in the scholarship of teaching and learning. Bass's case also had a disciplinary dimension with American literature, which, he told me, "may have gotten lost in the mythologization. To say that I got tenure on the scholarship of teaching isn't quite true. Unless you take it in its broadest sense, in which case it is."

Bass's point is well taken. He did not get tenure for the scholarship of teaching and learning, narrowly construed—for inquiring into his goals for student learning and revising a course, however systematically and insightfully done, or for writing it up and making it public, as he did in a Web-based course portfolio. To be sure, these played a role, because while no one could doubt his seriousness or success as a teacher, his choices were not those everyone would make. John Glavin noted that Bass's goals might look suspect to a teacher because excellence was not his only criterion for student achievement. He wanted risky work, even if the results were crude (as, for example, in class discussion). Leona Fisher pointed out that Bass's interest in making each choice intentional and in making that thinking visible could also rub people the wrong way. "This involves a fear of going outside the privacy of the classroom," she said, "and an elitist notion that anybody who does anything on process rather than product is spinning his wheels."

Like everyone else, however, Bass got tenure not just for his own teaching, but for the "whole package" of work he put on the table. That work, as we have seen, included a number of new media projects as well as participation in a host of organizations and forums devoted to exploring teaching and learning with new media, and, of course, there was *Border Texts*, his own multicultural anthology, as well. However, because most, if not all, of these projects bear on teaching American literature and related fields, it is also correct to say that they pertain to the scholarship of teaching and learning in the broad, "big canopy" sense of the term. Almost all of his work had a pedagogical dimension, and it was in this larger sense that the scholarship of teaching and learning was central to his case.

This sliding scale of scholarship, from course to big project to pervasive theme, is really little different whether talking about the scholarship of teaching or the scholarship of discovery. Take the vitae of any productive scholar, and often one can see in it a program of inquiry (a "project" in the larger philosophical sense) that builds over a period of time through a variety of initiatives (discovery, application, integration, and teaching), all of which both draw on and develop reputation and expertise. A more conventional scholar than Bass, with expertise in 19th- century literature, might take on several related research projects over the course of a career. For example, two of Bass's Victorianist colleagues have taken branching paths: Leona Fisher moving from women's to children's literature, and John Glavin from studies of Dickens himself to "after Dickens," that is, how Dickens played out on the stage and in film. Their publishing and teaching reflect these changes in focus, as do the communities with which they've engaged, and the audiences they've had the opportunity to address. In one sense, as both of these colleagues noted, Bass's path from 19th-century documentary narrative to modes of contextualizing such texts through the capacities of new media, and his pursuit of the opportunities this move offered in the classroom, on the Web, and on the road, is a similar kind of thing.

In another sense, however, Bass's new work diverged so sharply from his old work that in the eyes of many colleagues it was not the simple branching path so many English professors take in their own careers, but a real break in the road. The issue was not only that Bass had focused on new media and pedagogy as a subject for scholarly work. Indeed, if Bass had used these as grist for the familiar humanities mill, it is likely his case would have been more straightforward. That was not the world of new media scholarship as Bass found it. As we have seen, the new media world ran on a faster clock than that of traditional humanities scholarship; there was money for experimental projects; there was interest in it among high officials in the education establishment; and people outside the academy were involved. That this was a world beyond the experience of most faculty in Bass's department was best expressed, perhaps, in their puzzlement about the nature of Web-based projects, their quality, and how or even whether they are subject to "peer review."

In fact, according to both Bass and his colleagues, departmental deliberations involved something of a translation process: what were the conventional analogues to Bass's unconventional work? Clearly, *Border Texts* was a textbook, which in his case was taken seriously. What was the status of Bass's electronic scholarship, and in particular, his major effort, the American Studies Crossroads Project? James Sosnoski, professor of communication at the University of Illinois at Chicago, explained the problem. "In general, the majority of persons who inhabit English departments . . . know very little about electronic environments and tend to see them only in comparison to print," he said. "As a consequence, their evaluations are biased from the outset since when electronic environments are seen as simple equivalents to print, they have little to offer that print cannot match." For example, Bass noted that "as a publication, the Crossroads Project (like many others I could show you in digital form) commits all kinds of sins: it is . . . 'self-published'; it is highly collaborative; it is never 'finished' but ongoing; and it is very difficult to locate in its boundaries and extent" (1999b, section 2, paragraph 26). Hoping to avoid such comparisons, Bass himself presented Crossroads to his committee as work in the scholarships of integration, application, and teaching (but not discovery, or traditional research). He was grateful to his "mentors at Georgetown for their willingness to argue, in their words, that the Crossroads Project was 'the equivalent of, but not like, a book'" (1999b, section 2, paragraph 25).

If not exactly a book, then what was it? In speaking with me, Leona Fisher suggested that a resource like Crossroads is "a little bit like finding a brand new woman poet from the 1860s and all her manuscripts and archival stuff, putting it together with a certain level of scholarly apparatus and making it available to other scholars. The sophistication comes with more and more understanding of hypertext and the ways interactivity can work across websites."[14] Yet this is still faint praise in most humanities departments where, according to a leader in the field of textual scholarship, "a system of apartheid has marked literary and cultural studies. On the one hand we have editing and textual work and on the other theory and interpretation" (McGann, 2002, p. B7). In Bass's case, James Glavin added, "Crossroads was perceived as a new arrangement of information, but not new knowledge, although one could argue that in the very juxtapositions that it created, it was producing new knowledge and the possibility for even more new knowledge."[15]

It was recognized, of course, that whatever Crossroads was "kind of like"—for example, an editorial project or perhaps a book—it was also something else, a new kind of scholarship with which the profession was going to have to make its peace, if not now then sometime in the near future. Lucy Maddox noted, "The interests of faculty are changing, the nature of scholarship itself is changing, and the nature of publication is changing, with the published scholarly monograph becoming only one among many forms of publication." While Georgetown did not formally require a single-authored book for tenure, there was still a sense, according to Maddox, that "if you don't have one then there need to be reasons or signs of one on the way, and that just wasn't there in Bass's case." Could the kind of scholarship presented by Bass be an acceptable substitute? The case, Maddox said, made the department "think about new directions in the profession itself."

No matter how open-minded the members of the department or the profession might be about alternative forms and genres of scholarship, there remains a more fundamental problem of peer judgment. According to Glavin:

> The hard thing is for people to know how you consider achievement that doesn't come in the form of some kind of juried print. I think people are sincere. They [just] don't know what the equivalent is in order to make sure that what you are getting is material that in effect has been peer reviewed. I think that's the big issue. You know how a university press goes about choosing a book, you know how a journal does it. It's very hard to know what the equivalent evaluation process is for stuff that is coming out [on the Web].[16]

Where then does one look for assurance of quality? One colleague suggested to me that the grants Bass had received for the Crossroads Project could be considered a form of peer review. "How is getting grants different from getting a publisher? It's a different format but it's a valorization of the project in the same way." Another colleague said that Bass's external reviewers helped fill in the gap. "His outside evaluators were all people who have produced really significant literary and theoretical scholarship. Finding recognizable voices to speak to the work was very important in this department at that time." Indeed, Bass's reviewers appear to have been aware of this need. John Carlos Rowe, for example, believed that senior faculty "should make a real effort especially when we're outside reviewers to call attention to the fact that this innovative work is really crucial for the future of the profession."

With all these issues at play, it is not surprising that one participant described the proceedings about Bass as "difficult and tense; we felt that we were really groping our way. It was the longest discussion I've been part of, before anybody felt ready to take it to a vote." For Bass, this departmental end game was "an excruciating denouement of what had been a long, hard trip." His case came up in February, and while it usually takes two successive Wednesdays for a tenure review—one day on teaching and service, one day on research—it took the department four weeks to make a decision on him. People would stop by, he recalled, and tell him not to worry, it was just that he had done so much, that they wanted to discuss the case with a colleague who was in Italy for the year, or that his work looked so different from others' that they really didn't know how to evaluate it. Bass feared that the negative opinions would weigh more heavily than the positive ones as deliberations dragged on. However, when the votes were finally taken, on the fourth meeting, Bass got a call from his chair with the all-important numbers—not unanimous but strong enough, she thought, for the case for both tenure and promotion to succeed at the next level of review.[17]

The vote was encouraging, as were comments from colleagues aware of the anxiety that the process had caused. Leona Fisher, his chair, assured him that his supporters had been passionate. His friends dropped by to say "Congratulations! Great!" A most senior person in the department—a traditional scholar—called to say that he was proud to have a colleague in the department with such a strong national reputation. The same person had commented that Bass's outside letters were among the strongest he had ever seen. There was also hurt and irritation as he pieced together other arguments that might have been lodged against him by colleagues, for example, that his engagement with technology was a form of complicity with the corporatization of the university, and who demeaned the intellectual status of his work in pedagogy and faculty development. "If I'd written long, critically theorized articles on the Internet and technology and the body, things would have been fine," Bass said, "but they saw me working with technology in a way that pushed people to get into it. To them, I may have been seen as a patsy of the global techno-industrial complex, whereas I had thought of the kind of faculty development that I'd been doing as a kind of activist move to reclaim technology for faculty and students."[18]

The rest of Bass's tenure and promotion story is anticlimactic. The University's Rank and Tenure committee did not meet until May, where former provost Dorothy Brown told me, it was probably the first case in the humanities that committee had heard where the corpus of the work was so technology-based. Fortunately for Bass, his department chair Leona Fisher was on the committee that year and was able to present the case herself. Bass knew that he would have the support of the graduate dean and the president, who were both impressed with his contributions to technology. Indeed, Brown suggested that Georgetown's and the Jesuit traditional concern with teaching as well as its expanded commitment to technology both worked in Bass's favor. Of course, he was delighted to get a call from the President in June with the good news. But he realized that one lesson of his experience was that his future, much like his past, would be centered more in the world of technology and teaching than in what he calls "the top intellectual tier" of American cultural studies, and would unfold at Georgetown more on the campus level than in his own department. Indeed, for a brief moment, there was some question even about whether he would stay at Georgetown.

A NEW CENTER

Many faculty members who take up the scholarship of teaching and learning do so as a way of improving practice and enlarging their professional lives. The work will likely bring them into touch with others in their institution and in their discipline, and to new forums for intellectual exchange. For most, this sharpened attention to teaching and learning provides a welcome addition to their established interests. For some, however, the new work gives new direction to their careers. This is what happened to Randy Bass when, under stress in the tenure process, he synthesized the scholarship of teaching and learning with his previous work. As American studies scholar Gregory Jay put it, "I think Randy found in the scholarship of teaching and learning movement another way to push his thinking forward. It was a way to both encourage faculty to think and write reflectively about their teaching as a subject of scholarship, and to legitimize that in the academy to some extent."

As we have seen, Bass's work in technology and teaching had already spun him into webs of association far afield from those of most of his departmental colleagues, webs that were further extended as a new community began to form around the scholarship of teaching and learning. Bass's earlier involvement with various AAHE initiatives, particularly the Teaching, Learning, and Technology Group, had brought him in touch with Pat Hutchings. She invited him to work with on course portfolio development with the Peer Review of Teaching Project that she directed with Lee Shulman. In the winter of 1998, as the peer review project was drawing to a close, Hutchings and Shulman (who had become the new president of the Carnegie Foundation) invited Bass to join Dan Bernstein and Brian Coppola and 12 others that summer as the first class of Carnegie scholars in CASTL. This was an important step in the process of recentering Bass's career.

Another critical step took place closer to home. Among Bass's extensive network of admirers at this time was John O'Connor, then dean of the New Century College at George Mason University in Fairfax, Virginia.[19] O'Connor and Bass had come to know each other through intersecting circles of interest—both came out of literature backgrounds and moved more fully into American studies, shared a fascination with "cyberculture" and "hypertext," and got involved with the computers and writing community within composition and rhetoric. O'Connor, who (along with many others) was aware of Bass's situation, set wheels in motion at George Mason, thinking "that if Bass wasn't getting tenure at Georgetown, this would be a good opportunity to bring him to New Century before he got famous." Bass taught for a semester at George Mason while on sabbatical in fall 1998, met many like-minded people in cultural studies, history and the new media, and computers and writing. He left with a job offer from George Mason that O'Connor did not think Georgetown would come near. But Bass did get tenure and was invited by Georgetown's Chief Information Officer and by the Provost to create a center for teaching and technology.

It was the right time. Historian and former provost Brown recalled, all Catholic and Jesuit colleges and universities had been grappling with their identity as sectarian institutions and just what it means. At Georgetown, Brown explained, a presidential task force on the institution's Catholic and Jesuit identity suggested an institute on Jesuit pedagogy. As the members further analyzed Bass's proposal for CNDLS, it seemed that the exploration of Jesuit pedagogy could be carried on through CNDLS, which would also co-host workshops on teaching and diversity, rather than create a new institute. According to Brown, CNDLS would signify that teaching is important in a Jesuit research university and that technology would serve that end. "It's not about 'bells and whistles and machines,'" Brown said, but about "education and building a community of learners." The George Mason offer must have been "tempting," she concluded, "because at that point they already had six colleagues with comparable expertise, but Bass chose the challenge of building at Georgetown instead."

With this decision, Bass's academic life changed. Not suddenly or entirely, because he continued to teach, engage in the scholarship of teaching and learning, and tend old projects (including managing Crossroads, updating the Heath materials, and revising *Border Texts*), though often, now, with co-teachers, co-authors, and other colleagues. He continued to participate in his "old" communities, such as the American Studies Association; the Teaching, Learning, and Technology Group at AAHE; and CASTL.[20] He continued to travel and speak about new media and pedagogy. Now, Bass also had increasing administrative responsibilities, especially when, after a hectic year of grant writing, planning, and design, CNDLS officially opened in the fall of 2000.

CNDLS, not the first or the only unit at Georgetown concerned with technology and teaching, was seen as an integrative and collaborative venture from the start. As Bass wrote to the electronic mailing list of the Professional and Organizational Development Network:

> In putting CNDLS together, I have maintained that its purpose was not only to provide services (TA training, faculty development opportunities, etc.), but to create "a whole greater than the sum of the parts" from the various units on campus doing IT and other kinds of instructional support.

CNDLS, he wrote, "was not conceived as 'another center for teaching' on campus, but as a 'virtual organization' in that it is built out of partnerships with University Information Services (the IT folks), the Library, and the Provost's Office" (2000b). In early October 2000, when Bass and I had our first formal interview, he was meeting every week with the associate director of the library and the associate director of academic computing and struggling with the organizational challenges created by this "virtual" design. Who reports to whom, in what activities are people working through or for CNDLS, when is support for faculty work support for "research" or support for "teaching?" To these familiar but painful questions, Bass said, "There's something post-research, teaching, and service about the scholarship of teaching" that CNDLS would be trying, under his direction, to help get across.

From the beginning, CNDLS sought to support reflective practice in teaching, learning, and technology (a) to serve as a "general center for teaching, learning, and professional development, including attention to those values intrinsic to the Jesuit tradition"; (b) to "coordinate and make coherent the full array of information technology support services at Georgetown, and to advance the use of information technologies and new learning environments"; and (c) "to serve as a national institute for the advanced study of teaching and learning, supporting outside scholars and Georgetown faculty doing advanced work on teaching and learning, especially in connection with new learning environments."[21] In the same campus newsletter where Bass outlined this mission for his campus colleagues, he stressed the interdependence of its three parts:

> For example, we can only make the best use of new technologies if we take teaching and learning seriously; similarly, many faculty who begin to experiment with new technologies discover that they have to start asking questions about student learning that were not evident in more traditional settings. And we cannot take seriously new designs for learning and scholarship if we consider them only 'local' issues. This is why it is so important for CNDLS to foster the advanced study of teaching and learning, giving Georgetown faculty a place to reflect on the design and impact of teaching, and at the same time to bring faculty from other institutions doing innovative and thoughtful work on teaching and learning in residence at Georgetown." (Bass, 2000a, paragraph 3)

The centerpiece of CNDLS's efforts to foster the advanced study of teaching and learning was the externally funded (and beautifully named) Visible Knowledge Project (VKP), designed by Bass in 1999 as a scholarship of teaching and learning initiative. The problem Bass set for this effort was one that had animated his experience with technology in his own humanities classroom and in the classrooms of colleagues who had participated in the pedagogical work of the American Studies Crossroads Project (Bass, 1997b; Bass & Eynon, 1998). How can teachers best use the new cultural and historical materials that electronic technology has made possible?

The VKP was to address this question through an overlapping set of activities that would explore different aspects of what it might mean to make knowledge visible in today's electronic world:

> First, "visible knowledge" refers to ways that the World Wide Web and other digital resources are making visible—for both novice and expert learners—the cultural and historical record that has stayed largely out of reach in the archives, shelves, and basements of libraries and museums. Second, "visible knowledge" applies to . . . the opportunity to bring [them] into contact with primary historical and cultural materials through carefully crafted learning activities. . . . Third, just as new media technologies enable learners to think of their knowledge as "community property," these same multimedia and communication tools can help teachers make their own classroom practice—and reflective investigation of pedagogical suppositions— visible to their professional communities. (1999d, p. 3)

To pursue this work, Bass assembled a network of partner organizations. By late 2002, mid-way through the VKP's five-year timeline, 70 faculty from 21 institutions, including Bass, were involved, inquiring into teaching with technology in their own courses, documenting their findings, and sharing what they were finding out.[22]

In a conversation with me in the late fall of 2001, Bass mused that the unique thing about the VKP was its starting point—not technology, per se, but learning in the humanities:

> One of my operating hypotheses is that some of the greatest impact of technology will be on some of the dimensions of learning that we don't really have vocabulary for yet—not the end product, but the intermediate cognitive processes that [cognitive psychologist] Sam Wineburg talks about.[23]

For example, Bass said, he realized that in his own course, Reading the U.S. Cultural Past, he was interested not only in having students read more like experts, but also in developing "protocols for deferral—for deferring or not coming to understanding, in favor of a systematic way of continuing to open up questions." He went on to talk about the work of fellow VKP (and Carnegie) scholar Sherry Linkon, who is investigating what and how her students are learning as they work in teams to use their present knowledge of Youngstown, Ohio to zoom in and out of a 1880s city map. Our "current platitudes about 'critical analysis' or 'use of evidence' are just blunt objects for understanding whether or not there's a pay-off for using digital materials and activities or not."[24]

With CNDLS and the VKP, not to mention his own teaching, departmental responsibilities, and continuing outside commitments, Bass lives a hectic professional life—"overwhelming" is the term he used in our conversation. CNDLS itself has grown quickly. In the first 18 months, it has served Georgetown faculty who have come for assistance with technology and teaching, but also for other pedagogical advice, especially on assessment. CNDLS has run new faculty orientation sessions and assorted workshops; assisted in the preparation of the self-study documents for the University's re-accreditation; and, at the request of one of the deans, orchestrated a curriculum renewal effort, facilitating a retreat and mentoring 30 faculty projects. At the end of its first year of operation, the Department of Biology asked CNDLS to create a credit-bearing course on pedagogy for all their entering doctoral students, which, by providing a beachhead in the sciences, has "ratcheted up CNDLS' credibility" on campus—leading, of course, to more invitations and demands. The price of success, Bass joked with his staff, is that, "The honeymoon is over and the failed expectations period of our lives now begins."

It is doubtful that CNDLS will fail expectations at Georgetown, given sufficient support and funding, and presuming that Bass himself is not, as his former provost put it, "carried out on his shield."[25] But what about Bass's future at Georgetown as a faculty member in the English department, which he still is and wants to continue to be? He is teaching a course, participating as an active departmental citizen, bringing in money that helps fund English graduate students, and even involving some of his colleagues in VKP and CNDLS. Yet Bass is also beginning to think about promotion to full professor and how to meet departmental expectations for scholarship this next time around. Actually, Bass believed that the scholarly work that he is doing through VKP will count. He is thinking about other things as well. For example, he has some ideas for a course and possibly a publication about how the different documentary modes of the 19th century (his dissertation topic) imply different theories of learning in their audiences. More immediately, he is making progress on a book project that will deepen the themes he has been presenting on for several years regarding learning and technology, the impact of digital technologies on his discipline, and engaging various theoretical issues in the humanities. It is provisionally titled, *Hyper Activity and Under Construction: Learning Culture in the 21st Century.*

Conclusion

When Bass told me the title for his book, I laughed and said, "That sounds like the title for your autobiography!" In a way, he said, it is. I should not have been surprised, for Bass often uses stories about his own scholarship of teaching and learning as an occasion for reflection on broader issues. For example, we spoke together at a recent conference on the scholarship of teaching and learning at Duke University—my presentation was on disciplinary styles, but his was on the evolution of his own scholarship of teaching and learning, from his first redesign of his American Literary Tradition course in 1996–1997, with reduced reading and open-Web research; through his 19th-Century American Literature course in 1999–2000, which experimented with "rotation units" and "knowledge legacies" to get students to build on each others' work; to Reading the U.S. Cultural Past in 2000–2001, in which students explore their own learning with the use of videotaped "think alouds" and reflection to learn more about their own reading protocols (2002).

Bass's point is that a "simple" scholarship of teaching project can grow into a larger program of inquiry. What strikes *me* is the intellectual mileage Bass has gotten from the idea of "visible knowledge" over the years. Not only is he making learning visible to his students in ever new configurations and making his teaching visible to colleagues through rich new media representations, but he is also making the scholarship of teaching metaphorically visible through the oldest medium around, an oral narrative of his own career. What's important, of course, is to explore the potential of *all* media, however new or old, to advance knowledge in ways that respect its depth and complexity while also making it available and accessible to students, colleagues, and the larger communities that it can serve.

NOTES

1. This quotation is from Bass (1999b).

2. Many of the natural sciences are already making use of online publication, such as high-energy physicists who now use the e-Print Archive at Los Alamos instead of paper preprints. Many journals in the natural and social sciences are now available in online versions from their publishers, and the number of peer-reviewed online journals is growing. However, according to a recent roundtable report, "there remains a cultural resistance within many disciplines to acknowledge digital publication as a legitimate scholarly venue" (Knight Higher Education Collaborative 2001, p. 8). In his letter, MLA president Greenblatt (2002) noted, "a council subcommittee is considering actions the MLA and modern language and literature departments might take that would ease the current situation. For example, as a number of informed observers have noted, books are not the only way of judging scholarly achievement. Should our departments continue to insist that only books and more books will do?" (p. 1).

3. In some fields, pedagogical writing has been changing from largely anecdotal to evidence-based. See, for example, Bilimoria and Fukami (2002).

4. Although advocates of the scholarship of teaching and learning see it as a knowledge-building effort, few would want to see practitioner inquiry forced into the "publish or perish" mode.

5. Bernstein has made this point in a number of talks, though not yet in print (personal communication, May 9, 2003). For further information about the project

and portfolio examples, see the Peer Review of Teaching website, http://www. unl.edu/peerrev/index.html.

6. Jerome McGann makes a similar argument with regard to the advantages of Web-based textual editing, including the capacity to represent many versions of an original text and to link to as much other textual, pictorial, film, or audio material as one wants (2001). This argument is familiar from the work of Bass and others, discussed in the last chapter, on preparing hypertext and hypermedia resources for curricular use.

7. Over the next several years, MIT's OpenCourseWare initiative aims to make materials from more than 2,000 courses available for free on the Web. These materials will include lecture notes, course outlines, reading lists, assignments, experiments, and demonstrations. The initiative's Website is http://www.ocw.mit.edu. See also Johnstone and Poulin (2002) and Olsen (2002).

8. Bass's colleague, James Slevin, worried that the situation for higher education could become as regulated as K-12 with "the emphasis on student learning being too narrowly constrained as it merges with accountability models to make the consequences of a person's education assessable too early." He quips, only half-jokingly, that ignorance of these dangers is akin to what Catholics call a "vincible ignorance." "You can go to hell for it," he explained.

9. Foucault (1979) uses the figure of the Panopticon, and the penal system itself, as an image of the more diffuse techniques of self-discipline that emerged along with state power in the West. Indeed, Bass, too, finds the Panopticon an apt metaphor for conservative effects of accountability with regard to tenure and promotion. "[I]n the grand architecture of the academy," he wrote, "beginning in graduate school, and continuing at least through the day that one receives tenure, there is an imposing, mostly silent, force whose effect is to discipline the behavior of the faculty" (1999b, pp. 4–5). The title of the talk from which this quote is taken was "Discipline and Publish," a play on Foucault's *Discipline and Punish*.

10. Bushnell (1994) links "our own struggle to expand the canon while reading the text responsibly" to the discussion that took place among pioneer humanists of the 16th century. By the end of that century, she said, "when concern for argument and structure, or the 'body' of the text, came to dominate humanist rhetoric and grammar, conflict had begun to arise between the admiration of general education and a demand for the kind of close reading that construes a whole text" (p. 19). The tensions only deepen when, as in Bass's case, the aims of reading include historical and cultural contextualization.

11. Redesigning this course drew on all of Bass's skills. He explained, "It involved a large amount of overhead because I was using hypertext papers on *Moby Dick* and I had 30-some students. But a lot of the overhead was behind the scenes techno stuff."

12. Bass created the portfolio for the new course's second iteration over the fall semester of 1997. See http://www.georgetown.edu/bassr/traditions.html.

13. The fate of other scholars who integrate technology into their work indicates that the risks for junior faculty remain high. In reporting the results of a faculty survey administered by the National Education Association (NEA), *The Chronicle of Higher Education* presented interview comments from NEA's higher education coordinator, Christine Maitland. "Junior faculty need to invest their time in things

that are going to get them tenure," she said. "In most cases, spending time on cutting-edge digital projects will not have that payoff. It's still so new that it hasn't been worked into the criteria for promotion and tenure" (Kiernan, 2000, p. A45). Those interviewed for the article mentioned a series of barriers to recognizing digital scholarship, including the challenges of documenting and assessing such work. Similarly, in reviewing recent tenure decisions for five individuals working with digital media, *The Chronicle* reported three instances in which scholars who were denied tenure attributed the decision to their involvement with technology. A fourth, who did earn tenure, believed that his work with new media neither helped nor hurt his case. Only one of the five felt that her work with digital media had been recognized and rewarded (Young, 2000).

14. There is considerable ferment in the area of textual scholarship as the possibilities of digital technology are explored and the crisis in book publishing deepens. Jerome McGann, a leading theorist and practitioner in this area, recently published an article in *The Chronicle of Higher Education* predicting that, "In the next 50 years, the entirety of our inherited archive of cultural works will have to be re-edited within a network of digital storage, access, and dissemination. This system, which is already under development, is transnational and transcultural" (2002, p. B7; see also McGann, 2001).

15. It should not be a surprise that there is disagreement on this issue. Neither Bass nor Lucy Maddox, Bass's mentor, found it particularly useful to compare Crossroads to editing and translating and preparing work for the rest of the community. In our conversation, Maddox suggested "it was seen as something completely different because Randy had connected what he was doing so closely with teaching and pedagogy."

16. This concern is also embedded in the Modern Language Association's Guidelines for Evaluating Computer Related Work in the Modern Languages (1996), which, according to James Sosnoski, "basically . . . translate the criteria used for print environments into language that takes into account electronic texts but as a result the guidelines do not allow for innovative work. For example, electronic publications are acceptable for promotion or tenure on the condition that they are refereed by competent scholars, etc." These guidelines have since been revised, and now state that "faculty members who work with digital media should have their work evaluated by persons knowledgeable about the use of these media in the candidate's field" (Modern Language Association Committee on Information Technology, 2000, section 2, no. 2).

17. Tenure can be awarded without promotion at many institutions. At Georgetown, Bass said, "tenure was still sometimes awarded for service and teaching, but promotion to associate professor was considered to require a record of research or scholarship."

18. James Slevin suggested that while the grants and reputation that Bass had won were "plusses" in most people's estimation, they could also be seen as warning signs of the further intrusion of powerful government and corporate interests into the life of the university. According to Bass, other new media scholars who are also trying to empower faculty against the unthinking "technology rush" of those who manage or control their universities are often tarred with the same brush.

19. In its five-year existence as an autonomous college, New Century College gained a reputation for its interdisciplinary degree programs and for innovative teaching arrangements such as team-teaching and learning communities. In 1999, however, George Mason University's Board of Visitors voted to eliminate the college and move its programs into the College of Arts and Sciences ("George Mason U. Board Ends Experimental College's Autonomy," 1999; Magner, 1999).

20. Bass was a Carnegie Scholar in the pioneer class of 1998. This invitation came about through Bass's earlier association with the course portfolio group of AAHE's Peer Review of Teaching Project, led by Pat Hutchings and Lee Shulman, who organized CASTL when the latter became president of the Carnegie Foundation the following year.

21. CNDLS's mission has been variously phrased over time, but not in essence changed. For example, I have quoted a description from the CNDLS planning phase in the text. At the end of 2002, the center's Website stated the mission more economically, but the three parts were recognizably the same: (a) "to foster and comprehensively support an institutional focus on pedagogy and reflective teaching practice; (b) to advance faculty and student work in new learning environments, through professional development, curriculum development, research, and coordination of technology support; and (c) to engage in, and serve as a center for, research and scholarship on teaching and learning, especially in connection with new learning environments" (CNDLS, 2002).

22. The Visible Knowledge Project's partners are associations and groups with which Bass had already forged collaborations: the American Studies Crossroads Project, the American Social History Project of the CUNY Graduate Center, the Center for History and New Media of George Mason University, the TLT Group at AAHE, and The Carnegie Foundation for the Advancement of Teaching. See http://crossroads.georgetown.edu/vkp/.

23. Sam Wineburg, professor of education at Stanford University and consultant to the Visible Knowledge Project, is best known in higher education circles for his work on how students and professional historians interpret primary sources (Wineburg, 2001). He argued that the "intermediate cognitive processes" that professional scholars use to make sense of sources should be modeled and taught in the classroom. "Historians can model in class how they read by having students bring in unfamiliar texts and demonstrating how to interpret and assess them," he said:

> With a companion document, they can show the strategies they use to corroborate evidence and piece together a coherent context. Or professors could refer students to the useful website History Matters (http://www.historymatters.gmu.edu), whose section on making sense of evidence includes acclaimed historians' discussions of how they evaluate different genres of primary evidence (2003, p. B20).

24. See also the work of Mills Kelly, a historian at George Mason University, who is also a Carnegie Scholar and VKP participant. Kelly's special interest was on the effect of hypermedia on students' use of historical sources—an important aspect of historical expertise. His findings include the fact that "students employing hypermedia are more likely to go back to the earlier materials in the course"

(2000, p. 57). See also Kelly's course portfolio on the American Historical Association's website, http://www.theaha.org/teaching/aahe/welcome.htm.

25. Brown added that the phrase "carried out on a shield" referred not just to Bass's pace of work, but also "to his genuine commitment and remarkable generosity and openness to new ideas. In his commitment, Bass professionally epitomizes the Jesuit ideal of 'men and women for others.'"

10

Work in Progress

· ·

Members of professions take on the burden of their understanding by making public commitments to serve their fellow beings in a skilled and responsible manner. "Professors" take on a special set of roles and obligations. They profess their understanding in the interests of nurturing the knowledge, understanding, and development of others. They take learning so seriously that they profess it.[1]

Although Daniel Bernstein, Brian Coppola, Sheri Sheppard, and Randy Bass have faced challenges in making a place for their engagements in the scholarship of teaching and learning, they acknowledge their extraordinary good fortune. They attended excellent undergraduate and graduate programs. They became tenured faculty members at major universities. They work daily with gifted students and accomplished colleagues. They have gained recognition for the extent and quality of their work. They are experiencing the pleasures, as well as the pain, of taking learning so seriously that, in Lee Shulman's words, they "profess it"—not only in their own classrooms, but also in their departments, institutions, disciplines, and beyond. These four scholars *chose* to craft careers around the scholarship of teaching and learning and accepted the risks that choice entailed. Those pleasures and those risks are not over.

These scholars' careers are in progress, developing established lines of work and taking new directions. In the year or so that I have been writing this book, all four have become involved in new teaching and learning activities and have moved into new positions that were open to them because of the history and character of their education work. Bernstein left a faculty position at the University of Nebraska to join the faculty at the University of Kansas and direct its Center for Teaching Excellence. Coppola became associate chair for curriculum and faculty affairs in his department at the University of Michigan. Sheppard became associate chair of graduate curriculum and admissions of her department at Stanford. Bass, while still directing CNDLS at Georgetown, accepted a position as visiting senior scholar at The Carnegie Foundation for the Advancement of Teaching.

Bernstein, Coppola, Sheppard, and Bass are exceptional in the extent of their pedagogical activities, and their work has broad significance for others who are taking up the scholarship of teaching and learning. No one has taken a census or can give an exact account of how many and who these people are. If the hundreds of faculty members who have applied to the scholars program of CASTL since it began in 1998 can tell us anything, it is that people with these interests can be found across the institutional spectrum, across the disciplines, and across the ranks.[2] Some are long-time participants in the teaching and learning communities on their campuses or in their fields. Others have only recently become involved in curricular reform or pedagogical reflection. Many across this spectrum are newcomers to the central ideas of the scholarship of teaching and learning, exploring their own classroom practice and the character and depth of student learning that result (or do not) from that practice, and making public the results.[3]

Drawn to the scholarship of teaching and learning by a common purpose to improve the learning of students in their own courses, fields, and institutions, these people and others like them are seeking—and at the same time beginning to form—larger communities to inspire, support, and sustain their work. Pioneers like Bernstein, Coppola, Sheppard, and Bass are making contributions to knowledge that others are now building upon. They are explaining and exemplifying the work to others and leading initiatives in which colleagues can get involved. They are helping strengthen institutional conditions that will support the work. They are mentoring a next generation of scholars of teaching and learning. Through their own careers, they are providing visions of the possible, of what it can mean not only to profess learning, but also to make the scholarship of teaching and learning a viable "balancing point" for an academic career.

BUILDING THE FIELD

Scholarship is a deeply communal enterprise. It is, in essence, a conversation in which one participates by knowing what is now being discussed and what others in the past have said. It is common to talk of successful scholarship as "contributing to the field." If a project does not speak to current issues of theory, fact, interpretation, or method, it is unlikely that anyone would say that a contribution has been made. This is fairly uncontroversial with respect to established fields of scholarship. The catch with a "new" or "emerging" area, like the scholarship of teaching and learning is that, as the saying goes, "you can't jump if you've got no place to stand." One of the challenges in supporting the scholarship of teaching and learning on campus, in the disciplines, and across disciplines is not just to encourage those individuals who are interested in pursuing this work, although that is critical, but also to help develop the field itself. As Lee Shulman argued, the scholarship of teaching and learning can flourish only with the development of communities of scholars who share, critique, and build upon each other's work (1993, 2002).

When Dan Bernstein, Brian Coppola, Sheri Sheppard, and Randy Bass began their careers—from the early 1970s to the early 1990s—the scholarship of teaching and learning (at least as a name and a call to action) had not yet coalesced. Bernstein's early engagements with a teaching and learning community in the late 1960s and early 1970s are instructive in this regard, for he was first introduced by colleagues in graduate school to a literature on a particular philosophy of teaching—Keller's "personalized system of instruction"—that had emerged from (and gone beyond) his own discipline. By the time Bernstein got to Nebraska to teach introductory psychology, he found that he was part of a growing community of scholars from around the country experimenting with this kind of teaching, meeting to discuss it, and producing literature around it. For Bernstein, and no doubt many others, it was not yet part of a larger discourse community including people engaged with different philosophies and issues in teaching and learning.

Instead, it was Bernstein's efforts in the mid 1980s to enhance the quality and status of teaching at his own university that connected him to a national community that was developing its own forums and institutional life at about the same time. Coppola, Sheppard, and Bass all became involved in teaching and learning communities in the 1980s as well. Coppola, introduced in graduate school to the existence of a literature on teaching and learning, entered the chemistry education community just as practitioners were re-imagining chemistry education as a subject for scholarly inquiry and, more controversially, for specialized graduate degrees. The engineering education community was just taking shape in the mid to late 1980s when Sheppard joined one of the NSF-funded engineering education coalitions. Bass (though introduced to teaching and learning issues through participation as an undergraduate in a 1970s general education project with national connections) became, in essence, a charter member of the community that formed around new media pedagogy in the humanities in the mid to late 1980s. For each of these scholars, though grounded in their own discipline's forums, the journals, associations, conferences, and funding sources, connections to others multiplied as, in the mid to late 1990s, the new field of the scholarship of teaching and learning began to form (Huber, Hutchings, & Shulman, in press).

Still, one must use the term "field" rather loosely here because, as these scholars' careers illustrate, the scholarship of teaching and learning is emerging at the intersection of several more or less distinct communities in a variety of disciplinary, interdisciplinary, and institutional milieus. It may be helpful to think of this larger world in terms of the forums where people meet to discuss or exchange ideas—in person, in writing, or on the Web—about teaching and learning (Figure 1). These forums may draw scholars from a single campus, groups of campuses, or even nationally or internationally to discuss issues bearing on teaching and learning in a single discipline, a cluster of disciplines (like the STEM disciplines—science, technology, engineering and mathematics—or the humanities, or social sciences), or across all fields. One could add a third dimension, too, for topics, from specialized (say, problem-based learning, or case-based teaching) to comprehensive. No doubt, each of the resulting cells could be further divided and subdivided (Huber, 1999).

This world of discussion and debate has not, to my knowledge, been explored with the same care that historians or sociologists pay to the social worlds in which, say, scientific knowledge has developed and circulated. To be sure, you can find advertisements for national or international conferences, summer institutes, and publishers' offerings in *The Chronicle of Higher Education*, on electronic mailing lists like the one for professional and organizational developers in higher education, and on the websites of sponsoring organizations, like AAHE and the Association of American Colleges and Universities. One can find advertisements for the conferences, conference sessions, journals, and newsletters serving various disciplinary groups through the communications of scholarly societies and professional associations. Although they are not so widely advertised, one can also find out about forums for faculty at specific campuses or campus clusters on the websites of particular institutions or state systems. Still, we don't know the size of this world, how fast it has grown, or how many peo-

Forums for Discussions about Teaching and Learning			
	National	Campus Clusters	Single Campus
Comprehensive	National/ Comprehensive	Campus Clusters/ Comprehensive	Campus/ Comprehensive
Discipline Clusters	National/Discipline Clusters	Campus Clusters/ Discipline Clusters	Campus/Discipline Clusters
Single Discipline	National/ Single Discipline	Campus Clusters/ Single Discipline	Campus/Single Discipline

Figure 1

ple are participating in organized forums beyond the informal communications of practitioners (i.e., all those who teach or are concerned with teaching and learning in higher education).

Nor do we know that much about the content and style of discussion and debate about teaching and learning in these forums. What's important to note is that while only a few might identify themselves as forums specifically *for* the scholarship of teaching and learning, a number of them are in fact doing things that are in its spirit—making teaching public, to be sure, but also encouraging more systematic approaches to the improvement of teaching and learning by mainline faculty, an "ethic of inquiry" (Hutchings, 1999), and a more general appreciation of teaching as serious intellectual work. For example, it is now becoming more common for journals on teaching and learning to ask for evidence, not just assertions or anecdotes, about the quality of student learning (Bilimoria & Fukami, 2001; Chin, 1999); for teaching awards to ask for documentation, not just testimonials; for institutions to offer competitive stipends or time release for faculty to pursue classroom inquiry projects.[4]

One way of understanding the contribution of scholars of teaching and learning like Bernstein, Coppola, Sheppard, and Bass is to look not only at new forums they have organized for colleagues to work in this mode, but also to look at how they have helped move other forums in which they participate in a more scholarly direction. Thus, in his new position as director of the Center for Teaching Excellence at the University of Kansas, Dan Bernstein has the teaching seminar, a new forum for faculty to read course portfolios and decide on a research question to pursue in the next version of one of their own courses. He also has taken an existing forum, like his center's spring teaching workshop, and given it a more disciplinary-specific cast. Consider, too, Bass's efforts to provide occasions for faculty in the humanities to come together around the use of new media technology for teaching. In both the American Studies Crossroads Project and in the Visible Knowledge Project, faculty are documenting, discussing, and disseminating innovative teaching practices and exploring the kinds of student learning they appear to produce.

It may be helpful to consider this move towards the scholarship of teaching and learning as the development of a mode of discourse about teaching and learning that may crosscut and connect the different communities in which it is taking place. Consider, for example, the six defining characteristics of discourse communities identified by John Swales (1990). First, "a discourse community has a broadly agreed set of common public goals" (p. 25). This means that participants share not only an object of study, like teaching and learning, but also a goal—in this case, improving the practice of teaching and learning by treating it as serious intellectual work. Swales's example of people who share an object of study but not a goal is: "students of the Vatican in history departments, the Kremlin, dioceses, birth control agencies, and liberation theology seminaries" (1990, p. 25). While the goals of students of teaching and learning in higher education may not have been quite so diverse, there is no question that the emergence of a scholarship of teaching and learning is bringing professors of chemistry, sociology, and history with an interest in improving their own pedagogy closer together and also bridging some of the gap between themselves and faculty in their own fields and in schools of education whose research specialties are education.[5]

I have already touched on Swales's second and third characteristics of discourse communities—that they have "mechanisms of intercommunication" that people actually use "to provide information and feedback" (as opposed, say, to just sending in a check to support the work). In effect, these criteria might mean that faculty members who teach at a particular institution or in a particular discipline are not members of a discourse community in respect to their teaching unless they actually share their "discursive practice" and "admit or recognize that such a community exists" (1990, p. 25). The idea that teaching and learning might be areas of *scholarly* discourse and practice is, of course, only just beginning to take hold in many institutions and disciplines, as is its infusion into "mechanisms of intercommunication" that might bring together people under the flag of the scholarship of teaching and learning.

The relative newness of this discourse and its mechanisms of communication has consequences for the development both of the *genres* and the *lexicon* for the scholarship of teaching and learning, two additional features that distinguish established from emergent discourse communities in Swales's formulation. The traditional genres of scholarly communication such as books, journal articles, conferences, and conference sessions are available and in use in the larger teaching and learning community, as are some more specialized genres, like the "workshop." Establishing new genres, more friendly to the representation of classroom teaching and student learning, is still work in progress. As we have seen, Dan Bernstein and his colleagues are experimenting with electronic course portfolios *and* with ways of reading and reviewing them; Brian Coppola is experimenting with genres for engaging students in the scholarship of teaching and learning. Sheri Sheppard and Randy Bass, too, have been experimenting with new media as ways of making teaching public.

The issue of what Swales calls a "specific lexis" is more troublesome. This criterion refers to those special terms, names, and acronyms that make communication between professionals efficient and distinguish the different conversational communities to which people belong. For people who think teaching and learning are or should be transparent, even basic words like "pedagogy," "assessment," or "portfolios" can be off-putting, while more complex concepts like "chemical educator" or the "scholarship of teaching and learning" can be red flags.[6] The situation is complicated further by the fact that the scholarship of teaching and learning is emerging as a "trading zone" among people from different disciplines and fields, each with its own special terms of art for teaching and learning, for inquiry, and much else (Gallison, 1997; Huber & Morreale, 2002). Indeed, as I write, the issue of an acronym for the "field" itself is not settled. SoTL (pronounced "so-tul") appears to be gaining ground over the initials STL or those who would prefer not to have an acronym at all (myself included). Colleagues in the UK cleverly talk about the "scholarship of learning and teaching," which can be called SOLT (pronounced "salt").

Still, the lexis is forming. While learning a new way of thinking about teaching and learning, novices are likely to become familiar with names such as AAHE, journals like *Change*, publishers like Jossey-Bass, leaders like Lee Shulman, classics like Perry's *Forms of Intellectual and Ethical Development in the College Years* (1999 [1970]), concepts like "classroom assessment" (Angelo & Cross, 1994), methods like "the think-aloud" (Wineburg, 1991), and so on. Swales argued, "it is hard to conceive, at least in the contemporary English-speaking world, of a group of well-established members of a discourse community communicating among themselves on topics relevant to the goals of the community and not using lexical items puzzling to outsiders" (1990, p. 26).

The last criterion that Swales proposes as critical to a discourse community gets closest to the heart of this book. "A discourse community has a threshold level of members with a suitable degree of relevant context and discoursal expertise" (p. 26). In addition to a critical mass of participants, Swales is also suggesting the importance of a reasonable ratio between novices and experts, whatever the flux in community membership. Given the many different communities where people are taking up more scholarly and systematic approaches to teaching and learning, it is hard to know where and when and at what level critical mass is achieved. Many scholars of teaching and learning still feel isolated in their departments and sometimes in their institutions, finding their best colleagues in this venture elsewhere. However, there are also fields (such as composition, for example) and institutions (such as the CASTL Campus Program cluster leaders) where people do find colleagues close to home as well.[7]

Many other scholars of teaching and learning, including Bernstein, Coppola, Sheppard, and Bass have been active—even "hyper active," to use Bass's term—in spreading the word and attempting to involve colleagues in appropriate kinds of classroom activity and community forums. Many become tireless participants in (and organizers of) the kinds of programs and workshops and special events that the community uses to engage participants in new practices and reflection on those practices.

No less important, many also become activists for teaching and learning on their campuses and in their fields, recognizing that the future depends on what awaits faculty who begin to participate in this new discourse community and to weave the scholarship of teaching and learning into the fabric of their careers.

CAREERS IN PROGRESS

Faculty who take up the scholarship of teaching and learning often say that it gives them a new perspective on their lives as educators, a new language, new literature, new colleagues, and new work. They also note that it entails costs of time and, more significantly, support from colleagues who (as yet) have little familiarity with the scholarly discourse developing around teaching and learning. Both costs, of course, are proportional to the particular activities involved. For example, Dan Bernstein's course portfolio project has shown that modest efforts at documentation entail only modest investments of money and time.[8] It is also the case that engagements that stay close to the classroom do not seem to be hurtful to people's careers. While many faculty actually get involved in the scholarship of teaching and learning for its own sake, without planning to use their portfolios or classroom research projects as part of a case for tenure and promotion, the heightened profile of teaching in the academy today suggests that this work can actually be a plus.[9] Scholars of teaching may be a step in front of the band when it comes to taking learning seriously, but they are generally marching to the right tune.

This is not to deny that in their *teaching*, scholars of teaching and learning take risks. There are always hazards in classroom innovation, such as those encountered by Bass, whose students gave his early design for a technology-intensive course a thumbs-down in their end of term evaluations. However, students are not the only ones who may respond negatively to new responsibilities as learners or imperfectly realized innovations. One Carnegie Scholar, when still an assistant professor of history, received a formal review from colleagues who had observed his teaching that noted their disagreement with his preference for assessing student learning by means of essays and class discussion rather than via multiple choice tests. Emily van Zee, also a Carnegie Scholar, was a new assistant faculty member in a school of education at a large research university when a colleague advised that she close her classroom door for fear that senior faculty passing by would judge her poorly if they did not see her "teaching" up in front of the class. Of course, these are the kinds of "problems" that scholars of teaching and learning can recast as invitations to inquiry, discussion, and redesign. During her successful review for tenure, for example, van Zee summarized studies of her own teaching practices as an integral part of her research program. She included in her dossier a set of papers about her courses and her continued collaboration with interested graduates (van Zee, 1998a, 1998b, 2000; van Zee, Lay & Roberts, in press; van Zee & Roberts 2001).[10]

Indeed, it is in the nature of scholarship to raise new questions, take new paths, ramify, and grow, and this is where more serious career issues arise. What happens to faculty members who become more involved, for whom the work requires larger investments of time, money, and intellectual resources? What about scholars for whom one pedagogical project leads to another and another again? What about those who are presenting their work at conferences, organizing sessions, leading initiatives, publishing papers, and otherwise participating in the scholarly life of national teaching and learning communities, as well as those on their campuses and in their fields? These are the people most likely to face questions from colleagues about the wisdom of their scholarly commitments, and, if they are not yet tenured or promoted, they are also the most likely to face challenges to the normal progress of their careers.

There is a venerable tradition of senior scholars turning to questions of education toward the end of their careers. Nobel laureates who engage in the educational forums of their sciences and high-profile professors in the humanities who turn their pens to teaching (and occasionally learning) are the most visible.[11] But it is not uncommon. Certainly the Carnegie Scholars include a number who, like Dan Bernstein, have intensified their work in teaching and learning as senior faculty members after their tenure and promotion were secure. For them, the advantages are clear. During a panel presentation on careers at one of the CASTL summer residencies, one of these scholars talked about how this new work had not only refreshed her teaching and broadened her network but also given new life to her scholarly interests and renewed her commitment to academic life. Still, even senior professors can be unsettled by the incomprehension of colleagues. A senior scientist who had recently become principal investigator for a large, NSF-funded science education project commented that he was relatively new to this kind of work, but he could already see that he would be doing less of his science than normal over the course of the grant and could already imagine the puzzlement of those in the scientific communities with which he had engaged most closely before.

It is the issue of the evaluation of one's scholarly choices and commitments by colleagues that is the most troublesome for faculty who intensify their work on teaching and learning at earlier stages in their academic careers. To be sure, there will still be many whose scholarship of teaching and learning is a good fit within their institution. For example, one Carnegie Scholar, an accounting professor at a master's university, reported how he was awarded tenure with a record that included the "development of a unique approach to the instruction of intermediate financial accounting" that won an award from his professional association, and a grant from his own university to implement the approach in the business school. But others will face challenges, even at institutions where one would think such work would be welcome—as in the situation of a Carnegie Scholar who was initially turned down for tenure at his community college because he seemed *too interested* in scholarship: "We're here to teach. We're not here to think about teaching. You should find yourself a job at a four-year school where you have time to think about teaching." This scholar, a chemist, sought support from nationally known chemistry educators whom he had met through Project Kaleidoscope.[12] The case was eventually decided in his favor.

While every career is unique in its particular mix of personal histories, disciplinary traditions, and departmental and institutional circumstances, it is probably safe to say that the challenges to scholars of teaching and learning are greatest at colleges and universities that expect candidates for tenure and promotion not only to have a good teaching record, but also to establish major research programs in cutting-edge areas of their fields. This is because the scholarship of teaching and learning is so often placed in the "teaching" column, in large part because of its subject matter, but also because of its goals, methods, and classroom locale. As Sheri Sheppard's situation shows, the hazard can be especially great when the scholarship of teaching and learning involves differences both in method and subject matter from a field's historical core.[13]

Few faculty who become deeply involved in the scholarship of teaching and learning do so unaware of the fact that they are taking risks. They may not have considered all the subtleties that these case studies reveal—the choice of external reviewers or comparison candidates; slicing and dicing one's accomplishments into the procrustean bed of "teaching, research, and service"; the sense of being a prophet without honor in one's home department or institution. They may misjudge the politics when higher administrators, the faculty at large (as represented on college- or university-wide tenure and promotion committees), and departments are not of one mind on the value of educational activities.[14] Not all scholars are as fortunate as Brian Coppola in having such extraordinarily savvy mentors with whom to plan and prepare a path for tenure from department to provost.

Still, most scholars of teaching and learning and their mentors will have at least a general understanding of what it takes to progress normally through the ranks in their particular field and institution. They will have heard and shared the cautionary tales that circulate in their corners of the academy and serve to "discipline" scholars as they make choices about how to spend their time. They may consult one of the growing numbers of guides to how to succeed in the academy, where they will find good advice on how to be safe, not sorry (e.g., Boice, 2000; Goldsmith, Komlos, & Gold, 2001; Reis, 1997). But, unless they are in an institution or a discipline where there is already an established track record for this kind of work, if they really want to intensify their work the scholarship of teaching and learning and associated educational projects, they will have to go against much of the good advice they receive.

LESSONS LEARNED

What lessons can be drawn from the experience of our four extraordinary scholars that might ease the burden for others who wish to support the scholarship of teaching and learning or themselves get involved?

First, these cases underline the responsibility of scholars of teaching and learning and their supporters to educate their colleagues about the nature and significance of work they are doing. In my interviews, I often asked people what lessons *they* would draw from the career in question. At one end of the scale of responses were colleagues who suggested that untenured scholars in their fields at research universities would be best off waiting at least until they were tenured, because careers in academic science depend so heavily on getting a thriving research program up and running in the probationary (pre-tenure) years. Teaching was important, one colleague said, but the scholarship of teaching (at least in its more intense versions) could wait. Another colleague gave a little more ground, by advising untenured scholars who were truly inclined to pursue the scholarship of teaching and learning to use "stealth." If they are going to engage in serious work on the scholarship of teaching and learning, he said, they would be best off doing so under the radar screen of their senior colleagues.

Perhaps the most interesting answer I received, however, came from John Glavin of Georgetown's English department, who concluded just the opposite. "I would say that you'd have to go for absolute transparency," he said. "You have to let everybody in the department know in every possible way what it is you're doing, and why it is both intellectually and professionally serious. Another word for that is a kind of humility. I mean, you know more than most of your senior colleagues know at this point in this area, and you've got to, in a sense, make yourself available to them rather than expecting them to catch up with you." Glavin, of course, was talking about Randy Bass's exploration of new media pedagogy—a focus that engaged him in communities quite distinct in culture and style from that of his colleagues in the English department. But this, I think, is advice that many scholars of teaching and learning (regardless of focus) might find worth taking. Stealth may be best in truly adverse circumstances. But doing the scholarship of teaching and learning privately is almost a contradiction in terms. While it may bring real benefit to one's own students, one will not benefit from the comments and critique of peers, and it will do little to help bring one's departmental colleagues around.

The primary responsibility for communication, of course, should not be borne by the most vulnerable. The second lesson of these case studies concerns the responsibility of senior faculty (and academic administrators) to support the scholarship of teaching and learning and help create a culture where such work is understood and given due respect. There is every reason at any institution and in any field to encourage people to teach with questions about learning in mind and to tackle classroom problems as opportunities for informed inquiry. It makes sense, too, to create and support forums on campus and in the discipline where such work can be made public and a topic for intellectual exchange. As we have seen, all four of the scholars featured here have energetically embraced this responsibility, on their own campuses and beyond.

Senior faculty who are knowledgeable and sympathetic to the scholarship of teaching and learning have a special responsibility to serve as mentors, interlocutors, and external reviewers for junior colleagues engaged in this work. We have seen how important this kind of external support was in making the case for both Coppola and Bass. Of course, it is important that mentors continue to make sure that junior faculty understand the risks of taking the time to bring this kind of work to higher levels, especially at institutions where their scholarly records will be examined for promise of leadership in the traditional subject matter of the field. Still, if there is a young colleague who does have the interest, energy, and imagination, the right thing may be not to discourage them, but to help them do it well. They, like all young academics, will need all the help they can get, including lessons from the pioneers. Recall the words of Cornell's Tony Ingraffea, who came to know Sheri Sheppard during the Synthesis project, put it this way:

> I am now mentoring two of our younger faculty, and I think the best thing I've done in both cases was to recount history. Tell them stories about Synthesis, and tell them stories about Sheri, and others. And tell them to be what they are, be courageous, be brave. Follow their ideas and do the right thing. I have not advised them to just do research and then later when they're successful, then they can start doing teaching. No. Not at all. What I've advised is that there has to be balance.

Finally, these cases raise questions about the ways in which higher education determines the distinction of scholarly work, a problem posed by any kind of scholarship that comes via new media or unusual genres. Yet in the Carnegie Foundation's second report on faculty work, *Scholarship*

Assessed, my co-authors and I argued that the same criteria of excellence can be applied to *all* works of scholarship, be they in discovery, integration, application, or teaching. Our suggestions—clear goals, adequate preparation, appropriate methods, significant results, effective presentation, and reflective critique—have provided a starting point for many fruitful discussions on how to make visible and evaluate the scholarly dimension of academic activity of many kinds. The challenge is to start conversations on campuses and in disciplinary groups, to practice and to gain experience in evaluating emergent work that the community sees as worthwhile.

A word of caution: as long as colleges and universities, and the people whose lives and livelihoods they sustain, think of academic work as "teaching, research, and service," it will continue to be difficult to make an effective case for work that crosses the boundaries between them. It may be necessary to rethink old categories if the academy wants to produce new kinds and new forms of knowledge and see them thrive. It may also be necessary to rethink faculty assignments. *Scholarship Reconsidered* proposed that individual faculty might achieve balance among the scholarships of discovery, application, integration, and teaching over time— focusing on one or another during different three- or five-year "creativity contracts." Others have suggested that balance be sought at the level of academic units or even whole institutions, so that those who wished could concentrate their energies on the scholarly enterprises that interested them most (Rice, 2003).

Some combination of arrangements like these will help. None of these balancing acts will work, however, until more successful cases inspire more stories about the best ways to make a case for the scholarship of teaching and learning. It is likely that, as with other emergent areas of academic thought and practice, the best chance for scholars of teaching and learning will be the success of their scholarship itself. Will their work create better environments for student learning? Will they be suggestive for colleagues in other disciplines? I have seen all four of the scholars featured here engage mixed audiences in lively discussion of assessment of student learning (Bernstein), peer tutoring (Coppola), mechanical dissection (Sheppard) and expert–novice approaches to reading historical and cultural documents (Bass). These are just a few of the topics these scholars have explored, and their fellow scholars of teaching and learning have delved into many more.

Perhaps even more important, however, is how the ideas and methods these scholars develop play out among their own disciplinary colleagues. It is only by influencing them that the ways in which the field is taught will change. It is only by influencing them that the status of teaching in the field will change. It is only by influencing them that scholars of teaching and learning will find the deeply critical interlocutors they need for their educational work to advance. There are many advantages to working in the trading zone of interdisciplinary or cross-disciplinary exchange on matters of substance and method, but something is lost as well as gained. The new work can be exciting, and the new colleagues can be supportive. Still, without "sustained discussion" among one's disciplinary colleagues, who have their own professional views on what it means to know and learn the subject, the "close assessment of arguments and . . . claims [can be] curtailed."[15]

The future of the scholarship of teaching and learning in higher education is an open question right now. No one imagines (and few would advocate) that it will or should become a *discipline*, like economics or biology or even education (with a capital "E"). Will it become the vibrant, growing discourse community that its practitioners and friends would like it to be? People like Bernstein, Coppola, Sheppard, and Bass and many others are helping to make teaching and learning in higher education an area that advances through debate and demonstration, like other subjects and kinds of scholarship. They are showing that scholars who are trained and committed to the standard subject matter and methods of their fields and disciplines can use those same habits of mind to become informed and inquiring teachers. They are showing through the ups and downs of their own academic lives that it is possible to make the scholarship of teaching and learning a vital and viable part of an academic career.

NOTES

1. This quotation is from Shulman (1999), p. 12.

2. From 1998 to 2002, approximately 25 percent of the 765 applicants to CASTL worked in the social sciences (anthropology, communications, economics, geography, political science, sociology); 29 percent in the humanities (art and design, English, foreign language, history, interdisciplinary studies, performing arts, philosophy/religion); 19 percent in mathematics, science, and engineering; and 28 percent in professional fields (business, education, health services, and law). While 46 percent of the applicants came from doctoral/research universities; 32 percent were from masters colleges and universities; 12 percent from baccalaureate colleges; 6 percent from two-year colleges; and 4 percent from international institutions, specialized law or medical schools, and military academies.

3. Early CASTL brochures noted that most projects undertaken in the scholars' program shared the following features: (a) A focus on 'teaching for understanding.' That is, projects [that] explore not only teacher practice but also the character and depth of student learning that results (or does not) from that practice; (b) A commitment to the personal and social development of students. Projects [focus] not only on cognitive forms of learning but on learning in the areas of values and ethics, civic engagement, and commitment to principles and practices essential to democratic society; (c) Attention to issues that have broad relevance or implica-

tions; (d) Explicit links to prior and ongoing lines of work; and (e) A commitment to documenting and sharing results" (CASTL, 1999, pp. 4–5; see also CASTL, 1998).

4. The Carnegie Foundation's own teaching award (run in partnership with the Council for the Advancement and Support of Education), the national U.S. Professors of the Year program, began in 1981 and was recast in 1994. It has been revised several times since then to require better documentation of candidates' teaching accomplishments, and to explicitly allow recognition for faculty who shared their work on teaching and learning with colleagues through publication, workshops, and the like.

5. This is not to deny the sometimes tense state of relations between specialists in education and "regular" faculty who are scholars of teaching and learning, as we have seen in Brian Coppola's case. See also the essays on chemistry (Coppola & Jacobs) and mathematics (Banchoff & Salem) in *Disciplinary Styles in the Scholarship of Teaching and Learning* (Huber & Morreale, 2001).

6. Some campuses participating in the campus conversation phase of CASTL's Campus Program found it wiser to begin by using the ideas but not the term "scholarship of teaching."

7. In January 2003, the CASTL Campus Program initiated a distributed leadership model for the second phase of its work. Twelve campuses were selected as "cluster leaders" for a period of three years, working in partnership with core member campuses on special topics. The University of Michigan, for example, is cluster leader for work on the "scholarship of multicultural teaching and learning;" and Georgetown University is cluster leader for "Advancing the Scholarship of Teaching and Learning as a Networked Community of Practice." See the AAHE website for further information (http://www.aahe.org).

8. In materials for a session on "Supporting the Development and External Review of Course Portfolios," Bernstein and his colleagues described one of the main points:

> With a solid structure to guide it, the preparation of formal course portfolios will not compete with the other activities that are part of contemporary professorial life. As scholarship, however, this work is best done in the context of an intellectual community.

The authors go on to say:

> We have found several forms of support that generate a much improved rate of completion of the writing of course portfolios, and they are: identifying small steps that can be completed quickly and later combined into a portfolio, structured occasions for the completion of each piece of the work, maintenance of a strong local community of social and intellectual support for the work as it unfolds, technical and secretarial support for the actual compilation of the documents, and modest financial compensation that underscores institutional support for the enterprise. (Bernstein, Savory, Robinson, & Comer, 2002, p. 1)

Clearly, more intensive work involving classroom inquiry and course design involves greater expenditures of time and would benefit from greater institutional support (Huber, 2003).

9. National, system-based, and local reform initiatives are keeping the spotlight on critical issues in curriculum, assessment, and pedagogy. Forums for scholarly exchange about teaching and learning are multiplying in disciplinary and campus venues. New campus policies are giving greater attention to the ways in which teaching is represented for appointment, retention, tenure, and promotion. Faculty from all kinds of institutions are reporting on national surveys that teaching is being given greater weight (Huber, 2002).

10. Van Zee wrote about this incident (the warning to close her classroom door) to her fellow Carnegie Scholars shortly after getting tenure:

> Given this comment and the very low student evaluations from my first semester courses, I decided I needed to explain to my students, colleagues (and myself) what I was trying to do. I pass this paper out to my students each semester now and this seems to provide them with some confidence that my very weird ways of teaching have some credibility (mostly small group work, some whole group discussions, no lectures). In any event, there has been a steady climb in my student evaluations to an exemplary level as I have become better at articulating what I want the students to do and why.

Van Zee concluded, "I think this explanatory function is a very important reason to write about one's own teaching practices along the way to gaining tenure, even if such a paper can not be viewed as part of a coherent research program" (email message to CASTL Class of 2000 electronic mailing list, February 16, 2001; see also van Zee, 1998b).

11. Recent examples in the humanities include Booth (1988); Showalter (2003); and Tompkins (1996).

12. Project Kaleidoscope (PKAL) is described on its website as "an informal national alliance working to build strong learning environments for undergraduate students in mathematics, engineering and the various fields of science." The organization sponsors an array of workshops and events, some of which bring faculty and administrators together in team-building activities (see http://www.pkal.org/).

13. Indeed, even scholars in schools of education encounter colleagues who regard such "practitioner" or "action" research as inferior to "real" research (Anderson & Herr, 1999). For a consideration of how these methodological issues are experienced by scholars in different fields, see the essays in *Disciplinary Styles in the Scholarship of Teaching and Learning* (Huber & Morreale, 2001).

14. Although not focused on the scholarship of teaching and learning, a recent series of articles in *The Chronicle of Higher Education* by the chair of the English department at the University of Illinois at Chicago illuminates the politics of "making the case" at different levels of decision (see Barron, 2002a, 2002b, 2003a, 2003b).

15. The quotations here are from anthropologist George Marcus's discussion of what has happened in the last 20 years or so as anthropologists have moved into exploratory projects in new interdisciplinary areas like science studies (1998; see also Huber, 2000).

References

Abrams, M. H. (1997). The transformation of English studies: 1930–1995. In T. Bender & C. E. Schorske (Eds.), *American academic culture in transformation: Fifty years, four disciplines* (pp. 123–149). Princeton, NJ: Princeton University Press.

Academy of Distinguished Teachers, University of Nebraska–Lincoln. (2002). Envisioning education: Teaching and student learning at UNL. Lincoln, NE: University of Nebraska–Lincoln. Retrieved March 20, 2003, from http://tc.unl.edu/cansorge/academy/whitePaper.html.

Accreditation Board for Engineering and Technology. (2003). About ABET. Retrieved April 8, 2003, from http://www.abet.org.

———. (2000). *Criteria for accrediting engineering programs: Effective for evaluations during the 2001–2002 accreditation cycle.* Baltimore, MD: Author. (Available at http://www.abet.org.)

Adams, J. (2001). *Conceptual blockbusting: A guide to better ideas* (4th ed.). Cambridge, MA: Perseus Books.

Aglan, H. A., & Firasat Ali, S. (1996). Hands-on experiences: An integral part of engineering curriculum reform. *Journal of Engineering Education, 85*(4), 327–330.

Altbach, P. G. (2000). The deterioration of the academic estate: International patterns of academic work. In P. G. Altbach (Ed.), *The changing academic workplace* (pp. 1–23). Boston: Boston College School of Education, Center for International Higher Education.

American Association for Higher Education. (1995). *From idea to prototype: The peer review of teaching. A project workbook.* Washington, DC: Author.

———. (1996, January). Faculty careers for a new century [Conference program]. AAHE Conference on Faculty Roles and Rewards, Washington, DC: Author.

American Association of University Professors. (1940). Statement of principles on academic freedom and tenure [With interpretive comments, 1970]. Retrieved February 24, 2003, from http://www.aaup.org/statements/Redbook/1940stat.htm.

———. (1993). Report on the status of non-tenure-track faculty. *Academe, 79*(4), 39–46.

American Association of University Professors, Committee A on Academic Freedom and Tenure. (1997). Access to university records. *Academe, 83,* 44–48.

Amit, V. (2000). The university as panopticon: Moral claims and attacks on academic freedom. In M. Strathern (Ed.), *Audit cultures: Anthropological studies in accountability, ethics, and the academy* (pp. 216–235). London: Routledge.

Anderson, G. L., & Herr, K. (1999). The new paradigm wars: Is there room for rigorous practitioner knowledge in schools and universities? *Educational Researcher, 28*(5), 12–21, 40.

Anderson, L. W., & Krathwohl, D. R. (Eds.). (2000). *A taxonomy for learning, teaching, and assessing: A revision of Bloom's taxonomy of educational objectives.* New York: Longman.

Angelo, T. A., & Cross, P. K. (1994). *Classroom assessment techniques: A handbook for college teachers* (2nd ed.). San Francisco: Jossey-Bass Publishers.

Arnone, M. (2003, January 3). The wannabes: More public universities are striving to squeeze into the top tier. Can states afford these dreams? *The Chronicle of Higher Education,* pp. A18-A20.

Association of American Colleges. (1985). *Integrity in the college curriculum: A report to the academic community.* Washington, DC: Author.

Ayers, E. L. (2001). The valley of the shadow: Two communities in the American civil war. Retrieved October 26, 2003, from http://valley.vcdh.virginia.edu/.

Babcock, D. C. (1941). *History of the University of New Hampshire: 1866–1941.* Rochester, NH: The Record Press, Inc.

Baez, B., & Centra, J. A. (1995). Tenure, promotion, and reappointment: Legal and administrative implications. (ASHE-ERIC Higher Education Report No. 1). Washington, DC: The George Washington University, School of Education and Human Development.

Baker, P. J., & Zey-Ferrell, M. (1984). Local and cosmopolitan orientations of faculty: Implications for teaching. *Teaching Sociology, 12*(1), 82–106.

Banchoff, T., & Salem, A. (2002). Bridging the divide: Research versus practice in current mathematics teaching and learning. In M. T. Huber & S. P. Morreale (Eds.), *Disciplinary styles in the scholarship of teaching and learning: Exploring common ground* (pp. 181–196). Washington, DC: American Association for Higher Education and The Carnegie Foundation for the Advancement of Teaching.

Bank Street Corner. (n.d.). The voyages of the Mimi. Retrieved October 5, 2002, from http://www.bankstreetcorner.com/voyages_of_mimi.shtml.

Baron, D. (2002a, September 5). Getting promoted. *The Chronicle of Higher Education.* Retrieved January 7, 2003, from http://chronicle.com/jobs/2002/09/2002090501c.htm.

———. (2002b, November 7). A look at the record. *The Chronicle of Higher Education.* Retrieved January 7, 2003, from http://chronicle.com/jobs/2002/11/2002110701c.htm.

———. (2003a, January 7). External reviewers. *The Chronicle of Higher Education.* Retrieved January 7, 2003, from http://chronicle.com/jobs/2003/01/2003010701c.htm.

———. (2003b, February 14). The tenure files: Getting through the college. *The Chronicle of Higher Education.* Retrieved February 14, 2003, from http://chronicle.com/jobs/2003/02/2003021401c.htm.

Barrett, L. A., & Narveson, R. (1992). Rewarding teaching at research institutions: A dissemination plan (application to The Comprehensive Program, Fund for the Improvement of Postsecondary Education).

Bartlett, T. (2002, March 22). The unkindest cut. *The Chronicle of Higher Education.* Retrieved February 21, 2003, from http://chronicle.com/weekly/v48/i28/28a01001.htm.

Bass, R. (1981). The role of the student on a committee for academic reform. *Liberal Education, 67*(2), 125–128.

———. (1995, September). Crossroads: The release version. *ASA Newsletter.* Retrieved November 8, 2002, from http://www.georgetown.edu/crossroads/AmericanStudiesAssn/newsletter/archive/articles/xroads3.html.

———. (1996, December). Getting beyond linking: Or, how crossroads are always arrivals at beginnings. *ASA Newsletter.* Retrieved November 8, 2002, from http://www.georgetown.edu/crossroads/AmericanStudiesAssn/newsletter/archive/articles/xroads2.html.

———. (1997a). American literary traditions (course portfolio). Retrieved March 9, 1999, from http://www.georgetown.edu/bassr/traditions.html.

———. (1997b). Engines of inquiry: Teaching, technology, and learner-centered approaches to culture and history. In R. Bass (Ed.), *Introduction to engines of inquiry: A practical guide for using technology in teaching American culture.* Washington, DC: American Studies Association, American Studies Crossroads Project. Retrieved March 30, 2001, from http://www.georgetown.edu/crossroads/guide/engines.html.

———. (1997c). New canons, new media: American literature in the electronic age. In R. Bass (Ed.), *The Heath anthology of American literature online resources.* Boston: Houghton Mifflin. Retrieved August 6, 2001, from http://www.Georgetown.edu/bassr/heath/editorintro.html.

———. (Ed.). (1999a). *Border texts: Cultural readings for contemporary writers.* Boston: Houghton Mifflin Co. Online resources retrieved April 15, 2003, from http://www.georgetown.edu/bassr/bordertexts/web/.

———. (1999b). Discipline and publish: Faculty work, technology, and accountability. Plenary address presented at the AAHE Forum on Faculty Roles and Rewards. Retrieved April 21, 2003, from http://www.georgetown.edu/bassr/disc&pub.html.

———. (1999c). The scholarship of teaching: What's the problem? *Inventio: Creative Thinking about Learning and Teaching, 1*(1). Retrieved November 1, 2002, from http://www.doit.gmu.edu/Archives/feb98/randybass.htm.

———. (1999d). The 'visible knowledge' project: Modeling integrated approaches to technology-enhanced learning in the study of culture and history. Unpublished draft grant proposal.

———. (2000a). The Center for New Designs in Learning and Scholarship (CNDLS). Retrieved January 8, 2001, from http://www.georgetown.edu/users/boydsr/2000newsletter.html.

_____. (2000b, August 2). Re: Support units housed together. Message posted to pod@catfish.valdosta.edu.

———. (2002, September). Evidence of the journey: Six years in search of a scholarship of teaching. Paper presented at the Conference on the Scholarship of Teaching and Learning at a Research University, Durham, NC.

Bass, R., & Eynon, B. (1998). Teaching culture, learning culture, and new media technologies: An introduction and framework. In *Works and Days, 16,* 11–96.

Bass, R., & Young, J. (Eds.). (2003). *Beyond borders: A cultural reader* (2nd ed.). Boston: Houghton-Mifflin.

Batson, T., & Bass, R. (1996). Primacy of process: Teaching and learning in the computer age. *Change, 28*(2), 42–47.

Ben-Zvi, R. (1991). Chemistry programmes. In A. Lewy (Ed.), *The international encyclopedia of curriculum* (pp. 935–938). Oxford: Pergamon Press.

Bernstein, D. J. (1978). Reinforcement and substitution in humans: A multiple-response analysis. *Journal of the Experimental Analysis of Behavior, 30,* 243–253.

———. (1979). Reliability and fairness of grading in a mastery program. *Teaching Psychology, 6,* 104–107.

_____. (1998). Putting the focus on student learning. In P. Hutchings (Ed.), *The course portfolio: How faculty can examine their teaching to advance practice and improve student learning* (pp. 77–83). Washington, DC: American Association for Higher Education.

———. (2000). Peer review of teaching (Bernstein project summary). Retrieved January 14, 2002, from http://www.unl.edu/peerrev/examples/bernstein/.

———. (2001). Representing the intellectual work in teaching through peer-reviewed course portfolios. In S. Davis & W. Buskist (Eds.), *The teaching of psychology: Essays in honor of Wilbert J. McKeachie and Charles L. Brewer* (pp. 215–229). Mahwah, NJ: Lawrence Erlbaum Associates.

Bernstein, D. J., & Edwards, R. (2001, January 5). We need objective, rigorous peer review of teaching. *The Chronicle of Higher Education,* p. B25.

Bernstein, D. J., Goodburn, A., & Robinson, J. (2002, January 26). External peer review of the intellectual work in teaching [Session handout]. AAHE Faculty Forum on Roles and Rewards, Phoenix, AZ.

Bernstein, D. J., Jonson, J., & Smith, K. L. (2000). An examination of the implementation of peer review of teaching. In K. E. Ryan (Ed.), *Evaluating teaching in higher education: A vision for the future* (New Directions for Teaching and Learning No. 83, pp. 73–85). San Francisco: Jossey-Bass, Inc.

Bernstein, D. J., Savory, P., Robinson, J., & Comer, J. (2002, March). Supporting the development and external review of course portfolios [Session handout]. AAHE national conference, Chicago, IL.

Bilimoria, D., & Fukami, C. (2002). The scholarship of teaching and learning in the management sciences: Disciplinary style and content. In M. T. Huber & S. P. Morreale (Eds.), *Disciplinary styles in the scholarship of teaching and learning: Exploring common ground* (pp. 125–142). Washington, DC: American Association for Higher Education and The Carnegie Foundation for the Advancement of Teaching.

Blanpied, W. A. (1999). The National Science Foundation class of 1952. Retrieved May 13, 2002, from http://www.nsf.gov/od/lpa/nsf50/classof52.htm.

Bledstein, B. J. (1976). *The culture of professionalism: The middle class and the development of higher education in America.* New York: Norton.

Bloom, B. S. (Ed.). (1956). *Taxonomy of educational objectives: Cognitive domain.* New York: David McKay.

Blumenstyk, G. (2002, July 19). U. of Michigan finds good research is not enough. *The Chronicle of Higher Education,* p. A24. Retrieved July 18, 2002, from http://chronicle.com/weekly/v48/i45/45a02402.htm.

Bodner, G. M., & Herron, J. D. (1984). Completing the program with a division of chemical education. *Journal of College Science Teaching, 14,* 179–180.

Boice, R. (2000). *Advice for new faculty members.* Boston: Allyn & Bacon.

Bolgar, R. R. (1954). *The classical heritage and its beneficiaries.* Cambridge, England: Cambridge University Press.

Booth, W. (1988). *The vocation of a teacher: Rhetorical occasions, 1967–1988.* Chicago: University of Chicago Press.

Boston College. (1994). Jesuits and Boston College: B.C.'s mission, Jesuits' mission: Six propositions for a conversation. Retrieved February 24, 2003, from http://fmwww.bc.edu/SJ/sixpropositions.html.

Boyer, E. L. (1990). *Scholarship reconsidered: Priorities of the professoriate.* Princeton, NJ: The Carnegie Foundation for the Advancement of Teaching.

Boyer, E. L., & Levine, A. (1981). *A quest for common learning: The aims of general education.* Princeton, NJ: The Carnegie Foundation for the Advancement of Teaching.

Bronowski, J. (1974). *The ascent of man.* Boston: Little, Brown.

Brown, J. S, & Duguid, P. (1999). Mysteries of the region: Knowledge dynamics in Silicon Valley. In Lee, C.-M., Miller, W. F., Hancock, M. G., & Rowen, H. S. (Eds.), *The Silicon Valley edge: A habitat for innovation and entrepreneurship* (pp. 16–39). Stanford, CA: Stanford University Press.

Bucciarelli, L. L. (1994). *Designing engineers.* Cambridge, MA: The MIT Press.

Bushnell, R. (1994). From books to languages. *Common Knowledge, 3*(1), 16–38.

Calder, L., Cutler III, W. W., & Kelly, T. M. (2002). History lessons: Historians and the scholarship of teaching and learning. In M. T. Huber & S. P. Morreale (Eds.), *Disciplinary styles in the scholarship of teaching and learning: Exploring common ground* (pp. 45–67). Washington, DC: American Association for Higher Education and The Carnegie Foundation for the Advancement of Teaching.

Carnegie Commission on Higher Education. (1973). *A classification of institutions of higher education.* Berkeley, CA: The Carnegie Foundation for the Advancement of Teaching.

Carnegie Foundation for the Advancement of Teaching. (1994). *A classification of institutions of higher education.* Princeton, NJ: The Carnegie Foundation for the Advancement of Teaching.

Cartter, A. M. (1966). *An assessment of quality in graduate education.* Washington, DC: American Council on Education.

CASTL (The Carnegie Academy for the Scholarship of Teaching and Learning). (1998). The Carnegie teaching academy: The Pew scholars national fellowship program [Brochure]. Menlo Park, CA: The Carnegie Foundation for the Advancement of Teaching.

———. (1999). Information and applications for the Pew national fellowship program for Carnegie scholars, the teaching academy campus program, and work with the scholarly and professional societies [Brochure]. Menlo Park, CA: The Carnegie Foundation for the Advancement of Teaching.

Cerbin, W. (1994). The course portfolio as a tool for continuous improvement of teaching and learning. *Journal of Excellence in College Teaching, 5,* 95–105.

Chait, R. (1995, Spring). The future of academic tenure. *Priorities, 3,* 1–12. Washington, DC: Association of Governing Boards.

Chin, J. (1999). *Is there a scholarship of teaching in teaching sociology?* Unpublished manuscript.

CNDLS (Center for New Designs in Learning and Scholarship). (2002). What we are: Mission. Retrieved December 14, 2002, from http://cndls.georgetown.edu/about_us/mission.html.

Colby, A. (1994). Case studies of exceptional people: What can they teach us? *Journal of Narrative and Life History, 4*(4), 353–365.

Coleman, E. B., Rivkin, I. D., & Brown, A. L. (1997). The effect of instructional explanations on learning from scientific texts. *Journal of the Learning Sciences, 6*(4), 347–365.

———. (1998). Using explanatory knowledge during collaborative problem solving in science. *The Journal of the Learning Sciences, 7*(3&4), 387–427.

Coppola, B. P. (1998, January). Valuing multidimensional forms of scholarly excellence in appointment, promotion, and tenure policies & practices. Paper presented at the AAHE Conference on Faculty Roles and Rewards, Orlando, FL.

———. (1999, October). Teaching, scholarship, and the research university. Address presented to the Lilly Scholars Program at the University of Maryland, College Park, MD.

———. (2001a). Full human presence. In A. G. Reinarz & E. R. White (Eds.), *Beyond teaching to mentoring* (New Directions in Teaching and Learning No. 83, pp. 57–73). San Francisco: Jossey-Bass.

———. (2001b). Statement of recent and future teaching plans, Department of Chemistry, University of Michigan. Unpublished documents submitted for promotion to the rank of full professor.

————. (2002, August 9). Treating graduate students with dignity. *The Chronicle of Higher Education*, p. B16. Retrieved October 26, 2003, from http://chronicle.com/weekly/v48/i48/48b01601.htm.

Coppola, B. P., & Daniels, D. S. (1998). Mea culpa: Formal education and the disintegrated world. *Science and Education, 7.* 31–48.

Coppola, B. P., Daniels, D. S., & Pontrello, J. K. (2001). Using structured study groups to create chemistry honors sections. In J. E. Miller, M. S. Miller, & J. E. Groccia (Eds.), *Student-assisted teaching: A guide to student-faculty teamwork* (pp. 116–122). Bolton: MA: Anker Publishing Company.

Coppola, B. P., Ege, S. N., & Lawton, R. G. (1997). The University of Michigan undergraduate chemistry curriculum 2. Instructional strategies and assessment. *Journal of Chemical Education, 74*(1), 84–94.

Coppola, B. P., & Jacobs, D. C. (2002). Is the scholarship of teaching and learning new to chemistry? In M. T. Huber & S. P. Morreale (Eds.), *Disciplinary styles in the scholarship of teaching and learning: Exploring common ground* (pp. 197–216). Washington, DC: American Association for Higher Education and The Carnegie Foundation for the Advancement of Teaching.

Coppola, B. P., & Pearson, W. H. (1998). Heretical thoughts II – On lessons we learned from our graduate advisor that have impacted our undergraduate teaching. *Journal of College Science Teaching, 27,* 416–421.

Coppola, B. P., & Smith, D. H. (1996). A case for ethics. *Journal of Chemical Education, 73,* 33–34.

Crane, G. (Ed.). (2002). The Perseus digital library. Retrieved November 13, 2002, from http://www.perseus.tufts.edu.

Craver, L. W., Jr., Schroder, D. C., & Tarquin, A. J. (1987). *Introduction to engineering.* New York: Oxford University Press.

Cuban, L. (1999). *How scholars trumped teachers: Change without reform in university curriculum, teaching, and research: 1890–1990.* New York: Teachers College Press.

Diamond, R. M. (1999). *Aligning faculty rewards with institutional mission: Statements, policies, and guidelines.* Bolton, MA: Anker Publishing Company, Inc.

Diamond, R. M., & Adam, B. E. (Eds.). (1995). *The disciplines speak: Rewarding the scholarly, professional, and creative work of faculty.* Washington, DC: American Association for Higher Education.

————. (1997). Changing priorities at research universities: 1991–1996 [Prepublication copy]. Syracuse, NY: Center for Instructional Development, Syracuse University.

————. (2000). *The disciplines speak II: More statements on rewarding the scholarly, professional, and creative work of faculty.* Washington, DC: American Association for Higher Education.

Downey, G. L., & Lucena, J. C. (1995). Engineering studies. In S. Jasanoff, G. Markle, J. Petersen, & T. Pinch (Eds.), *Handbook of science and technology studies* (pp. 167–188). Thousand Oaks, CA: Sage Publications.

————. (1997). Engineering selves: Hiring in to a contested field of education. In G. L. Downey & J. Dumit (Eds.), *Cyborgs and citadels: Anthropological interventions in emerging sciences and technologies* (pp. 117–141). Santa Fe, NM: School of American Research Press.

————. (2003). When students resist: Ethnography of a senior design experience in engineering education. *International Journal of Engineering Education, 19*(1), 168–176.

Dym, C. L. (1999). Learning engineering: Design, languages and experiences. Retrieved October 26, 2000, from http://www.2.hmc.edu/~dym/EngrngEd.html [A more current (2002) version of the paper is located at http://www2.hmc.edu/~dym/LearningEngrng.pdf].

Ege, S. N., Coppola, B. P., & Lawton, R. G. (1997). The University of Michigan undergraduate chemistry curriculum 1: Philosophy, curriculum, and the nature of change. *Journal of Chemical Education, 74*(1), 74–83.

Eisenhart, M. A., & Finkel, E. (1998). *Women's science: Learning and succeeding from the margins*. Chicago: University of Chicago Press.

Epstein, J. (2003, February). Goodbye, Mr. Chipstein. *Commentary, 115*, 40–45.

Etzkowitz, H., Kemelgor, C., Neuschatz, M., Uzzi, B., & Alonzo, J. (1995). Gender implosion: The paradox of "critical mass" for women in science. Paper presented at the NACME research and policy conference on minorities in mathematics, science and engineering, Wake Forest, NC.

Ewell, P. T. (1987). Assessment: Where are we? The implications of the new state mandates. *Change, 19*(1), 23–28.

————. (1991). Assessment and public accountability: Back to the future. *Change, 23*(6), 12–17.

Finkelstein, M. J., Seal, R. K., & Schuster, J. H. (1998). *The new academic generation: A profession in transformation*. Baltimore: The Johns Hopkins University Press.

Flowers, W. (2001). New media's impact on education strategies. In M. Devlin, R. Larson, & J. Meyerson (Eds.), *The internet and the university: 2001 forum* (pp. 24–27). Retrieved March 10, 2003, from http://www.educause.edu/ir/library/pdf/ffp0204s.pdf.

Foltin, R. W., Fischman, M. W., Brady, J. V., Bernstein, D. J., Capriotti, R. M., Nellis, M. N., & Kelly, T. H. (1990). Motivational effects of smoked marijuana: Behavioral contingencies and low-probability activities. *Journal of the Experimental Analysis of Behavior, 53*, 5–19.

Foltin, R. W., Fischman, M. W., Brady, J. V., Bernstein, D. J., Nellis, M. N., & Kelly, T. H. (1990). Marijuana and behavioral contingencies. *Drug Development Research, 20*, 67–80.

Foltin, R. W., Fischman, M. W., Brady, J. V., Kelly, T. H., Bernstein, D. J., & Nellis, M. N. (1989). Motivational effects of smoked marijuana: Behavioral contingencies and high-probability recreational activities. *Pharmacology, Biochemistry, and Behavior, 34*, 871–877.

Foucault, M. (1979). *Discipline and punish: The birth of the prison*. New York: Vintage Books.

Freeland, R. M. (1992). *Academia's golden age: Universities in Massachusetts, 1945–1970.* New York: Oxford University Press.

Gaff, J. G. (1980). Avoiding the potholes: Strategies for reforming general education. *Educational Record, 60,* 50–59.

Gallagher, C. (1997). The history of literary criticism. In T. Bender & C. E. Schorske (Eds.), *American academic culture in transformation: Fifty years, four disciplines* (pp. 151–171). Princeton, NJ: Princeton University Press.

Galle, W. P., Jr., & Koen, C. M., Jr. (1993, September/October). Tenure and promotion after Penn v. EEOC. *Academe, 79,* 19–26.

Gallup, H. F. (1998, May). Tribute to Fred Keller: Variations on a theme. Paper presented at Association for Behavior Analysis Annual Convention, Orlando, FL. Retrieved October 26, 2003, from http://ww2.lafayette.edu/~allanr/keller.html.

Gallup, H. F., & Allan, R. W. (1996). Concerns with some recent criticisms of the personalized system of instruction (PSI). Retrieved December 7, 2001, from http://ww2.lafayette.edu/~allanr/psiart.html.

Ganss, G. E. (1989). St. Ignatius and Jesuit higher education. In R. E. Bonochea (Ed.), *Jesuit higher education: Essays on an American tradition of excellence* (pp. 154–159). Pittsburgh: Duquesne University Press.

Gardner, H. (1991). *The unschooled mind: How children think and how schools should teach.* New York: Basic Books.

———. (2002, July 18). Test for aptitude, not for speed. *New York Times,* p. A23.

Geiger, R. L. (1999). The ten generations of American higher education. In P. G. Altbach, R. O. Berdahl, & P. J. Gumport (Eds.), *American higher education in the 21st century: Social, political, and economic challenges,* (pp. 13–44). Baltimore, MD: The Johns Hopkins University Press.

———. (2002). The American university at the beginning of the twenty-first century: Signposts on the path to privatization. In R. McC. Adams (Ed.), *Trends in American and German higher education* (pp. 33–84). Cambridge, MA: American Academy of Arts and Sciences.

Gelmon, S., & Agre-Kippenhan, S. (2002). Promotion, tenure, and the engaged scholar: Keeping the scholarship of engagement in the review process. *AAHE Bulletin, 54*(5), 7–11.

George Mason U. board ends experimental college's autonomy. (1999, June 25). *The Chronicle of Higher Education,* p. A14.

Gibbons, J. F. (2000). The role of Stanford University: A dean's reflections. In C.-M. Lee, W. F. Miller, M. G. Hancock, & H. S. Rowen (Eds.), *The Silicon Valley edge: A habitat for innovation and entrepreneurship* (pp. 200–217). Stanford, CA: Stanford University Press.

Gilbert, S. W. (2002, November 1). Ten most obvious cost-effective strategies for improving teaching and learning with technology. Retrieved October 26, 2003, from http://www.tltgroup.org/costeffective/TenBest.htm.

Gilgen, A. R. (1982). *American psychology since World War II: A profile of the discipline.* Westport, CT: Greenwood Press.

Glassick, C. E., Huber, M. T., & Maeroff, G. I. (1997). *Scholarship assessed: Evaluation of the professoriate.* San Francisco: Jossey-Bass Publishers.

Glidden, H. (1997, May/June). Does confidentiality ensure the educational mission? *Academe, 83,* 32–34.

Gold, M. J. (1988). A simple quantitative synthesis: Sodium chloride from sodium carbonate. *Journal of Chemical Education, 65,* 731.

Goldenberger, M. L., Maher, B. A., & Flatteau, P. E. (1995). *Research-doctorate programs in the United States: Continuity and change.* Washington, DC: National Academy Press.

Goldsmith, J. A., Komlos, J., & Gold, P. S. (2001). *The Chicago guide to your academic career: A portable mentor for scholars from graduate school through tenure.* Chicago: University of Chicago Press.

Gombrich, E.H. (1984). *The sense of order: A study in the psychology of decorative art.* Ithaca, NY: Cornell University Press.

Gouldner, A. W. (1957). Cosmopolitans and locals: Toward an analysis of latent social roles-I. *Admin. Sci. Quarterly, 2,* 281–306.

———. (1958). Cosmopolitans and locals: Toward an analysis of latent social roles-II. *Admin. Sci. Quarterly, 2,* 444–480.

Graff, G. (1987). *Professing literature: An institutional history.* Chicago: University of Chicago Press.

Grafton, A. (2002). *Bring out your dead: The past as revelation.* Cambridge, MA: Harvard University Press.

Graham, H. D., & Diamond, N. (1999, June 18). Academic departments and the rating game. *The Chronicle of Higher Education,* p. B6. Retrieved March 24, 2003, from http://chronicle.com/prm/weekly/v45/i41/41b00601.htm.

Grant, G., & Reisman, D. (1978). *The perpetual dream: Reform and experiment in the American college.* Chicago: The University of Chicago Press.

Grayson, L. P. (1977). A brief history of engineering education in the United States. *Engineering Education, 68*(3), 246–64.

———. (1993). *The making of an engineer: An illustrated history of engineering education in the United States and Canada.* New York: John Wiley & Sons.

Greater University Tutoring Service (GUTS). (n.d.). More about GUTS. Retrieved March 26, 2002, from http://guts.studentorg.wisc.edu.

Green, K. C. (1998, November). *The 1998 national survey of information technology in higher education: Colleges struggle with IT planning.* Retrieved October 26, 2003, from http://www.campuscomputing.net/summaries/1998.

Greenblatt, S. (2002, May 28). A special letter from Stephen Greenblatt. (Available from the Modern Language Association of America, http://www.mla.org/scholarly_pub).

Grieder, T. (1996). *Artist and audience.* (2nd ed.). Madison, WI: Brown and Benchmark, Publishers.

Guernsey, L. (1999, February 26). With Web skills and now tenure—a professor promotes improved teaching. *The Chronicle of Higher Education,* p. A24. Retrieved October 26, 2003, from http://chronicle.com/prm/weekly/v45/i25/25a02401.htm.

Gumport, P. J. (2002a). *Academic pathfinders: Knowledge creation and feminist scholarship*. Westport, CT: Greenwood Press.

_____. (2002b). Universities and knowledge: Restructuring the city of intellect. In S. G. Brint (Ed.), *The future of the city of intellect: The changing American university* (pp. 47–81). Stanford, CA: Stanford University Press.

Hannan, A., & Silver, H. (2000). *Innovating in higher education: Teaching, learning, and institutional cultures*. Buckingham, England: The Society for Research into Higher Education and the Open University Press.

Hastorf, A. H., & Cantril, H. (1954). They saw a game: A case study. *Journal of Abnormal and Social Psychology, 49*, 129–134.

Hatch, T., Bass, R., Iiyoshi, T., & Pointer, D. (2003). Building knowledge for teaching and learning: The promise of scholarship in a networked environment. Unpublished manuscript, The Carnegie Foundation for the Advancement of Teaching.

Hatch, T., Pointer, D., & Iiyoshi, T. (2001). In the acts of teaching: Using multimedia and new technologies to advance the scholarship of teaching and learning. (Available from the Knowledge Media Lab, The Carnegie Foundation for the Advancement of Teaching, http://kml.carnegiefoundation.org/resources/new/text.pdf)

Herman, P. C. (2000). '60s theory/'90s practice. In P. C. Herman (Ed.), *Day late, dollar short: The next generation and the new academy* (pp. 1–24). Albany: State University of New York Press.

Hopkins, N., Bailyn, L., Gibson, L., & Hammonds, E. (2002). The status of women faculty at MIT: An overview of reports from the schools of architecture and planning; engineering; humanities, arts, and social sciences; and the Sloan School of Management. Retrieved April 2, 2002, from http://web.mit.edu/faculty/reports/.

Huber, M. T. (1998). *Community college faculty: Attitudes and trends, 1997*. Stanford, CA: National Center for Postsecondary Improvement.

_____. (1999a, March). Developing discourse communities around the scholarship of teaching. Paper presented at the Colloquium on Campus Conversations, national meeting of the American Association for Higher Education, Washington, DC.

_____. (1999b). Evaluating outreach: *Scholarship assessed's* approach. In *Best practices in outreach and public service: The "scholarship of engagement" for the 21st century* (pp. 37–42). State College, PA: Outreach and Cooperative Extension Program of The Pennsylvania State University. (Available at http://www.outreach.psu.edu/C&I/Monograph/eval.html).

_____. (2000). Disciplinary styles in the scholarship of teaching: Reflections on The Carnegie Academy for the Scholarship of Teaching and Learning. In C. Rust (Ed.), *Improving student learning: Improving student learning through the disciplines* (pp. 20–31). Oxford, UK: Oxford Centre for Staff and Learning Development, Oxford Brookes University.

_____. (2002). Faculty evaluation and the development of academic careers. In C. L. Colbeck (Ed.), *Evaluating faculty performance* (New Directions for Institutional Research No. 114, pp. 73–83). San Francisco, CA: Jossey-Bass Publishers.

———. (2003, January). Patterns of support for the scholarship of teaching and learning. Paper presented at the American Economics Association annual conference, Washington, DC.

Huber, M. T., Hutchings, P., & Shulman, L. S. (in press). The scholarship of teaching and learning today. In K. A. O'Meara & R. E. Rice (Eds.), *Encouraging multiple forms of scholarship: Voices from the field.* Washington, DC: American Association for Higher Education.

Huber, M. T., & Morreale, S. P. (2002). Situating the scholarship of teaching and learning: A cross-disciplinary conversation. In M. T. Huber & S. P. Morreale (Eds.), *Disciplinary styles in the scholarship of teaching and learning: Exploring common ground* (pp. 1–24). Washington, DC: American Association for Higher Education and The Carnegie Foundation for the Advancement of Teaching.

———. (Eds.). (2002). *Disciplinary styles in the scholarship of teaching and learning: Exploring common ground.* Washington, DC: American Association for Higher Education and The Carnegie Foundation for the Advancement of Teaching.

Hutchings, P. (1994, November). Peer review of teaching: "From idea to prototype." Lessons from a current AAHE teaching initiative project. *AAHE Bulletin, 47,* 3–7.

———. (1996). *Making teaching community property: A menu for peer collaboration and peer review.* Washington, DC: American Association for Higher Education.

_____. (1998a). How to develop a course portfolio. In P. Hutchings (Ed.), *The course portfolio: How faculty can examine their teaching to advance practice and improve student learning* (pp. 47–55). Washington, DC: American Association for Higher Education.

———. (1998b). Defining features and significant functions of the course portfolio. In P. Hutchings (Ed.), *The course portfolio: How faculty can examine their teaching to advance practice and improve student learning* (pp. 13–18). Washington, DC: American Association for Higher Education.

———. (2000). Approaching the scholarship of teaching and learning. In P. Hutchings (Ed.), *Opening lines: Approaches to the scholarship of teaching and learning* (pp. 1–10). Menlo Park, CA: The Carnegie Foundation for the Advancement of Teaching.

———. (Ed.). (2002). *Ethics of inquiry: Issues in the scholarship of teaching and learning.* Menlo Park, CA: The Carnegie Foundation for the Advancement of Teaching.

Hutchings, P., & Shulman, L. S. (1999). The scholarship of teaching: New elaborations, new developments. *Change, 31*(5), 10–15.

Jay, G. (1999, June). WWW.AMERICANSTUDIES.COM? Strategies and challenges in high-tech teaching. Paper presented at the Dartmouth Institute on the Futures of American Studies, Darmouth, MA. Retrieved February 10, 2001, from http://www.uwm.edu/~gjay/dartmouth/.

JEITA (Japan Electronics and Information Technology Industries Association). (2002, December). Representative organizations from Japan, United States and Europe begin preparing the world lead-free soldering roadmap and agree to eliminate lead by 2005 [Press release]. Tokyo: JEITA. Retrieved March 4, 2003, from http://www.jeita.or.jp/english/press/2002/1217/index.htm.

Johnstone, S., & Poulin, R. (2002). What is OpenCourseWare and why does it matter? *Change, 34*(4), 48–50.

Joncas, R., Neuman, D. J., & Turner, P. V. (1999). *Stanford University: An architectural tour.* New York: Princeton Architecture Press.

Keller, F. S. (1968). Good-bye, teacher. . . . *Journal of Applied Behavior Analysis, 1,* 79–89.

Kelly, T. M. (2000). For better or worse? The marriage of Web and classroom. In P. Hutchings (Ed.), *Opening lines: Approaches to the scholarship of teaching and learning* (pp. 53–61). Menlo Park, CA: The Carnegie Foundation for the Advancement of Teaching.

Kemper, J. D. (1990). *Engineers and their profession* (4th ed.). New York: Oxford University Press.

Keniston, H. (1959). *Graduate study and research in the arts and sciences at the University of Pennsylvania.* Philadelphia: University of Pennsylvania Press.

Kerr, C. (in association with M. L. Gade & M. Kawaoka). 1993. *Troubled times for American higher education: The 1990s and beyond.* Albany: State University of New York Press.

Kiernan, V. (2000, April 28). Rewards remain dim for professors who pursue digital scholarship. *The Chronicle of Higher Education,* pp. A45-A46.

Knight Higher Education Collaborative. (2001). Op.Cit. *Policy Perspectives, 10*(3), 1–12.

———. (2002). Who owns teaching? *Policy Perspectives, 10*(4), 1–9.

Knoll, R. E. (1995). *Prairie university: A history of the University of Nebraska.* Lincoln, NE: University of Nebraska Press.

Kohn, A. (2002, November 8). The dangerous myth of grade inflation. *The Chronicle of Higher Education,* p. B7.

Kornberg, A. (1997). Basic research, the lifeline of medicine. Retrieved July 2, 2002, from http://almaz.com/nobel/medicine/1959b.html.

Krathwohl, D., & Bloom, B. S. (1984). *Taxonomy of educational objectives, handbook 1: Cognitive domain.* New York: Addison-Wesley Publishing Company.

Krathwohl, D. R., Bloom, B. S., & Masia, B. B. (1964). *Taxonomy of educational objectives: Affective domain.* New York: David McKay.

Kroto, H. (2002, November 22). Untitled essay. *The Times Higher Education Supplement,* 15.

Kuper, A. (1992). Post-modernism. Cambridge and the great Kalahari debate. *Social Anthropology, 1*(1A), 57–71.

Landow, G. P. (1995). The death of Intermedia and the migration to Storyspace. Online supplement to G. P. Landow, *Hypertext: The convergence of contemporary critical theory & technology.* Baltimore, MD: The Johns Hopkins University Press.

Retrieved October 27, 2003, from http://www.victorianweb.org/cpace/ht/jhup/int2.html.

Langer, J. A. (1992). Speaking of knowing: Conceptions of understanding in academic disciplines. In A. Herrington & C. Moran (Eds.), *Writing, teaching, and learning in the disciplines* (pp. 69–85). New York: The Modern Language Association.

Lave, J., & Wenger, E. (1991). *Situated learning: Legitimate peripheral participation.* Cambridge: Cambridge University Press.

Lazerson, M., Wagener, U., & Shumanis, N. (2000). Teaching and learning in higher education, 1980–2000. *Change, 32*(3), 12–19.

Leahey, T. H. (1991). *A history of modern psychology.* Englewood Cliffs: Prentice Hall.

Lederman, D., & Mooney, C. J. (1995, April 14). Lifting the cloak of secrecy from tenure. *The Chronicle of Higher Education,* p. A17.

Levine, A. E. (1978). *Handbook on undergraduate curriculum* (1st ed.). San Francisco: Jossey-Bass.

———. (2000, October 27). The future of colleges: 9 inevitable changes. *The Chronicle of Higher Education,* p. B10. Retrieved October 26, 2003, from http://chronicle.com/weekly/v47/i09/09b01001.htm.

Levine, J. (1996). The long way home: Once her focus was on faraway places. Now Sherry Ortner looks for anthropology in her own backyard. *The University of Chicago Magazine, 88.* Retrieved January 4, 2002, from http://www2.uchicago.edu/alumni/alumni.mag/9602/9602Ortner.html.

Levy, D. (2000, March 1). David Kelley elected to National Academy of Engineering. *Stanford News.* Retrieved July 31, 2001, from http://www.stanford.edu/dept/news/pr/00/000301Kelley.html.

McCaughy, R. A. (1994). *Scholars and teachers: The faculties of select liberal arts colleges and their place in American higher learning.* New York: Conceptual Litho Reproductions.

McGann, J. (2001). *Radiant textuality: Literature after the World Wide Web.* New York: Palgrave.

———. (2002, December 13). Literary scholarship in the digital future. *The Chronicle of Higher Education,* pp. B7-B9.

McLemee, S. (2001, June 15). A star of American studies (or is that 'Un-American studies'?). *The Chronicle of Higher Education,* p. A12. Retrieved October 26, 2003, from http://chronicle.com/prm/weekly/v47/i40/40a01201.htm.

Magner, D. K. (1999, June 18). Battle over academic control pits faculty against governing board at George Mason U. *The Chronicle of Higher Education,* p. A14.

Manis, J. D., Thomas, N. G., Sloat, B. F., & Davis, C. (1989). An analysis of factors affecting choice of majors in science, mathematics, and engineering at the University of Michigan. (Research report #23, Center for the Education of Women). Ann Arbor, MI: Center for the Education of Women, University of Michigan.

Manuel, D. (1998, May 20). Senators, others debate status of women faculty. *Stanford Online Report.* Retrieved April 16, 2003, from http://www.stanford.edu/dept/news/report/news/may20/facsen520.html.

Marcus, G. E. (1998). *Ethnography through thick and thin*. Princeton, NJ: Princeton University Press.

Marsh, H. W. (1987). Students' evaluations of university teaching: Research findings, methodological issues, and directions for future research. *International Journal of Educational Research, 11*(3), 253–388.

Mazuzan, G. T. (1994, July 15). *The National Science Foundation: A brief history* (Report NSF8816). Washington, DC: The National Science Foundation. Retrieved May 13, 2002, from http://www.nsf.gov/pubs/stis1994/nsf8816/nsf8816.txt.

Merton, R. K. (1968). *Social theory and social structure*. New York: Free Press.

———. (1973). Recognition and excellence: Instructive ambiguities. In R. K. Merton (Ed.), *Sociology of science: Theoretical and empirical investigations* (pp. 419–438). Chicago: University of Chicago Press.

Metzger, W. P. (1987) The academic profession in the United States. In B. R. Clark (Ed.), *The academic profession: National, disciplinary, and institutional settings* (pp. 123–208). Berkeley, CA: University of California Press.

Miller, M. A. (1998). Preface. In P. Hutchings (Ed.), *The course portfolio: How faculty can examine their teaching to advance practice and improve student learning* (pp. v-vii). Washington, DC: American Association for Higher Education.

———. (2002). The Fund for the Improvement of Postsecondary Education: 30 years of making a difference. *Change, 34*(5), 4.

MIT Committee on Engineering Design. (1961, April). Report on engineering design. *Journal of Engineering Education, 2*, 645–660.

Modern Language Association. (n.d.). MLA job information list. About the MLA's studies of PhD placement. Retrieved January 26, 2003, from http://www.mla.org/resources/jil/jil_career/jil_phd_survey.

Modern Language Association Committee on Computers and Emerging Technologies in Teaching and Research. (1996). Guidelines for evaluating computer-related work in the modern languages. *Profession, 1996*, pp. 217–219.

Modern Language Association Committee on Information Technology (2000, May). Guidelines for evaluating work with digital media in the modern languages. Retrieved October 26, 2003, from http://www.mla.org/resources/documents/rep_it/guidelines_evaluation_digital.

Mooney, C. J. (1995, April 12). At branch campuses, teaching matters more. *The Chronicle of Higher Education*, p. A22.

Muramatsu, B., & Agogino, A. M. (1999, April). The national engineering education delivery system: A digital library for engineering education. *D-Lib Magazine, 5*(4). Retrieved January 27, 2003, from http://www.dlib.org/dlib/april99/muramatsu/04muramatsu.html.

Nasar, S. (1998). *A beautiful mind: The life of mathematical genius and Nobel Laureate John Nash*. New York: Simon & Schuster.

National Research Council. (1995a). *Engineering education: Designing an adaptive system*. Washington, DC: National Academy Press.

———. (1995b). *Reshaping the graduate education of scientists and engineers*. Washington, DC: National Academy Press.

————. (1996). *From analysis to action: Undergraduate education in science, mathematics, engineering, and technology.* [Report of a Convocation]. Washington, DC: National Academy Press.

————. (1999). *Transforming undergraduate education in science, mathematics, engineering, and technology.* [Committee on Undergraduate Science Education, Center for Science, Mathematics, and Engineering Education]. Washington, DC: National Academy Press.

————. (2000). *Enhancing the postdoctoral experience for scientists and engineers: A guide for postdoctoral scholars, advisors, institutions, funding organizations, and disciplinary societies.* Washington, DC: National Academy Press.

National Science Foundation. (1997). *Guide to programs, fiscal year 1997: A compilation of NSF funding opportunities.* Washington DC: National Science Foundation.

————. (1996). *Shaping the future: New expectations for undergraduate education in science, mathematics, engineering and technology* (NSF 96–139). Washington, DC: National Science Foundation.

Noble, D. (1998). Digital diploma mills: The automation of higher education. *First Monday, 3*(1). Retrieved November 1, 2002, from http://www.firstmonday.dk/issues/issue3_1/noble/.

North, S. M. (2000). *Refiguring the Ph.D. in English studies: Writing, doctoral education, and the fusion-based curriculum.* Albany: State University of New York Press.

Nummedal, S. G., Benson, J. B., & Chew, S. L. (2002). Disciplinary styles in the scholarship of teaching: A view from psychology. In M. T. Huber & S. Morreale (Eds.), *Disciplinary styles in the scholarship of teaching and learning: Exploring common ground* (pp. 163–179). Washington, DC: American Association for Higher Education and The Carnegie Foundation for the Advancement of Teaching.

Olsen, F. (2002, December 6). MIT's open window: Putting course materials online, the university faces high expectations. *The Chronicle of Higher Education,* p. A31.

O'Meara, K. A. (2000). Climbing the academic ladder: Promotion in rank. In C. A. Trower (Ed.), *Policies on faculty appointment: Standard practices and unusual arrangements* (pp. 141–179). Bolton, MA: Anker.

Ortner, S. (1993, Summer). Ethnography among the Newark. *Michigan Quarterly Review, 32*(3), 410–429.

————. (1996). *Making gender: The politics and erotics of culture.* Boston: Beacon Press.

————. (1998, Spring). Identities: The hidden life of class. *Journal of Anthropological Research, 54*(1), 1–17.

————. (2003). *New Jersey dreaming: Capital, culture, and the class of '58.* Durham, NC: Duke University Press.

Ory, J. C. (2000). Teaching evaluation: Past, present, and future. In K. E. Ryan (Ed.), *Evaluating Teaching in higher education: A vision for the future* (New Directions in Teaching and Learning No. 83, pp. 13–18). San Francisco: Jossey-Bass.

Oxford English Dictionary (The Compact Edition). (1971). "Balance" (Volume I, A-O), p. 158. Oxford: Oxford University Press.

Perry, W. R. (1999 [1970]). *Forms of intellectual and ethical development in the college years: A scheme*. San Francisco, CA: Jossey-Bass Publishers.

Peterson, M. W., & Einarson, M. K. (1997). Analytic framework of institutional support for student assessment (NCPI Technical Report). Stanford, CA: Stanford University, National Center for Postsecondary Education, School of Education.

Petroski, H. (1992). *To engineer is human: The role of failure in successful design*. New York: Vintage Books.

Phelps, L. W. (1997, January). Interference patterns: Making the transition to the new paradigm. AAHE Faculty Roles and Rewards Conference, San Diego, CA.

Phillips, S. (2002, November 8). Take away the books and the chairs collapse. *The Times Higher Education Supplement*. Retrieved November 8, 2002, from http://www.thes.co.uk.

Portland State University. (1997). Promotion and tenure guidelines. Retrieved April 8, 2002, from http://oaa.pdx.edu/PromotionAndTenureGuidelines.

————. 1999. Mission: Portland State University. Retrieved February 3, 2003, from http://www.pdx.edu/psumission.phtml.

Rabinow, P. (1996). *Making PCR: A story of biotechnology*. Chicago: University of Chicago Press.

Reamon, D. T., & Sheppard, S. D. (1997). The role of simulation software in an ideal learning environment. *Proceedings of the 1997 ASME Design Engineering Technical Conference*, 1–6.

————. (1998). Motor workshop: The role of interactivity in promoting learning. *Frontiers in Engineering Conference Proceedings*.

Regan, M., & Sheppard, S. D. (1996). Interactive multimedia courseware and hands-on learning experience: An assessment study. *ASEE Journal of Engineering Education, 85*(2), 123–130.

Reis, R. (1997). *Tomorrow's professor: Preparing for careers in science and engineering*. New York: IEEE Press.

Rice, R. E. (2003). Rethinking scholarship and new practice: A central AAHE priority (AAHE Special Report). Retrieved March 4, 2003, from http://www.aahe.org/specialreports/part4.htm.

Richards, B. P., Levoguer, C. L., Hunt, C. P., Nimmo, K., Peters, S., & Cusack, P. (1999). An analysis of the current status of lead-free soldering. Retrieved January 20, 2003, from http://www.npl.co.uk/ei/documents/pbfreereport.pdf.

Richards, B.P., & Nimmo, K. (2000). An analysis of the current status of lead-free soldering: Update 2000. Retrieved March 4, 2003, from http://www.npl.co.uk/ei/documents/pbfreereport.pdf.

Romberger, J. (2000). Writing across the curriculum and writing across the disciplines. Retrieved January 26, 2002, from http://owl.english.purdue.edu/handouts/WAC/index.html.

Roose, K. D., & Andersen, C. J. (1970). *A rating of graduate programs*. Washington, DC: American Council on Education.

Roth, P. (1997). *American pastoral*. New York: Vintage International.

Roth, P. (1998). *I married a communist*. Boston: Houghton Mifflin.

Ruark, J. K., & Montell, G. (2002, July 2). A wake-up call for junior professors. *The Chronicle of Higher Education*, Career Network. Retrieved October 27, 2003, from http://chronicle.com/jobs/2002/07/2002070201c.htm.

Ruskin, J. (1856). Modern painters, Vol. 3, containing part 4, of many things. London: Smith Elder & Co.

Saldivar, J. D. (1997). Tracking English and American literary and cultural criticism. In T. Bender & C. E. Schorske, *American academic culture in transformation: Fifty years, four disciplines* (pp. 173–192). Princeton, NJ: Princeton University Press.

Salvatori, M., & Donahue, P. (2002). English studies in the scholarship of teaching. In M. T. Huber & S. P. Morreale (Eds.), *Disciplinary styles in the scholarship of teaching and learning: Exploring common ground* (pp. 69–86). Washington, DC: American Association for Higher Education and The Carnegie Foundation for the Advancement of Teaching.

Schwab, J. (1964). Structure of the disciplines: Meanings and significances. In G. W. Ford & L. Pugno (Eds.), *The structure of knowledge and the curriculum* (pp. 1–30). Chicago: Rand McNally & Company.

Scott, J. W. (1995). Academic freedom as an ethical practice. *Academe, 81*(4), 44–48.

Searle, J. (1990, December 6). The storm over the university. *New York Review of Books*. Retrieved May 7, 2002, from http://www.nybooks.com/articles/3428.

Seely, B. E. (1999). The other re-engineering of engineering education, 1900–1965. *Journal of Engineering Education, 88*(3), 285–294.

Seldin, P. (1984). *Changing practices in faculty evaluation*. San Francisco: Jossey-Bass Publishers.

———. (1993, October). How colleges evaluate professors 1983 v.1993. *AAHE Bulletin, 46*, 6–12.

Seymour, E. (2002). Tracking the Processes of Change in US Undergraduate Education in Science, Mathematics, Engineering, and Technology. *Science Education, 85*, 79–105.

Seymour, E., & Hewitt, N. M. (1997). *Talking about leaving: Why undergraduates leave the sciences*. Boulder, CO: Westview.

Sheppard, S. D. (1990). Statement of work in NSF engineering coalition: Stanford University. Unpublished manuscript.

———. (1992, January). Mechanical dissection: An experience in how things work. *Proceedings of Engineering Education: Curriculum Innovation & Integration Conference* (sponsored by the Engineering Foundation), Santa Barbara, CA. (Available at http://www-adl.stanford.edu/images/dissphil.pdf.)

———. (2001). The compatibility (or incompatibility) of how we teach engineering design and analysis. *International Journal of Engineering Education, 17*(4), 440–445.

———. (2002). S. Sheppard activities at Stanford University. Unpublished manuscript.

Sheppard, S., & Jenison, R. (1997). Freshman engineering design experiences: An organizational framework. *International Journal of Engineering Education, 13*(4), 190–197.

Sheppard, S. D., Johnson, M. & Leifer, L. (1998). A model for peer and student involvement in formative course assessment. *ASEE Journal of Engineering Education, 87*(4), 349–354.

Sheppard, S. D., Jones, K., & Jeremijenko, N. (1998). Developing 'text learning capture' to examine how students learn from text and how text learns from students. *ASME 10th International Design Theory and Methodology Conference Proceedings.*

Sheppard, S., & Tsai, J. (1992). A note on mechanical dissection with pre-college students. Paper presented at New Approaches to Undergraduate Engineering Education IV, Santa Barbara, CA.

Sherman, J. G. (Ed.). (1974). *Personalized system of instruction: 41 germinal papers.* Philippines: W.A. Benjamin Inc.

Sherman, J. G., Ruskin, R. S., & Semb, G. B. (Eds.). (1982). *The personalized system of instruction: 48 seminal papers.* Lawrence, KS: TRI Publications.

Showalter, E. (2003). *Teaching literature.* Malden, MA: Blackwell Publishers.

Shulman, L. S. (1986). Those who understand: Knowledge growth in teaching. *Educational Researcher, 15*(2), 4–14.

———. (1993). Teaching as community property: Putting an end to pedagogical solitude. *Change, 25*(6), 6–7.

———. (1998). Course anatomy: The dissection and analysis of knowledge through teaching. In P. Hutchings (Ed.), *The course portfolio: How faculty can examine their teaching to advance practice and improve student learning* (pp. 5–12). Washington, DC: American Association for Higher Education.

———. (1999). Taking learning seriously. *Change, 31*(4), 10–17.

———. (2002a). If we build it, who will come? The scholarship of teaching and learning as a field and a trading zone. Plenary address presented at the CASTL reunion.

———. (2002b). Making differences: A table of learning. *Change, 34*(6), 36–44.

Sikora, A. C. (2002b). *A profile of participation in distance education:1999–2000* (NCES 2003–154). Washington, DC: U.S. Department of Education, National Center for Education Statistics.

Slaughter, S., & Leslie, L. L. (1997). *Academic capitalism: Politics, policies, and the entrepreneurial university.* Baltimore: Johns Hopkins University Press.

Smith, V. B. (2002). FIPSE's early years: Seeking innovation and change in higher education. *Change, 34*(5), 10–16.

Spencer, J. (2000). British social anthropology: A retrospective. *Annual Review of Anthropology, 29,* 1–24.

Stanford University. (n.d.). History of the school of humanities and sciences. Retrieved December 21, 2001, from http://www.stanford.edu/dept/humsci/about/history.html.

————. (n.d.). History of Stanford and the School of Engineering: 77 years of innovation, School of Engineering. Retrieved August 14, 2002, from http://soe.stanford.edu/soe_timeline.

————. (1993, November). Report of the provost's committee on the recruitment and retention of women faculty. Stanford, CA: Author.

Stevenson, H. W., & Stigler, J. W. (1992). *The learning gap: Why our schools are failing and what we can learn from Japanese and Chinese education*. New York: Touchstone.

Strathern, M. (1995). The relation: Issues in complexity and scale. *Prickly Pear Pamphlets, 6,* Cambridge: Prickly Pear Pamphlets.

Swales, J. (1990). *Genre analysis: English in academic and research settings*. Cambridge: Cambridge University Press.

Synthesis Coalition. (n.d.). The Synthesis Coalition. Retrieved August 28, 2000, from http://www.synthesis.org.

The Columbia Encyclopedia (5th Ed.). (1993). New York: Columbia University Press.

Theall, M., & Franklin, J. (2000). Creating responsive student ratings systems to improve evaluation practice. In K. E. Ryan (Ed.), *Evaluating teaching in higher education: A vision for the future* (pp. 95–107). San Francisco: Jossey-Bass.

Tillotson, G. (1996). A short history of WAC. Retrieved February 25, 2002, from http://www.engl.niu.edu/wac/histwac.html.

Tirelli, V. (1998). Adjuncts and more adjuncts: Labor segmentation and the transformation of higher education. In R. Martin (Ed.), *Chalk lines: The politics of work in the managed university* (pp. 181–201). Durham, NC: Duke University Press.

Tobias, S. (1990). *They're not dumb, they're different: Stalking the second tier*. Tucson, AZ: The Research Corporation.

————. (1992). *Revitalizing undergraduate science: Why some things work and most don't*. Tucson, AZ: The Research Corporation.

Tompkins, J. (1996). *A life at school: What the teacher learned*. New York: Addison Wesley Longman.

United States Bureau of the Census. (1975). *Historical statistics of the United States, part 2*. Washington, DC: Author.

U.S. Department of Education, National Commission on Excellence in Education. (1983). *A nation at risk: The imperative for educational reform: A report to the nation and the secretary of education, United States Department of Education*. Washington, DC: U.S. Department of Education.

U.S. News & World Report. (2001). Best graduate schools: Programs in psychology. Retrieved October 27, 2003, from http://www.usnews.com/usnews/edu/grad/rankings/phdhum/brief/psych_brief.php.

————. (2004). Best undergraduate engineering programs (at schools whose highest degree is a doctorate). Retrieved October 27, 2003, from http://www.usnews.com/usnews/edu/college/rankings/brief/engineering/phd/topprogs_withphd_brief.php.

University of Colorado at Denver. (n.d.). New urban university. Denver, CO: Author.

University of Michigan. (n.d.). Faculty promotion guidelines, attachment A: Qualifications for appointment and promotion in the several faculties of the University of Michigan. Retrieved October 26, 2000, from http://www.umich.edu/~provost/promotions/promatt_a.html.

University of Nebraska–Lincoln. (2001). University of Nebraska–Lincoln enrollment, fall semester 1932–33 to 2001–02. Retrieved January 5, 2002, from http://factbook.unl.edu/factbook/enrl32–03.html.

_____. (2002). Historical notes. Retrieved January 5, 2002, from http://www.unl.edu/unlpub/special/history/history.shtml.

University of Wisconsin–Madison. (2003). Institute for Chemical Education overview. Retrieved January 27, 2003, from http://ice.chem..wisc.edu/Overview.htm.

Van Duzer, E. (1999, June). Talking teaching in engineering: A discourse community in higher education. Background paper prepared for the program on Cultures of Teaching and Learning in Higher Education. Menlo Park, CA: The Carnegie Foundation for the Advancement of Teaching.

———. (2000). ABET engineering criteria 2000: A guarantor of quality? (Doctoral dissertation, University of California, Berkeley, 2000). *Dissertation Abstracts International, 61* (07), 2628A.

Van Zee, E. H. (1998a). Fostering elementary teachers' research on their science teaching practices. *Journal of Teacher Education, 49,* 245–254.

_____. (1998b). Preparing teachers as researchers in courses on methods of teaching science. *Journal of Research in Science Teaching, 35,* 791–809.

_____. (2000). Analysis of a student-generated inquiry discussion. *International Journal of Science Education, 22,* 115–142.

Van Zee, E. H., Lay, D., & Roberts, D. (in press). Fostering collaborative inquiries by prospective and practicing elementary and middle school teachers. *Science Education.*

Van Zee, E. H., & Roberts, D. (2001). Using pedagogical inquiries as a basis for learning to teach: Prospective teachers' perceptions of positive science learning experiences. *Science Education, 85,* 733–757.

Wankat, P. C., Felder, R. M., Smith, K. A., & Oreovicz, F. S. (2002). The scholarship of teaching and learning in engineering. In M. T. Huber & S. P. Morreale (Eds.), *Disciplinary styles in the scholarship of teaching and learning: Exploring common ground* (pp. 217–237). Washington, DC: American Association for Higher Education and The Carnegie Foundation for the Advancement of Teaching.

Warburton, E. C., Chen, X., & Bradbum, E. M. (2002). *Teaching with technology: Use of telecommunications technology by postsecondary instructional faculty and staff in fall 1998* (NCES 2002–161). Washington, DC: U.S. Department of Education, National Center for Education Statistics.

Wasserman, E. (2000). *The door in the dream: Conversations with eminent women in science.* Washington, DC: Joseph Henry Press.

Weimer, M. (1993). The disciplinary journals on pedagogy. *Change, 25*(6), 44–51.

Western Michigan University, Department of Psychology. (n.d.). Dr. Jack Michael. Retrieved October 27, 2003, from http://www.wmich.edu/psychology/faculty/michael.html.

Whitman, N., & Weiss, E. (1982). *Overview of faculty evaluation: The use of explicit criteria for promotion, retention, and tenure.* Washington, DC: American Association for Higher Education.

Wilson, R. (2001, January 5). A higher bar for earning tenure. *The Chronicle of Higher Education,* pp. A12–13.

Wineburg, S. (2001). *Historical thinking and other unnatural acts: Charting the future of teaching the past.* Philadelphia, PA: Temple University Press.

_____. (2003). Teaching the mind good habits. *The Chronicle of Higher Education,* p. B20.

Winslow, W., & the Palo Alto Historical Association. (1993). *Palo Alto: A centennial history.* Palo Alto, CA: Palo Alto Historical Association.

Wubbels, G. G., & Girgus, J. G. (1996). The natural sciences and mathematics. In J. Gaff, J. L. Ratcliff, & Associates (Eds.), *Handbook of the undergraduate curriculum: A comprehensive guide to purposes, structures, practices, and change* (pp. 280–300). San Francisco: Jossey-Bass.

Yaskin, D, & Gilfus, S. (2002). *Blackboard 5TM: Introducing the blackboard 5: Learning system.* (Information available at www.blackboard.com.)

Young, J. R. (2002, February 22). Ever so slowly, colleges start to count work with technology in tenure decisions. *The Chronicle of Higher Education,* p. A25. Retrieved February 19, 2002, from http://chronicle.com/prm/weekly/v48/i24/24a02501.htm.